D0385245

East Meadow Public Library
1886 Front Street, East Meadow, NY 11554
(516) 794-2570
www.eastmeadow.info

CAPITAL OF THE WORLD

ALSO BY DAVID WALLACE

Lost Hollywood
Hollywoodland
Dream Palaces of Hollywood's Golden Age
Exiles in Hollywood
A City Comes Out: How Celebrities Made Palm Springs a Gay and Lesbian Paradise
Malibu, A Century of Living by the Sea (contributor)

DAVID WALLACE

CAPITAL OF THE WORLD

A PORTRAIT OF NEW YORK CITY IN THE ROARING TWENTIES

LYONS PRESS
Guilford, Connecticut
An imprint of Globe Pequot Press

For Chris

Lyons Press is an imprint of Globe Pequot Press.

Photo on the title page is courtesy of the Library of Congress.

Text design: Sheryl Kober
Layout artist: Kevin Mak
Project manager: Ellen Urban

Library of Congress Cataloging-in-Publication Data is available on file.

ISBN 978-0-7627-7010-6

Printed in the United States of America

10 9 8 7 6 5 4 3 2 1

CONTENTS

INTRODUCTION

Curfew shall not ring tonight!
—Legendary speakeasy proprietor Texas Guinan's exhortation to her patrons in the 1920s to party on!

The 1920s were, simply speaking, the most transformative and probably the most exciting decade in American history. So much changed in our culture, our lifestyles, and our economy that it seemed a new world had been born. With the exception of Hollywood, where the world's most powerful entertainment industry was being built, the city that was setting the pace for American and global change was New York.

While the automobile was to play a leading role in transforming America from a largely rural culture into an urban and suburban one, the growing national numbers of horseless carriages was less important in New York City, then nearly as jammed with vehicles as today. It was in New York that everything else seemed possible through modern thinking, new philosophies emancipated from generations of Victorian strictures by the "war to end all wars," population changes, and, of vast importance, the economic boom. Along with these catalysts was the arrival of modern technology that brought about—besides the ubiquitous Model T—radio, motion pictures, hundred-story skyscrapers, nonstop trans-Atlantic airplane flights, and, yes, bathtub gin, the Tommy gun, and the call girl.

Before 1920 one's lifestyle was largely limited by one's job income; during the decade, buoyed by New York's exploding stock market, elevator operators became millionaires. And those little elevator cages were going higher and higher as the New York skyline began rising dramatically toward the end of the decade.

Before 1920 communication was basically limited to local newsprint and a few national general-interest magazines; by 1930 radio was on its way to linking millions with world events, and such magazine tastemakers as *Time* and the *New Yorker* had been born. Before 1920 literature was still largely bound by Victorian sentimentality. In the 1920s realism took over both novels and the theater with an output of memorable writing rarely matched anywhere else at any other time. Outside the theater and literature, the language itself was being modified by the spirit of the '20s, reflected in a bountiful harvest of slang, some of which is still with us—*hair of the dog* (all too descriptive of much of the era's homemade *hooch*), and *necking* and *petting* (no explanation necessary). You could *frame* someone for a crime, and if someone wasn't *on the up and up*, you could always tell them to *scram*!

Before 1920 most African Americans lived in hopeless servitude in the South; during the 1920s hundreds of thousands of black job seekers migrated north, thousands rediscovering their own roots in the cultural explosion called the Harlem Renaissance.

Before 1920 women were second-class citizens, denied the right to vote and largely confined to careers as wife and mother; after the Nineteenth Amendment took effect in 1920, they not only joined men in the voting booth, but with their emancipation women would overnight set startling new standards in fashion and behavior. They began taking on the roles of doctors, bankers, lawyers, and other occupations that were usually reserved for men. Their styles changed from clothes that went all the way down to their ankles, and long hair all pinned up, to short skirts and short "bobbed" haircuts.

Before 1920 the only sport that *really* counted in America was baseball; at the end of the decade, it was joined by football, tennis, golf, and boxing. Before 1920 popular music was defined largely by sentimental ballads. In fact, Jimmy Walker, New York's mayor from 1926 to 1932, wrote one of the most popular. During the decade, evangelized in such New York clubs as the Cotton Club and by radio, jazz became a universal passion.

And the modern celebrity was born, although, unlike today when many are famous only for being famous, most actually *did* something. Among the first was opera singer and film star Geraldine Farrar, and then Charles Lindbergh, who became an overnight hero the like of which we have never seen since by flying solo from an airfield adjacent to the city across the ocean to Paris. And his fame was first acknowledged with the greatest of New York's public honors, the ticker-tape parade. It was also the era when celebrity's handmaiden (or nemesis), the gossip column, was born.

In a time of seismic cultural changes, not all of them were edifying. With the passage of the Eighteenth Amendment, also in 1920, the sale of alcohol in America was made illegal. By filling the public's bottomless highball glasses (and teacups in clandestine speakeasies) with "hooch," small-time outlaws became kings of crime as the Mafia became a major player in urban life, most notoriously in New York and Chicago. And as the telephone came more and more into use in the decade, so too did the "call girl."

Politics were also famously subject to corruption, and indeed, it was a murder and mounting scandals that brought down Mayor Walker.

On a less lethal note, before 1927, when the Holland Tunnel was opened (it would be the longest underwater tunnel in the world), cars coming into an already congested Manhattan from the west had to be carried across the Hudson River by ferry.

One of the most telling changes, and one often overlooked, was educational—at least in name. Before the 1920s few people other than the children of the wealthy attended college (and then they were almost universally men). In the 1920s, effectively freed from tradition by World War I, young people began flooding into colleges—to learn, but also, for the first time for many, simply to have fun. By the end of the decade, 20 percent of American college-age youth were on campuses; a popular limerick of the time went: *She doesn't drink, She doesn't pet. She hasn't been to college yet*. But it was more than that; a good case could be made that, other than the economic boom, the social upheavals of the 1920s were largely caused, for the first time in history, by young people instead of their parents.

It was a time and, in New York, a place out of mind when, as one writer has written, "people laughed more often than cried, partied more often than worked, and dreamed more often than facing reality. Athletes [except in one tragic example, as we will see] were looked up to as heroes, authors helped people escape into a different life [sometimes tragic but most often jolly], and women dressed as flappers and started voting." It was, as Paul Johnson wrote in his landmark book, *Modern Times*: "America's most fortunate decade."

For three administrations (those of Harding, Coolidge, and Hoover), American presidents were Republican, and each one cozied up to big business, which suited most New Yorkers as just fine (other than the anarchists, socialists, and Communists who still populated Greenwich Village). Money, rather than tourism, culture, or an unusual lifestyle, has always been the city's main occupation.

Readers will notice that I probably shortchanged some weighty aspects of life in the Twenties. Perhaps I should have mentioned the city's most respected actors, the Barrymores. Ethel Barrymore actually had a theater named for her in 1928 but found few roles worthy of her talent. By the middle of the decade, brother Lionel deserted the New York stage for Hollywood, where he became a star. And brother John—the "great profile" himself—famously starred in a Broadway production of *Hamlet* in 1922, took it to London, then decamped for the film capital where he would become an even bigger star than Lionel.

Modern art had exploded on the public in the previous decade, most famously (or infamously to many) through the 1913 Armory Show, which introduced cubism to a skeptical audience. Perhaps I also should have paid some attention to the years that Georgia O'Keeffe spent honing her art in New York City (during which she was also living with Alfred Stieglitz, who, essentially, created respect for photography as an art form in the following decade). The problem, at least as I saw it, was that, as noted, the Barrymores were phasing New York out of their lives and careers, and as seminal as was the work of O'Keeffe, hers was essentially a lonely craft, at least in the 1920s.

As the theme of this book is to present the extraordinary, the "Capital" characteristics of the decade—the politics, the sports, the crime, the explosion in communications—personified by individuals who were particularly identified with them, some difficult choices had to be made.

The writer Edmund Wilson once wrote that he was struck by the fact that so many of the books and plays of the 1920s seemed to tell only what "a terrible place America is." There was Edith Wharton's *Age of Innocence*, Sinclair Lewis's *Main Street*, certainly Theodore Dreiser's *An American Tragedy*, and many more. But isn't exploring the downside as well as the gloss of a culture exactly what great writers do? F. Scott Fitzgerald's *The Great Gatsby*, unquestionably the most famous book about the 1920s, is not a celebration of the era; it is his criticism of it, albeit lyrically written.

Despite the manifold examples of the downside of the era—the bad taste and danger of homemade hooch, the lethality of the newly powerful Mafia, the sexual license found in Harlem, the political corruption of the times, and its brassiness (illustrated by both the early blonde hair dye then available to flappers and nightclub queen Texas Guinan's quips)—life in New York was like none other, before or since.

To use another slang expression of the time, for many New Yorkers, life in the 1920s was *the bees' knees*.

November 1925. James J. Walker, a former songwriter and Democratic political machine-backed candidate for New York City mayor, is about to vote, presumably, for himself. He would become New York's most popular mayor as well as the city's most scandal-laden during his tenure. Just to the right of the mayor-to-be is his wife Allie, whom he would leave for a Broadway chorus girl before his first term was finished.

Photography Collection, Miriam and Ira D. Wallach Division of Art, Prints and Photographs, The New York Public Library, Astor, Lenox and Tilden Foundations

CHAPTER 1

"Gentleman Jim," Part I, The Good Times

Mayor Jimmy Walker

The reason for his vast popularity was that Jimmy Walker somehow or other seemed to be New York brought to life in one person.

— Ed Sullivan, then a pretelevision New York newspaper columnist

On November 9, 1946, few noticed the slim, dapperly dressed man who climbed slowly to his inexpensive seat high above the twenty-yard line for the Army–Notre Dame football game at Yankee Stadium. The game, which many have hailed since as "the college football game of the century," matched the number-one college team (Army) against number two (Notre Dame). It was, at the time, effectively the national championship game.

The teams tied 0–0, and Notre Dame was awarded the National Championship by the Associated Press.

Two decades before, that lonely man's arrival and progress to what would have been a far better seat would have been greeted with near hysteria; during those earlier days (and in retrospect), his millions of admirers considered him the Mayor of the Century. But time, scandal, and the capriciousness of fate had by '46 rendered him more or less invisible to legions of heretofore devoted followers.

But forgotten? No, he was not, as events would remind the city the following week. On November 18 James John Walker,

New York's once-beloved bad-boy, Jazz Age mayor, died of a cerebral thrombosis at Manhattan's Doctors Hospital. His passing was marked with the kind of banner headlines that limned his every move two decades earlier. "Gentleman Jim," the jaunty, silk-hatted symbol of the Roaring Twenties, was gone, like the era he had come to personify. But for hundreds of thousands of New Yorkers—maybe millions—"Gentleman Jim" was, as Viking Press rhapsodized in promoting *Beau James*, his friend (and Hearst journalist) Gene Fowler's biography of the mayor, ". . . a pageant, a panorama, a fable. His good deeds were as varied as New York's population; his misbehaviors as famous as its skyline. He outraged many, he delighted more, he never bored a human being in his life. He was 'Mr. New York.'"

Fowler's *Beau James*—as Walker was called by many in his heyday—served as the basis of a 1957 film starring Bob Hope and *Jimmy*, a short-lived 1969 Broadway musical. "Beau" was an appropriate term, colloquially evoking both the affection in which Walker was held as well as the image of England's early 1800s dandy Beau Brummell, known for his sartorial elegance as well as his amorous adventures. Jimmy was also a sharp dresser who was known to often change his outfits five times daily and reportedly owned seventy suits that cost an average of $165 apiece ($1,900 today). He didn't really care that many Englishmen, more comfortable with the conservative Savile Row styles of the time, sniffed at his slimly tapered, pinch-waisted, cuffless style. He was chauffeured around town in a black, silver-trimmed Duesenberg, the era's ultimate American automobile, although Walker never learned to drive and preferred speeds under 20 miles per hour. The vehicle cost $17,000 at the time, the equivalent of some $200,000 today.

And like the historic Beau, Jimmy also fancied the ladies. Although married, his affairs with "chorus girls" were widely known. Eventually, he left his wife, Janet—known as "Allie" by all—for a series of showgirls, most publicly one named Betty Compton (who would become his second wife) without impairing his popularity. Well beyond the time when he was forced to resign by New York governor Franklin D. Roosevelt in 1932 amid corruption scandals and go into self-imposed exile in Europe, he still could do no wrong as far as the vast majority of the city's six million inhabitants were concerned.

Later in life Jimmy said that the two people he most admired were his father and Charles Francis Murphy, the boss or "Grand Sachem" of Tammany Hall from 1902 until 1924. Then the nation's most powerful political machine, Tammany's support would launch Walker's political career. (The character Jim Gettys in Orson Welles's celebrated film *Citizen Kane* was based on Murphy, of whom Walker would later say: "The brains of Tammany Hall lie in Calvary Cemetery." Located across the 59th Street Bridge in Queens, Calvary is also the resting place for most of the Walker clan and his wife's family, as well as a number of 1920s personalities including—in this book—the Mafia's Joe Masseria, nightclub queen Texas Guinan, and Governor Al Smith.)

Jimmy Walker was born June 19, 1881, in a flat at 101 Leroy Street in Greenwich Village. To put the era in context, there was then no Washington Square Arch (that would come in 1889), France's gift of the Statue of Liberty had not yet arrived, and, other than two massive piers in the East River, the Brooklyn Bridge was still a blueprint. The city was still gas lit, although Thomas Edison's electric lights would soon arrive on lower Broadway; transportation was by horse-car or by cars pulled by smoky steam engines on the elevated railroads; and baseball, which would soon be a national obsession (Walker was a passionate fan of the sport), was only a generation old.

But how fast things would change. Within forty years, bustle-clad matrons parading up Broadway, once more of a shopping street than now, had been replaced by the flappers who drank and smoked indiscriminately; horses had been replaced by the Model T and then the Model A; and skyscrapers, New York's signature contribution to urban architecture, were rising everywhere. A world war had been fought and won, and the stock market, which only reached its first million-share day in 1886, had soared to heights undreamed of by the most optimistic investors.

When Jimmy was five he and his family moved up the street into a three-story brick townhouse at number 6 St. Luke's Place. It would remain his home for decades. His father, William Henry Walker ("Billy" to everyone), whom he adored, had emigrated from Ireland in 1857. He made his living as a lumber dealer. More importantly, as a creature of the Tammany Hall Democratic political machine, he became the Democratic assemblyman and alderman from Greenwich Village when it was still an enclave of German and Irish immigrants like himself. Eventually, he became New York City's Commissioner of Public Buildings. Jimmy's mother, Ellen Roon, was the daughter of a local saloonkeeper. Jimmy grew up, as *Time* once pointed out, "with the cigar smoke of Tammany Hall in his nostrils."

After attending St. Francis Xavier High School, La Salle Academy (a business school), and New York Law School, Jimmy's career took a sharp turn—over the objections of his father, who wanted him to take the bar. He had often confided in a fellow law student, Harry Carey, who would go on to become a famous Hollywood movie star, that he wanted to be a songwriter. At the time America's popular music industry was centered on Manhattan's West Twenty-Eighth Street, then (and since, in legend) known as Tin Pan Alley, so it was not surprising that Walker was drawn there. He soon found sporadic work as a lyricist and, in August 1908 hit the big time with his ballad "Will You Love Me in December (As You Do in May)?" He didn't know it at the time, but the title could have been a metaphor for his career.

Jim was twenty-seven when the sheet music for his "December/May" song was published, and the first thing he did when it became clear that it would become a hit was to borrow five hundred dollars from his publisher and buy three custom-made suits, four pairs of shoes, a dozen silk shirts, three fedora hats, and a walking stick. The second thing he did was to accept the Tammany sponsorship for a run for the state assembly (which he won in November 1909). Two years later, and after fulfilling his father's dream of passing the bar, he married Janet "Allie" Allen, a singer who plugged his songs.

As happened with most events throughout his life, Walker was late for his wedding; two hours in fact. His best man was to take him to the church, he explained, but had been diverted by watching a fire. The organist kept the congregation diverted by playing Jimmy's "December/May" song slowly, explaining that since he was in a church, he was playing it in Latin. After the couple's return from their Atlantic City honeymoon, Jimmy was summoned by the Tammany leader, Charles F. Murphy, who announced that he would be supporting the former songwriter for a state senate seat the following year. As far as Murphy was concerned, the move was entirely political. "You have many friends on Broadway and in the sports world," he told Walker. "Tammany Hall has long neglected these interesting people. I believe you are making us popular there."

Walker served in the New York State Senate for eleven years, from 1914 until he became mayor in 1926. From the start it was apparent to all that he was a far different breed of politician. For one thing, unlike most newly elected solons, when Walker joined the New York State Assembly in 1910, he didn't sit around learning the ropes but dove right into the legislative maelstrom, debating issues and displaying an aptitude for parliamentary tactics. Al Smith, his mentor and then an assembly leader, said of him: "This boy is a greater strategist than General Sheridan, and he rides twice as fast."

Walker's style, then and later, was always more that of an actor than a politician; he was, in fact, possibly the greatest actor that ever trod the staid stage of the state capitol in Albany. He had a spontaneous wit and also spoke extemporaneously, using the floor of the assembly and later the senate chamber as a personal theater. His soft tones could be heard in the farthest reaches of the senate chamber; his louder tones shook the rafters. Like a great actor, Walker also had a full range of stage business, toying with his handkerchief, tugging at his waistcoat (he would always wear three-piece suits), and playing to the galleries packed with growing admirers by gazing upward to them while speaking. David Belasco, the legendary Broadway playwright, director, and producer, occasionally sent his actors to Albany during the January-to-April sessions, "to learn something from the little master." Walker was acutely aware of his talent, once remarking to his older brother, George, that he was merely an actor in a play and that he had to give the kind of performance that was expected of him.

In fact, all this hoopla over his bouncy personality tended to shade his real accomplishments in Albany. Although he sponsored hundreds of bills in his fourteen years upstate (most involving the welfare and rights of the underprivileged), he is mostly remembered for sponsoring bills to legalize boxing in New York and to permit baseball games and the operation of motion picture houses on Sundays. His habit of being late was also escalating. When most of his colleagues were going to sleep, Jimmy, as would be his lifetime habit, was only just getting going. He subscribed to the code of the writer Richard Harding Davis, who once remarked that a civilized man never went to bed on the same day he rose from sleep. Jimmy was also an excellent dancer. He had a reputation for being a heavy drinker, but according to his long-time friend and biographer, Gene Fowler, the rumor was due more to his natural flushed complexion and public antipathy to Prohibition as a blue-nose violation of personal liberty than to drinking too much. According to another close friend, he was a drinker but not a drunkard, in his younger days at least drinking only an occasional glass of beer or wine. For social events while in Albany he drank mostly wine and, as mayor, had an occasional highball but liked champagne best.

Possibly his most important battles in his senate years occurred during the ratification of the Eighteenth Amendment. He opened his speech in opposition to Prohibition with "this measure was born in hypocrisy and there it will die." He was right, of course, as he was when he predicted that Prohibition would cause widespread disrespect of the law and would be impossible to enforce, adding: "In fact, even the army and navy of the United States are not large enough to enforce this unenforceable mockery." How correct this prediction turned out to be will be gone into more detail in the next chapter.

Seeing his son become a state senator was the proudest moment in Billy Walker's life; he even dreamed that his Jimmy would become president one day. Sadly, Billy Walker died in 1916, a decade before Jimmy came as close as he would to the presidency by becoming the mayor of New York; nevertheless, it should be remembered that at the time the New York mayor's job was considered the second most powerful in America.

Jimmy Walker and Al Smith began to part ways as early as 1913, and Walker's carousing, which the staid Smith despised, wasn't the only reason. One thing that really griped the future governor was Walker's pet name for him, "Algie," as well as Smith's belief that when he gave a political Tammany member a command, he should obey it. But what really deepened the divide between the pair of Democratic and Roman Catholic politicians, was Smith's support of an increase in the New York City subway fare from a nickel to seven cents, which he ordered Walker, then senate majority leader, to bring about. Walker defused the situation with one of his trademark humorous parables and won undying popular support in New York City by fighting to keep the five-cent fare.

Another problem between the pair was Walker's opposition to what was called the clean books bill, designed by the blue noses in the legislature to "protect womanhood and the home from ruinous prose" (D. H. Lawrence's works were most frequently cited by the bill's supporters). Although opposed to smut, Walker strongly believed that the creative artist should be kept free from bigotry, and he succeeded in killing the bill with a stinging phrase that became famous: "Why all this talk about womanhood? I've never heard of a girl being ruined by a book."

Speaking of girls . . . by 1928, a little more than two years into his first term as mayor, it was an open secret that Jim was, as Fowler says, "finding romantic interests away from St. Luke's Place," although until they finally divorced five years later, the long-suffering Allie refused to speak about his dalliances. Apparently, the affair had begun many years before, when the then-mayor, John P. Mitchel, introduced Jim to a petite Ziegfeld Follies star named Vonnie Shelton. Follies colleagues of Shelton included the later Hollywood star Billie Burke, who was married to Florenz Ziegfeld, and W. C. Fields, the company's star comedian. Fields would soon become famous as both an actor and the era's greatest curmudgeon, and he became a close friend of the future mayor.

Although in 1925 there was no evidence of a movement to make Jim mayor of New York, it was clear to many that the end was at hand for the old order, most prominently personified by Mitchel's successor, the long-winded, stuffy John F. Hylan, whom the *New York Times* called "an imperfect demagogue." After the state senate adjourned in April, Jim returned to the city, spending his evenings in the theater district and his days at his law office, a small room in a partnership of a friend's law office at 61 Broadway. Although he apparently had a lot of opportunities to defend clients in criminal cases—mostly Prohibition lawbreakers—he avoided doing so most of the time. Apparently, the reason was to avoid the reputation of being a "mouthpiece" for the gangsters who, after enforcement of the Eighteenth Amendment began in 1920, were making millions supplying liquor for the city's speakeasies, eventually to number some thirty thousand.

It was Governor Al Smith (with, of course, Tammany backing) as well as Mayor Hylan's lackluster record that propelled Walker into City Hall (Vonnie Shelton was told in no uncertain terms to get out of sight and "out of Jim's mind" during the campaign; she hid out in Cuba). His Republican opponent in the November 1925 election was Frank D. Waterman of the Waterman Pen Company. Like the campaign that followed, their initial debate at a union-organized luncheon still stands out as one of the most gentlemanly contests in American political history; no epithets were thrown, there was no name-calling and none of the personal attacks that have come to poison contemporary politics. Walker even went so far as to comment that Waterman was so superior to him (especially in business, as Walker had by then spent sixteen years doing the "business of government") that he was tempted to vote for Waterman himself. He didn't, of course, and won a landslide victory over Waterman, who by election time was crippled by, among other things, the revelation that a Florida hotel he owned banned Jewish guests.

One of Walker's first decisions was where he would live, since, until Mayor Fiorello LaGuardia's occupancy of Gracie Mansion, New York's mayors had no publicly owned residence. During the campaign Walker lived at the Commodore Hotel, but after his inauguration, his wife, Allie, was determined that they would live in the St. Luke's Place townhouse. When Jim countered that it was really too run down, a political supporter stepped in and offered to pay the estimated twenty-five-thousand-dollar remodeling cost. The same month the house was adorned with the two things the city then provided its mayors: One was a pair of tall iron pedestals flanking the mayor's front door, topped by lights with spiked crowns that burned all night. The other freebie was a police booth at the front door that was removed when the mayor left office. The lights remained, unlighted, unless the former mayor paid for the electricity.

After becoming mayor Jim saw no reason to change his daily routine. He would arise about 10 a.m., read the newspaper headlines (he would rarely read an entire news story) while sipping a cup of tea at a nearby table, get back in bed, begin making telephone calls, and continue scanning the newspaper headlines. He would then get up, have a light breakfast, and retire to the bathroom for an hour or so while his valet dressed a mannequin in the clothes selected for the day. The valet kept a flatiron on a hot plate just outside the bedroom so that, after Walker okayed the outfit, any slight wrinkle could be immediately removed.

Despite such a seemingly lazy start to the day and his partying at night, Walker managed to accomplish a lot, according to a *New York Times* editorial a month and a half after he entered office. Mayor William O'Dwyer, a successor, explained why to Gene Fowler: "He played hard, but he worked harder . . . after some personal experience with City Hall, and after a close study of the records of my distinguished predecessors, I must admit that Jim Walker as mayor got more things done in two hours than any of the rest of us could do in ten."

Walker had no choice.

In its day the amount of work for the New York mayor—bills, petitions, complaints, requests, and the rest of the paraphernalia of governance—was second only to that of the White House. And there were also endless official recognitions and receptions. During his six years in office, Walker hosted three hundred open-air events on the steps outside City Hall and awarded keys of the city, scrolls, and medals to honored visitors—three times to Admiral Richard Byrd (Queen Marie of Romania was his first royal honoree). As a sort of city greeter at such occasions, Walker chose a former Wanamaker's department store general manager named Grover Whalen to be more or less the "official" face for the city (chapter 20). Whalen had built the two-mile runway at Roosevelt Field on Long Island—then said to be the longest runway in the world—from which Charles Lindbergh, with Whalen's grudging approval, launched his flight to Paris and immortality on May 20,

1927 (Lindy needed the lengthy runway as his Ford Tri-motor was overloaded with fuel). On the night of Lindy's triumphant return and ticker-tape parade, Whalen brought the twenty-five-year-old hero to a party given by William Randolph Hearst at the Warwick Hotel. Lindy sat on the floor with actress Jeanne Eagels while Mayor Walker played the piano for two hours.

Gentleman Jim's problems began creeping up early in his first term as mayor, although few saw them as such—certainly not Walker himself, who by then was riding such a publicity wave that journalist Douglas Gilbert wrote in the *World-Telegram* that "New York wore James J. Walker on its lapel." While he was vacationing in Florida, the news got out that a bus contract, awarded by the Board of Estimate, had been obtained with bribes. So far, no one was paying much attention to how his many trips—including a highly publicized European trip featuring a visit to Castlecomer, Ireland, where his father had been born—were financed. That would come later.

As a perfect example of how unimportant his use of power and government money seemed at the time, when Jimmy left for Europe in August 1927 (with forty-three suits plus dozens of shirts and baskets of shoes), he was seen off by a crowd of New York powerhouses, including Cardinal Hayes, both New York senators (Robert F. Wagner and Royal Copeland), Congressman LaGuardia, Al Jolson, and a crowd of Tammany members and policemen, along with the police glee club, which, on the pier, sang Irving Berlin's musical salute to Walker, "Gimme Jimmy for Mine." In Europe he was hosted by everyone from the president of Ireland to Mussolini. In Paris, where the American Legion was having their convention, he reviewed a parade of the veterans with French Marshal Foch and America's General Pershing, who had commanded the American forces in World War I.

The previous December, a millionaire publisher named Paul Block became the foremost of Walker's group of rich admirers. No one asked—then—why Block provided Walker with a private railway car for his travels, why he paid many of the mayor's hotel bills and personal expenses, or why, as it would explosively be unveiled during former Judge Samuel Seabury's probe of municipal malfeasance in 1932, the pair opened a joint stock brokerage account from which Walker, who contributed nothing to the account, later admitted he had made $246,692 after taxes (some $3.9 million today).

But the thing that would change his life, then and ever afterward, was an invitation to attend a musical titled *Okay* at the Imperial Theater. Invited to go backstage to meet the show's star, Gertrude Lawrence, Jimmy was immediately attracted to one of the showgirls, a dimpled brunette named Betty Compton. Initially, she dismissed Walker's invitations to join him at various social functions, but when Jim, knowing how hard it would be to find a taxi following a three-thousand guest dinner honoring Mrs. William Randolph Hearst's charity work, gave her a ride home in his Duesenberg with its newly mounted siren screaming, Betty admitted that she was impressed. Although the romance took several months more to get off the ground, both acknowledged that this was the beginning. The following year, 1928, Jim decided to leave his wife and St. Luke's Place and moved into the Ritz (where Paul Block also lived).

By then Walker's absences from City Hall were also attracting the notice of the press. Still, his public didn't care, excusing seven excursions to destinations that included Paris, Havana, and Hollywood, as goodwill trips. But it was bothering his supporters. After Jim repeatedly ducked Governor Al Smith, who wanted to confer with him about the city's growing transit problems to free himself to run for president, Smith said in a sarcastic pun on Jimmy's song: "If you make a date with Jim in December, he will keep it next May."

And then serious problems began when, on November 4, 1928, Arnold Rothstein, considered New York's most notorious gambler, mob banker, and fixer famous for manipulating the outcome of the 1919 World Series (also considered Broadway's biggest banker), was assassinated. Walker, with Betty, was dining at a suburban nightclub when someone whispered in his ear. The famous bandmaster Vincent Lopez was appearing at the club and recalled asking Walker, who seemed upset: "Are you all right, Jim?" "Not exactly," the mayor replied. "Rothstein has just been shot, Vince. And that means trouble from here in."

Prohibition ,which arrived in 1920, would dramatically change the lives of most Americans by forcing them to break the law to get liquor. Nowhere was this more dramatically evident than in New York City, where thousands of speakeasies served up illegal hootch to thirsty patrons. After Prohibition ended in 1933, many "speaks" became nightclubs; the longest lasting was the Stork Club, originally backed by mob money and run by a former bootlegger named Sherman Billingsley (center). By the 1930s the Stork Club had become the most famous nightclub in the country, patronized by the likes of writers Ernest Hemingway (l) and John O'Hara (r).

Courtesy of Stork Club Enterprises, LLC

CHAPTER 2

Prohibition

Sherman Billingsley's Stork Club

"You'll be the doorman, keep out everybody you know. . . ."

— Stork Club owner Sherman Billingsley cautioning a new employee who had bragged about his underworld connections to refuse admittance to "low-life" gangsters (mob bosses like Frank Costello were welcomed)

At the stroke of midnight, January 16, 1920, with the ratification of the Eighteenth Amendment to the U.S. Constitution by the legislature of Utah, the thirty-sixth state to do so and therefore a mere formality, Prohibition became the law of the land. From that moment until 1933, when the law was repealed, every citizen of the United States was denied the right to buy or sell alcoholic drink. But instead of regulating social behavior and eliminating the scourge of what "dry" supporters called "the Devil's Brew," Prohibition incited Americans to bend or break the law by any and all means possible.

Formerly law-abiding citizens frequented speakeasies—clandestine "clubs" where people drank often dangerous concoctions often brewed by other formerly law-abiding citizens in homemade stills or mixed up by the gallon in their bathtubs (hence the famous "bathtub" gin of the era; whiskey was faked by coloring alcohol with iodine or caramel). Druggists found their business booming; in fact the number of drugstores in the country burgeoned because of an exception in the new law that permitted them to dispense "medicinal quantities" of alcohol. Everyone, from petty criminals to the most upstanding citizens, found Prohibition a license to get rich quick. Even the clergy, allowed to purchase communion wine, found themselves in the bootlegging business. It was not by accident that the opportunity spawned the growth of the Mafia in New York from neighborhood crime operations to citywide—indeed national—power (chapter 3).

Pioneer America was always a hard-drinking place. Even in 1630 saloons constituted one-quarter of all the businesses in Peter Stuyvesant's New York City, then known as New Amsterdam. But that was the city; in some parts of rural America (and America was basically a rural nation until the early twentieth century), liquor was so prized that it was often used as the local currency, with prices for goods displayed in pints and gallons of whiskey.

Nevertheless, from Kansas, where Carrie Nation began axing saloons to splinters in the 1890s, to Detroit, where teetotaler (and, incidentally, violently anti-Semitic) Henry Ford had his workers' homes searched to make sure they were dry, the temperance movement grew in strength. Preachers shouted of the dangers of drink from the pulpit, claiming "John Barleycorn" (slang for liquor at the time) as the cause of everything from melancholy to madness. And naturally, as the Reverend Mark Matthews of Seattle's First Presbyterian Church warned: "The saloon . . . takes your sweet, innocent daughter, robs her of her virtue, and transforms her into a brazen, wanton harlot." Some physicians even claimed that excessive drinking would lead to a body's spontaneous combustion, citing case after fictional case of people bursting into flames kindled by internal alcohol fumes.

But Prohibition was at best a Pyrrhic victory for the temperance crowd. More than one observer has pointed out that Prohibition was, in fact, the last gasp of ruralism, which finally fell to the demand for liquor, especially among the vast numbers of immigrants from Europe. Most immigrants never understood the point of Prohibition, especially the many new arrivals of German descent who loved their beer, the beer-and-whiskey-swilling Irish, and the wine-drinking Italians. Prominent in leading the "dry" charge was the Women's Christian Temperance League, mostly made up of middle-class wives of doctors, lawyers, and wealthy farmers who wanted to do nothing more than better the lives of the working class—even if it didn't especially want to be reformed. A perfect example of how out of touch the reformers were with the people they wanted to "better" was a plan to replace the hated saloons with coffeehouses.

And then there was the Anti-Saloon League, made up primarily of Protestant businessmen. Wayne Wheeler, an amoral entrepreneur, was drawn to the league not for religious or social reasons but solely because it offered a way for him to become powerful, and he did so by appealing directly to many people's jingoistic prejudices. "God made the country, but man made the town; un-American, lawless and wet." He reserved his loudest scorn for the "Irish, the continentals with their beer and wine, and the guzzling wet Democrats in the North and East." It was Wheeler, in fact, who conceived and wrote (and rewrote) the bill that would become the Eighteenth Amendment to the Constitution, although it was (and still is) commonly called the Volstead Act.

Andrew J. Volstead was an obscure Republican senator from Minnesota who, as chairman of the Senate Judiciary Committee, oversaw the passage of the bill in the Senate after three months of debate before it was then adopted by the House of Representatives. President Woodrow Wilson, then seriously ill and weakened in Congress by his unsuccessful campaign to keep America in the League of Nations, vetoed the bill twice on both constitutional and ethical grounds but was overridden. Mississippi was the first state to ratify the amendment, which, to become law, required ratification by a two-thirds majority of the then forty-eight states. A year later Nebraska was the last state needed for ratification, and one year later (a year of grace was provided to implement the new law) it went into effect.

When Wheeler was writing the bill, he made a number of mistakes that would make the amendment completely ineffective and would spur the greatest growth in crime the country had or has ever seen. For one thing, the bill hopelessly underestimated people's determination to get alcoholic beverages, whatever the risk, and the ingenuity displayed to get around the law's provisions could not have been imagined. The law allowed some exceptions that opened doors for exploitation, among them that industrial alcohol was allowed to be manufactured and sold, as well as sacramental wine, some patent medicines, and toiletries. Alcohol could also be obtained with a doctor's prescription, provided it was for no more than a pint and no oftener than every ten days. The act, which banned any advertising of alcohol and authorized the destruction of liquor stored for sale and the vehicles that transported it, said nothing about consumption in private homes. Nevertheless, Billy Sunday, the most famous evangelist of the day, echoed Wheeler's optimism: "The reign of tears is over," he shouted to a huge revival gathering in Norfolk, Virginia, soon after the ratification "The slums will soon be only a memory. We will turn our prisons into factories and our jails into storehouses. Men will walk upright now, women will smile and children will laugh. Hell will be forever for rent." As he was celebrating, six armed masked men in Chicago held up a pharmacy warehouse and made off with $100,000 ($1,090,000 today) worth of whiskey classified for "medicinal use"; i.e., to be dispensed only with a prescription.

Adding to the turmoil, to supplement the real thing smuggled in from Canada or overseas (Joseph Kennedy, President Kennedy's father, was one of the many powerful businessmen who couldn't resist an occasional bootlegging flutter, albeit usually behind the mask of a dummy company), illegal manufacturers sprang up everywhere, mixing sometimes weird concoctions to pass for real "hooch," as slang called it. We mentioned mixing alcohol with iodine or burnt sugar to pass—visually, anyway—for whiskey; something called "sweet whiskey" was made with nitrous ether, alcohol mixed with nitric and euphoric acid. Instead of grain alcohol, some makers even used wood alcohol, which is poisonous. The cocktail was born of Prohibition because the additions—usually fruit juices—were found to be the only way to disguise the often horrible taste of homemade or manufactured fake booze. Not surprisingly, the results were often tragic. It has been estimated that during the thirteen "dry" years, tens of thousands were poisoned by bad liquor.

But given the "anything goes" mood of the 1920s, drinking—whatever you drank—became the thing to do; as much as quenching a thirst for alcohol, drinking was seen as defying the law and a statement of personal freedom.

Most of the real stuff was smuggled across the border from Canada, but nearly as much was brought in at night along America's thousands of beach miles from Maine to Malibu. Records from the famous French champagne firm Moët et Chandon show that its shipments to Canada increased twofold between 1922 and 1929; following Prohibition's repeal in 1933, they dropped precipitously. The Bahamas became a sort of halfway (ware)house between European and Caribbean (rum) manufacturers and the United States. So profitable was the liquor traffic through Nassau that more than a million dollars (about $13 million in today's currency) was spent on harbor improvements alone.

One essential thing the smugglers needed, though, was boats, and this problem solved itself after the stock market crash. Sally Rand, the famous fan dancer, explained that on the West Coast alone: "Beautiful yachts that cost a million dollars apiece were being sold to bootleggers for five or ten thousand dollars. They had been owned by people who jumped out of windows." In New England even humble fishermen were involved—smugglers simply dumped barrels of booze overboard, and fishermen from Long Island Sound to Cape Cod netted them and delivered the haul along with their legitimate catch to waiting customers ashore. Part of the entertainment at East Hampton's exclusive

Maidstone Club was to watch Coast Guard vessels chasing rum-running fishing boats; as a perfect example of the hypocrisy surrounding Prohibition, the club, which served any kind of liquor a guest wanted, was never once raided during Prohibition . . . its members were too influential.

The most famous rumrunner (as those smuggling liquor by boat were usually called) was Bill McCoy, who bought whiskey in the Bahamas for eight dollars a case and took it on his ship, the *Arethusa*, to Martha's Vineyard, where he sold it for an average net profit of some $300,000 ($3.8 million today) per trip. When competitors began copying his way of wrapping whiskey kegs in burlap pyramids to pack more into his boat, the phrase "the real McCoy" came to denote authentic, quality hooch.

Ex-president William Howard Taft immediately spotted the problem with Prohibition and accurately predicted the future. He wrote, "Those who think that an era of clean living and clear thinking is at hand are living in a fool's paradise." The law had been passed, "against the views and practices of a majority of people who live in many of the large cities," Taft continued. "The business of manufacturing alcohol, liquor and beer will go out of the hands of law-abiding members of the community and will be transferred to the quasi-criminal classes." There would be no "quasi-" about it, as time would quickly show.

The plan also had another fault that few saw at the time. Wheeler's amendment placed the Prohibition Bureau under the Treasury Department, not, as logic would have suggested, as part of the Justice Department. Worse, it exempted Prohibition Bureau employees from civil service; thus, across the nation recruitment of enforcement personnel became a political rather than a career issue and in the hands of local politicians. As the jobs paid only $2,300 a year, corruption was built in. In Philadelphia in 1921 it was discovered that the local director of the Prohibition Bureau was part of a plot to remove seven hundred thousand gallons of whiskey with a street value of $4 million ($49 million today) from a government-bonded warehouse (before the case came to trial, the evidence, all seven hundred thousand gallons, mysteriously disappeared).

Some agents rose above temptation, of course; the most famous was probably the "Untouchable" Eliot Ness in Chicago. Among New York's "Untouchables" were an unlikely pair who, for a time, became the most famous Prohibition agents in America: Izzy Einstein and his partner Moe Smith. The five-foot, 225-pound Izzy, called "the man of a thousand disguises" for his ability to infiltrate bootlegging operations, alone accounted for 20 percent of all cited violations of the Volstead Act in Manhattan between 1920 and 1925. Variously disguised as a fisherman (on Long Island) or a German, a football player, or an Italian immigrant, he would buy illegal liquor (secreting the evidence in a bottle in the lining of his coat), then arrest the seller. He sometimes made twenty to thirty arrests a day, eventually totaling (according to him) 4,932 arrests.

He and his partner, Moe, would often visit the city's top restaurants—Moe playing a naïve out-of-towner, and Izzy the knowledgeable native—to get the owner to serve them liquor and then make an arrest. Izzy, who spoke Yiddish, would even wheedle sacramental wine out of compliant rabbis before taking them in. As it turned out, "Izzy and Moe" were too successful for their own good. By November 1925 they had offended so many in the police, state, and federal government that Roy Haynes, the Prohibition commissioner, fired them both under the pretext of an "administrative reorganization."

The illegal profits by bootleggers became so huge and commonplace that, as hypocritical as it seems, twenty months after Prohibition became the law of the land, the Internal Revenue Service was trying to figure out how to get millions of dollars in excess profits tax from the lawbreakers.

It took a while for the country to realize that Prohibition simply wasn't workable. As Mabel Willebrandt wrote in 1928, after having served eight years as the deputy attorney general in charge of Prohibition enforcement: "Other than the slavery issue in the nineteenth century, no political, economic, or moral issue had so engrossed and divided all the people of America as did Prohibition." Politicians—especially politicians—were part of the problem. "The truth is," Willebrandt added, "in New York as in other cities, it is immensely profitable to the politicians to let the speakeasies flourish." But, she also said when predicting the repeal of the Eighteenth Amendment four years later, "the people of America do not want and will not permit an army of officers of the federal government to enforce law and order in local counties and cities . . . it is repugnant to the basic principles of our form of government." In the minds of millions, the problem wasn't the bootleggers—they were doing nothing more than filling a demand, a good, old-fashioned tenet of capitalism in an era when even the president, Calvin Coolidge, claimed "the business of America is business. . . ." People simply couldn't stand the feds meddling in their lives, whether they were on the take or not.

Al Smith, New York governor and president wannabe who lost in 1928 to Herbert Hoover and whose dreams were finally ended when FDR trounced him at the Democratic nominating convention in 1932, was one of the few impeccably honest "wet" politicians. Another was Congressman Fiorello LaGuardia, who would, by running on a fusion ticket, become the city's mayor in 1934. Three years earlier, after tipping off the press, he marched into Room 150 of the Old House of Representatives Building in Washington in a bartender's uniform and proceeded to demonstrate how easy it was to make beer with legally purchased ingredients. The Prohibition bureau was furious, and the branch in Albany, New York, said that anyone caught making the LaGuardia–formula beer would be arrested.

LaGuardia, tipping off the press again, later walked into a drugstore at 95 Lenox Avenue in Albany, purchased the necessary ingredients for making his illegal beer, and waited to be arrested. Of course, no Prohibition agent showed up, and a lone city policeman refused to arrest him. The story was carried in newspapers across America, but if you think he did it as a political stunt, you'd be wrong. The "Little Flower," as he was called, was convinced that Prohibition was destroying the country by creating contempt and disregard for the law, and this was his way of proving it.

By the time Willebrandt and LaGuardia were explaining why Prohibition couldn't work (LaGuardia, while in congress, often complained that Prohibition was in direct conflict with the Fourteenth Amendment, which "deals with human rights and liberties and is as dead as a doornail in certain sections of the country"), deaths from bad liquor were piling up. On New Year's Day 1927, there were forty-one deaths from adulterated alcohol in New York City, and it was estimated that by then more than fifty thousand people had died in the country at large, plus countless thousands more paralyzed or blinded by the stuff.

By then organizations supporting repeal (or modification) of Prohibition were forming. Even the American Bar Association, as well as several state bar associations, was challenging the legality of the Volstead Act, and the then giant American Federation of Labor had never stopped lobbying for 2.5 percent beer (instead of the 0.5 percent "near beer" that was permitted). The American Legion, to which millions of World War I veterans belonged, would soon come out for an end to it all.

By 1932 when, in the middle of the Great Depression, Herbert Hoover ran again for the presidency, he was overwhelmed by FDR. Although Prohibition wasn't the issue—the economy was—by then repeal had become moot, but not for the reason many people think. The government needed money. And one way to get it, as FDR said to a cheering audience in St. Louis, would be to "increase the federal revenue several hundred million dollars a year by placing a tax on beer."

It turned out to be rather easy to get rid of the law. On December 6, 1932, three months before FDR would be inaugurated, a resolution was passed to void the Eighteenth Amendment. It had been delayed only a few days by the filibuster of one senator, Morris Sheppard of Texas, which shows how weak the dry lobby had become. As with the passage of the Volstead Act, the Twenty-third Amendment, which would render the Eighteenth Amendment null and void, required the ratification of two-thirds of the states. That occurred in December 1933, when Utah voted for it. By then President Roosevelt had already taken the lead by successfully asking Congress to amend the act's provisions and raise the legally allowed alcoholic content of beer from 0.5 percent to 3.2 percent.

The celebrating on the night of December 5, 1933, the day the sale and consumption of liquor became legal again, didn't last long . . . there were no liquor stores, and reputable hard liquor was difficult to come by (there is a picture from the era showing the interior of a New York bank transformed into a temporary liquor store).

But it was over. The journalist H. L. Mencken was a curmudgeon and a humorist whose Swiftian style of irony is largely lost today. He was exaggerating—but not by much when you consider the overall impact on American lives—when he wrote: "Prohibition [lasted] twelve years, ten months, and nineteen days. It seemed almost a geologic epoch while it was going on, and the human suffering that it entailed must have been a fair match for that of the Black Death or the Thirty Years War."

For one thing, Prohibition changed American attitudes about organized crime; the nation had become passive about breaking the law. Prohibition, as we will see, turned the New York Mafia, as well as organized crime in other cities, including, of course, Chicago, into big-business operations. Along the way many mob bosses have even been transmogrified into cultural icons, as witnessed by the tremendous popularity of the *Godfather* films, which were more true to real life than people admit. One writer said that Prohibition "made outlaws into kings." Prohibition, as author Edward Behr said in his book *Prohibition: Thirteen Years*

That Changed America, was the beginning of organized crime in America.

Some major bootleggers went legit. Joseph Kennedy became the official distributor of Haig and Haig scotch and Gordon's gin even before Prohibition's end; Sam Bronfman, Canada's biggest bootlegger (and mafioso Lucky Luciano's biggest supplier) founded Seagram's; Frank Costello and his friends founded Alliance Distributors selling the same brands they smuggled during the 1920s (King's Ransom, House of Lords whiskey). Meyer Lansky, along with Luciano and Bugsy Siegel, set up Capitol Wines and Spirits and became the leading importer of French wines, scotch, and Canadian whisky.

In 1929 a bootlegger named Sherman Billingsley opened a speakeasy in a brownstone at 132 West Fifty-Eighth Street, just down the block from his apartment at 152 West Fifth-Eighth Street, and a legend was born. Billingsley had begun selling illegal liquor in a drugstore and to local Native Americans back home in Enid, Oklahoma, when he was twelve and later ran bootleg liquor from Canada while managing three speakeasies in Detroit. He named his second location the Stork Club and soon moved it to East Fifty-First Street (after all, the money was then on the East Side). When Prohibition agents closed his new place, the Stork Club found its permanent home for more than the next thirty years when, in 1934, it opened at 3 East Fifty-Third Street.

Billingsley had come to New York looking for his brother and liked the place so much he decided to stay. But no one, not even Billingsley himself, could have imagined that, even during Prohibition and after repeal when the place went "legit" as a nightclub, his Stork Club would reign for so long as the city's—which is to say probably the world's—swankiest and most glamorous watering hole. It was, for most of its life, the place to see and be seen by film and theater stars, sports icons, society wannabes (real society would rarely go to a club) and, in its early days, more than a few gangsters. The Stork Club, along with its equally sophisticated younger rival, El Morocco, became the stages on which an entire social phenomenon was nurtured and grew famous (or notorious, if you will): "café society."

Today the original East Fifty-Third Street site, where, for a generation, the street was clogged nightly with Rolls-Royces and Cadillacs, is now a pocket park, bought from Billingsley after "the Stork" (as everyone called it) closed, by CBS chairman William Paley, who turned it into a park and dedicated it to his parents.

Of course, Billingsley didn't make it happen all by himself. It was an era when, astonishingly (according to writer Ralph Blumenthal in his book *Stork Club*), one in ten New Yorkers had criminal records. So it isn't surprising that the ex-bootlegger's financing was said to have come from Mafia boss Frank Costello. Maybe it did; it is a known fact, however, that three of Billingsley's partners in the club were gangsters, and Costello was a business partner with one of them, named Owney Madden. Madden, a former English child star turned protection enforcer who gained the nickname "Clay Pigeon of the Underworld" for taking a dozen bullets in a 1912 dance-hall shoot-out, was the main partner in Harlem's Cotton Club. He also owned a block-long brewery on Tenth Avenue that illegally brewed "Madden's Number One" beer, which was sold to the city's illegal speakeasies.

Another of Billingsley's partners (and also a partner of Madden), whom most people at the time thought supplied Billingsley's capital, was William "Big Bill" Dwyer. He had recently served a couple of years in Atlanta's federal prison for running the country's largest liquor-smuggling fleet before becoming part of the Stork Club partnership. The third partner was George Jean (Frenchy) DeMange, who looked so much like the popular image of a gangster that Billingsley had to turn him down when the man asked to be made a member of Billingsley's golf club. Nicknamed "the Frog" by the police because his arms and legs seemed too long for his body; his head was huge, with deeply sunk small eyes;

a large, flat nose; and prominent cheekbones . . . think James Bond's nemesis Jaws.

The partnership was never enshrined in writing, and aside from enjoying the profits from the club, the trio also promised protection whenever Billingsley needed it; it's a little-known fact that, at least in the 1920s and '30s, Billingsley carried a pistol in his tuxedo pocket. His partners also arranged for the club to buy liquor for fifteen dollars under the going rate but added, "We'll tell you who to buy it from." Billingsley knew that anyone who crossed mobsters (by 1929, the Mafia had, through its bootlegging business, become all powerful in New York) usually ended up dead. Realizing that probably the safest thing for his health was to never handle any of the vast sums of cash the club would bring in, he insisted that his partners put in their own money man.

Aside from a prewar cover charge of $20 (more than $240 today) and tap water priced at $2 a carafe ($24), an idea of how really profitable the club could be may be gleaned from an incident that occurred one night in 1940, years after Prohibition had ended and the Stork Club had evolved into its glamorous, East Side persona. Seems that Ernest Hemingway, back in New York from Paris and a Stork Club regular, had grandiosely tried to pay his bar bill with a $100,000 royalty check he had received from Paramount for the film rights of his novel *For Whom the Bell Tolls*. In today's money that would be over $1,500,000; Billingsley shook his head and said he couldn't cash it then, but that Hemingway should wait around until closing time. And at 2:00 a.m. apparently enough cash had come in and he cashed the check, at a time when, by Billingsley's own account, the club was grossing only $3,500 nightly.

But there was more to it than taking care of the patrons' needs. Aside from knowing the right gangsters, Billingsley had another break, and this one would make his place the most famous speakeasy (and later nightclub) in the country. Again according to Blumenthal, another club owner, Mary Louise ("Texas") Guinan (celebrated by posterity as "the Queen of the Nightclubs";

chapter 6) introduced Billingsley to a rising young gossip columnist named Walter Winchell, who in 1929 plugged the Stork Club while it was still at its West Side location as "New York's New Yorkiest place." Billingsley called the plug "a blessed event."

It was a gift that kept on giving as the Stork Club became a regular late-night stop for Winchell to gather news for his column. More than anything else, Walter Winchell made the Stork Club the place to be and be seen. Like El Morocco, which had its prime seating location (up front, so everyone would see you) and its "Siberia," (in back by the kitchen), so too did the Stork Club have its prime spot: the wood-paneled Cub Room. It was overseen by a haughty host whom everyone called St. Peter; those to whom he refused to open its gates often referred to it as the "snub room." Several movies were made there, perhaps most memorably, 1950's *All About Eve*, which featured Bette Davis, George Sanders, and Celeste Holm in the Cub Room.

As the '20s moved into the 1930s and then into the '40s and '50s, more and more celebrities flocked to the place, so many that one might suppose some may have actually become celebrities by being seen there; it was that kind of place. George Burns and his wife Gracie Allen were patrons; so were Frank Sinatra, the Bing Crosbys, Red Skelton, and Marilyn Monroe, with her husband Joe DiMaggio. John Kennedy celebrated his thirty-ninth birthday at the Stork with Jackie in 1956, and Prince Rainier wooed Grace Kelly at a table in the Cub Room. The legendary singer Ethel Merman was not only enamored of the place, she was so taken with Billingsley himself she once reportedly offered him a half million dollars to leave his wife Hazel and their three children for her. Her passion was clearly reciprocated; the pair were lovers for a time before Merman married Robert Six, CEO of Continental Airlines in 1953, and Billingsley sent a bottle of the club's private-label champagne to her dressing room every night during the late '40s run of the musical *Annie Get Your Gun*.

More than its presence during the 1920s—it started right at the end of the decade, ironically, hand in hand with the stock market crash—what the Stork Club represented defined the era as much as the career of Mayor Jimmy Walker. "Gangsters running amok in New York coupled with elegance as crystalline as a polished diamond do not seem to go together at all," said one historian of the decade, "but there was a time when they did." In the Stork Club's heyday, it blended movie stars, politicians, writers, debutantes, heiresses, and mobsters in what has been called a "Gatsby-esque extravaganza." The club was torn down in 1966, the same year Sherman Billingsley died.

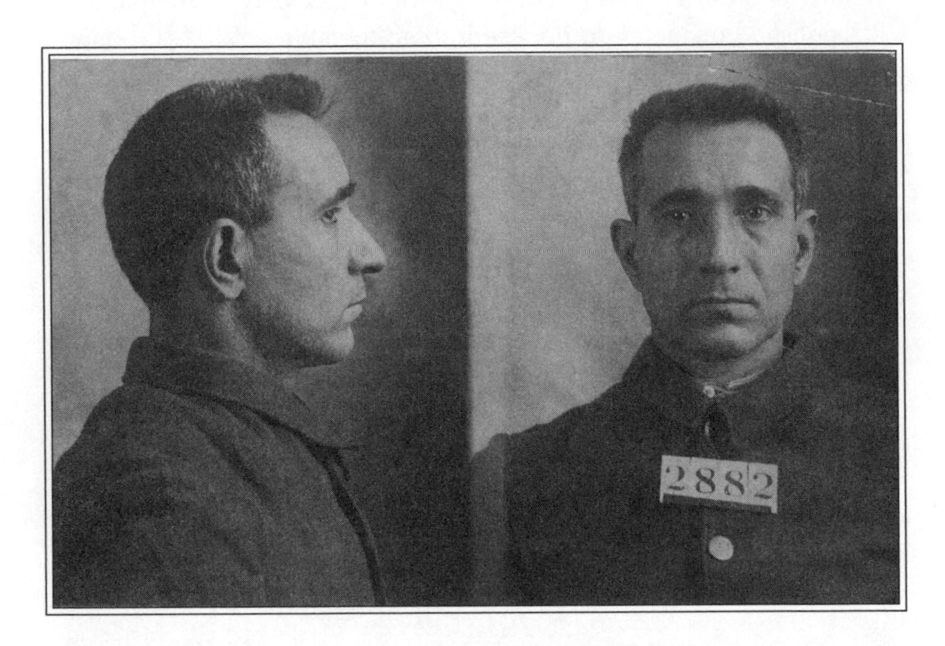

While Prohibition may have been a pain in the side for most New Yorkers (as well as most Americans), it provided an environment where a once small-time New York crime organization of largely Southern Italian gangsters known as the Mafia grew into a national phenomenon. One of its first boss of bosses was Giuseppe Morello, here shown in a 1910 mug shot when he was arrested for counterfeiting. He would be assassinated in 1930 during the many years when Mafia family rivalries and wars turned the city into a crime capital and mob battleground.

Courtesy of the U.S. National Archives

CHAPTER 3

The Rise of the Mafia, Part I

The Three "M"s: Morello, Masseria, and Maranzano

**"Goodfellas don't sue goodfellas.
Goodfellas kill goodfellas,"**
— ***Salvatore Profaci***

Undoubtedly, among the members of "café society" populating the Stork Club, one might notice the presence of a few Latin-appearing gentlemen throwing money around with abandon. They might have been members of a newly powerful organization that grew directly out of the Stork Club's original operation, the speakeasy, and a time when millions of Americans would pay anything for liquor—Prohibition. The organization was known as the Mafia; it became a household word. It was the American version of the (usually) Sicilian secret criminal organization and has remained known as the Mafia ever since.

True, the term is used loosely these days, as in "Russian Mafia" or "Jewish Mafia" or is unrelated to crime at all but slang for JFK's political crowd, "Kennedy Mafia." Then and now, its members usually refer to it as La Cosa Nostra—"our thing."

Unlike many of the extraordinary events that took place in New York in the 1920s, the explosive rise of the city's Mafia to national prominence during the decade still looms large in our collective consciousness, as do the names of many of the mobsters who began their careers in the Roaring Twenties. The decade's mafiosi are as familiar to people as many contemporary celebrities—familiar to filmgoers, certainly. Mafia-themed films and television specials have had huge international success.

Although the names of its characters were changed from those of their models, one reason for the *Godfather* films' success is that the story of the rise and fall, the betrayals and survivals, the gang wars and the secret deals of the mob were largely based on historic events. Another key to the movies' permanence is that, however lethal the events may have been, they—as well as the people involved—were so, well, theatrical. Just the nicknames of the mobsters sound like they were made up for a Dick Tracy comic strip: Vincent "The Chin" Gigante, Vincent "Mad Dog" Coll, and the like. But don't be fooled; as comic as the nicknames sound these days, the people bearing them were deadly and powerful, and by the 1930s they basically ran New York City by controlling everything from the waterfront to the Teamsters union to politicians and, of course, the supply of the liquor that millions were clamoring for.

Assassinating rivals and enemies was done with apparent legal impunity in busy restaurants and barbershops, and mob connections were even used by the U.S. government in the 1940s to make inside deals protecting war production and, in the case of the Allies' invasion of Italy, getting crucial intelligence. Even J. Edgar Hoover, the head of the FBI, who first gained national fame by catching John Dillinger, "Public Enemy Number One" (then a newly coined FBI term), chose to look the other way for more than thirty years when it came to Mafia activities, diverting attention from the big organized crime picture by chasing after petty criminals like Bonnie and Clyde in 1934. The American public, at least during and after Prohibition, when dealing with the Mafia to get illegal booze was commonplace in many major U.S. cities, was transfixed for decades; in 1957, when the U.S. Senate hearings into organized crime were televised, they were watched by one of the largest television audiences of the time and made household names of the Senate committee's general counsel, Robert Kennedy, and Teamsters union boss Jimmy Hoffa.

The New York Mafia, which would grow to become the largest, most powerful, and richest crime organization in America during the 1920s, first emerged (as memorably presented in the flashbacks in the *Godfather II* film) in the area of Manhattan's lower East Side, still known as "Little Italy." It basically was a small, neighborhood-based organization helping the newly arrived immigrants to cope with a new and far different lifestyle in America, as well as continuing a heritage of criminal activities. The January 1920 arrival of Prohibition opened the door to supplying something not just a few hundred immigrants needed but, in the case of liquor, something everybody demanded. Consequently, the size, power, and influence of the New York Mafia, as well as similar organizations in (especially) Chicago, Philadelphia, and New Orleans, exploded, turning what were previously small-time criminals into millionaire crime bosses.

It wasn't just money that these men accumulated, but also fame. So powerful did America's crime organizations become during the nearly thirteen years of Prohibition that America's traditional respect for the law began to wear away. Citizens were daily forced to break the law to get the liquor, beer, and wine they wanted, as well as constantly encountering law enforcement officials and politicians on the take. Eventually, some Mafia bosses, the "hooch" enablers, actually gained a sort of perverted celebrity, which continues to this day.

Unlike Charles "Lucky" Luciano, the first celebrity mob boss, his predecessor was not accorded public notoriety. The man who was the head of the New York Mafia during much of the 1920s is largely unremembered, but his influence and especially the vast profits he made under Prohibition would set in motion everything that would follow; among the most important was the eventual division of New York gangs into the still-famous "Five Families" in an attempt to reduce lethal rivalry (it was not too successful, as related in Mario Puzo's novel *The Godfather* and the later films based on it). His name was Joseph Masseria.

First, a little background on the New York crime scene that Masseria inherited when he became the boss of bosses. Fifty years earlier a Sicilian named Giuseppe Esposito and six associates apparently were the first members of the Sicilian Mafia to arrive in America when they fled to New Orleans after committing multiple murders back home (Esposito would be arrested in 1881 and extradited to Italy). But by the 1890s Sicilian as well as members of other Italian crime families, including the Neapolitan Camorra and Calabrian 'Ndrangheta crime organizations, were coming to New York, along with thousands of Italian immigrants. Many of the new arrivals, at least those from Sicily, soon formed the Five Points Gang, which was very powerful in Little Italy (often warring with the Jewish Eastman gang in the same area). The new arrivals also formed a Mafia family in East Harlem (which was then largely Italian) and in Brooklyn, where the territory was controlled not by the Sicilians but by veterans of the Camorra.

From 1895 until 1910, when he was jailed for counterfeiting, the boss of the New York Mafia was Giuseppe Morello, head of a gang of extortionists in East Harlem, Brooklyn, and Little Italy. He was succeeded in Italian Harlem by Fortunato "Charlie" Lo Monte, who was killed by rivals in 1914 when he tried to take over the rackets in Lower Manhattan. The leadership of the original Morello Family then passed to the late Joseph Morello's half brothers, Vincent and Nicholas Terranova; Vincent became sole boss of East Harlem after Nicholas was assassinated on his way to a so-called "Peace Conference" with the Brooklyn Camorra gang. Vincent was himself killed in 1922.

That left the road open for Giuseppe ("Joe the Boss") Masseria. When Vincent Terranova was shot, Masseria rallied the Morello-Terranova Family, as well as Sicilian and non-Sicilian Mafia families in Chicago, Detroit, and Cleveland, in a war with the Brooklyn family that was led by Salvatore D'Aquila. When D'Aquila was killed in 1928, Masseria, basically a hard-drinking, profane thug, assumed complete control.

But conflict continued, now between Masseria and a 1925 arrival from Sicily named Salvatore Maranzano, who was born in the village of Castellammare del Golfo. In all ways (other than his criminal activities), he was the opposite of Masseria: an elegant, vain, fairly well-educated man who had once studied for the priesthood.

After arriving in America Maranzano set up a bootlegging, extortion, and gambling operation that directly competed with Masseria's business. But whether or not you loathed a rival—and Masseria and Maranzano passionately hated each other—survival in the Mafia demanded pragmatism. So it isn't surprising that in 1930, when Masseria set himself up as a sort of underworld Mussolini demanding absolute obedience from the other families, Maranzano's Castellammare Family paid the ten thousand dollar tribute Masseria demanded.

Which didn't mean that they were at all happy about accepting Masseria as a "boss of bosses" and paying the tribute money. The next year, when a number of Maranzano Family members in Detroit, Chicago, and New York were killed, Maranzano decided he had had enough and declared war on Masseria and his allies, mobsters whose names became as familiar to millions as those of movie stars during the 1920s and long thereafter. They included Frank Costello, Charles "Lucky" Luciano, Vito Genovese, Joe Adonis, Albert Anastasia, Carlo Gambino, Bugsy Siegel, and Meyer Lansky. On Maranzano's side were Joseph "Bananas" Bonanno, Joseph Profaci (who headed his own family), and a number of Masseria turncoats, including Gaetano "Tommy" Gagliano and Gaetano Lucchese. New York's subsequent gangland shootout, remembered as the Castellammare War, after Maranzano's Sicilian hometown, would rage for nearly two years, cost more than sixty lives, and devastate both sides' bootlegging and racket operations.

The younger generation—Costello, Luciano, and their buddies, as well as their rivals Joseph Bonnano and members of the Profaci clan, were known as the "Young Turks," a term that originally described a reform movement in Turkey at the end of the Ottoman Empire, which has since come to refer to any young, ambitious, impatient group.

Regardless of the enmity between them, they realized that the only way to get the profits from their operations back on track was to make peace, end the Castellammare War, and form a national crime syndicate. They were also convinced that the only way to do so was to get rid of both Masseria and Maranzano, who were known as "Mustache Petes"—as the jargon of the times identified old-school Mafiosi who wanted to preserve the traditional Sicilian underworld codes of honor, respect, and dignity in America (the Mafia titles capo [boss], sottocapo [underboss], caporegime [captain], and soldato [soldier] were presumably taken from ancient Roman military designations).

To the Mustache Petes the traditional codes also meant never working with anyone who wasn't Italian and, preferably, Sicilian. Luciano, whose criminal creativity had carried him up the crime ladder to the job of Masseria's top aide, was particularly incensed at their dismissing of his friend and business partner Frank Costello as "the dirty Calabrian." Obviously, they didn't much approve of another of Luciano's friends, either, the Polish Jew Meyer Lansky.

Then one day in 1929, Luciano was forced into a limousine at gunpoint by three men, beaten, stabbed, and dumped on a remote beach. He somehow survived, but for the rest of his life, Charles Luciano carried both the marks of the assassination attempt (a long scar on his face and a droopy eye) and the nickname for surviving it: "Lucky." No secrets lasted forever in the underworld, so it wasn't long before Lansky discovered that the man behind the attempt on Luciano's life was Masseria's rival, Salvatore Maranzano. Survival in the underworld also demanded biding your time and striking only when the time was ripe, so Luciano, now "Lucky" to everyone, in a calculated (and eventually successful) move to end the gang war, secretly switched his loyalty to Maranzano and waited. He was soon made second in command to the man who had tried to kill him in return for now agreeing to engineer the death of his previous boss, Joseph Masseria.

On April 15, 1931, Luciano invited his ostensible boss, Giuseppe Masseria, to lunch at Scarpato's Restaurant in Coney Island, and when he excused himself to go to the restroom, his associates Albert Anastasia, Vito Genovese, Joe Adonis, and Bugsy Siegel entered the restaurant and gunned down Masseria. As planned, Maranzano then became the boss of bosses . . . but only briefly. Five months later, on September 10, 1931, Luciano's strategy became apparent when Maranzano was killed in his ninth-floor office in Manhattan's Helmsley Building at 230 Park Avenue by gunmen hired by Lansky and Luciano (including a member of Lansky and Siegel's Murder Incorporated organization) posing as IRS agents.

Following the killings of Mafia bosses Joe Masseria and Salvatore Maranzano, Luciano also became the leader of his own crime family, with Vito Genovese as underboss and Frank Costello as consigliere (the Mafia term for a legal "counselor"). Luciano and the Young Turks had taken over the New York underworld and would run it for decades. What they decided to do to get a national crime syndicate set up was to first establish a Mafia family in each major city (New York, being the largest market would have five families; originally they were the Profaci, Bonanno, Mangaro, Gagliano, and Luciano families). "Luciano was a genius," one surviving member of his family has recalled. "He could have been the CEO of a major corporation which, in effect, he was."

But there was no such thing as equal opportunity in the New York Mafia. To be a "made man" (baptized into a family via solemn oaths and deeds, which occasionally required killing someone), you had to be 100 percent Italian—better yet, 100 percent Sicilian—as we've seen was demanded by the Young Turks' predecessors, the Moustache Petes. Non-Italians such as Meyer Lansky, however powerful they became, could never be more than an "associate."

Aside from Luciano, Frank Costello was probably the most interesting member of the new Mafia family, if for no other reason than that he, unlike most other mafiosi, moved as comfortably within the noncriminal world as he did among mobsters. Because of his "legit" friends and contacts, he made it reasonably easy for Luciano and his people to buy favors and influence from judges, politicians (he was close to the Tammany Hall machine), and businessmen. He was so effective that he was later nicknamed the "Prime Minister of the Underworld." (In later life, Costello liked to reminisce about his criminal bootlegging partnership with Joe Kennedy, father of JFK.) In addition, by the mid-1930s Costello controlled a vast gambling empire spread across America; in New York, besides controlling slot machines and other gambling ventures, he also controlled the betting at Aqueduct Racetrack. He would eventually head the Luciano Family after Lucky went to jail.

Born Francesco Castiglia in a mountain village in Calabria in 1891, Costello emigrated to New York in 1900 with his mother and brother and settled in East Harlem, where his father had earlier opened a small Italian market. When Frankie Costello (his newly adopted name) was thirteen, he began his life of crime with petty thefts. Before his twenty-seventh birthday he had been jailed four times; three times for assault and robbery and the fourth a ten-month sentence for carrying a concealed weapon. Costello learned a lesson, but hardly the one the law hoped for; after his release from his weapons conviction, he decided to use his brains instead of his brawn to make money unlawfully, and he never carried a gun again. It would be thirty-seven years before he saw the inside of another jail.

The rising gangster joined the Morello-Terranova Family and quickly gained a reputation for creative toughness in his work involving the family's gambling and loan-sharking business. There he met Luciano, who was leading his own gang in Manhattan's Little Italy, and they became close friends. When Prohibition became law, they immediately broadened their operations into bootlegging, financed by the criminal financier Arnold Rothstein, as well as worked with Irish and Jewish criminals, including Dutch Schultz (whose real name was Arthur Flegenheimer). But they weren't powerful enough yet to overcome the competition, and their established rivals, who included Vincent "Mad Dog" Coll and Jack "Legs" Diamond, eventually put them out of business in a gang war.

In spite of defeat Costello and Luciano continued their gambling rackets—punch cards, slot machines, bookmaking, and floating casinos—with Lansky and Siegel. In 1927, along with former Chicago gangster Johnny Torrio (Al Capone's mentor), they organized the Big Seven Group, an association of top bootleggers who realized that pooling their Canadian and European liquor sources could give them a major advantage over their competition. When the Group, plus other top gangsters from across the country, met in Atlantic City two years later, it would be the first national underworld get-together and a major step toward forming the national crime syndicate dreamed of by the Young Turks movement. Masseria and Maranzano were obviously not invited because of their resistance to sharing authority with others, but it is suspected that the earlier-mentioned assassination attempt on Luciano was the result of Maranzano's learning of the meeting.

After Luciano succeeded Maranzano as boss in 1931, Costello, in addition to his responsibilities as Lucky's consigliere, also became responsible for an important part of the profits of the Luciano Family through his control of their slot machine and bookmaking business. Costello placed approximately 25,000 slot machines in bars, restaurants, cafés, drugstores, gas stations, and bus stops throughout New York. In 1934 the new mayor, Fiorello LaGuardia, confiscated thousands of them and dumped them into the East River. Costello then accepted Louisiana governor Huey Long's invitation to put slot machines throughout his state in exchange for 10 percent of the take; it was one of Costello's first steps in broadening his gambling empire nationwide and one that, in addition to starting the layoff and odds system still used by bookies and gamblers, brought millions into the Luciano Family coffers.

Luciano went to prison in 1936, as a result of one of the biggest frame-ups of the era, and named Costello as his underboss and Vito Genovese as acting boss (Luciano retained his title even when in jail). But Genovese was indicted for murder the following year and fled to his hometown of Naples, Italy, where he was safe, thanks to a payment of $250,000 to Benito Mussolini. Lucky, from his prison cell, then appointed Costello as acting boss of the Luciano Family,

Not only did Frank Costello have the best political connections of any boss in the United States, he was an extremely popular boss because he wasn't greedy and shared fairly the profits from the family business. He also owned legitimate businesses, including a large New York poultry company and a meat-market chain.

In the *Godfather* book and films, a major controversy arises between the family of the Godfather, Vito Corleone (whose character was based on the lives of both Lucky Luciano and Frank Costello), and their rivals over getting into the narcotics business; Corleone spoke of it in the film as "a dirty business." This was taken directly from the growing rivalry between Luciano Family members; Costello was determined not to go into drug dealing, and Vito Genovese dealt in drugs on the side throughout his career.

During World War II in Italy, where he had gone to avoid going to prison for a 1934 murder, Genovese was appointed to a position of interpreter/liaison officer in the U.S. Army headquarters and quickly became one of the most trusted employees of the American Military Government of Occupied Territories). After the war Vito Genovese returned to New York from his self-exile in Italy and set out to regain the leadership of the Luciano Family by, among other things, lending money to the family "soldiers." Nevertheless, Costello's continuing popularity among the family rank and file plus the support of other underworld leaders kept him safe from any assassination attempt, as did the support of the new underboss, Guarino "Willie Moore" Moretti, a Costello cousin who had a small army of soldati in New Jersey.

Move forward in the Costello story to 1950, when the U.S. Senate opened a now-famous investigation of organized crime generally known, from the name of its head, Senator Estes Kefauver of Tennessee, as the Kefauver Hearings. It was the first major event of its kind to be seen on television, which was then in its infancy, and the country was transfixed as more than six hundred gangsters, lawyers, and politicians testified. The star witness was Frank Costello, by then the most famous Mafia figure in the country and billed as America's number-one gangster and the power behind the Tammany Hall (Democratic) political machine.

Costello agreed to testify and to not take the Fifth Amendment if his face wasn't shown on television, and the committee agreed (there is a similar hearing in *The Godfather, Part II*, with Michael Corleone, the family boss, played by Al Pacino, testifying). Oddly, for someone as self-assured as Costello, he turned in a poor performance before the committee, appearing nervous and evasive (which he undoubtedly was, since his words were being heard by a huge television audience). He did get a big laugh from the hostile committee, though, when he was asked what he had done for his country; he replied in his raspy voice, "Paid my taxes!" and walked out.

The hearings brought him media and law attention, but what soon did him in was the assassination of his cousin and underboss, Willie Moretti. Because Moretti had violated the Mafia code of silence by cooperating with the Kefauver Hearings, Costello ordered his elimination. It took place in a New Jersey restaurant on October 4, 1951. (One fascinating aside: Marlon Brando, who played Vito Corleone in *The Godfather*, used tapes from Costello's testimony during the Kefauver Hearings as the basis for his famous slurred speech in the movie.)

In August 1952, in addition to being found guilty for Moretti's death, Costello was convicted on contempt of Senate charges for his hearings walkout and went to jail for eighteen months. Released after fourteen months, despite his quip before the Senate committee, he was then charged with tax evasion and sentenced in 1954 to five years' imprisonment. He served eleven months before it was overturned on appeal. In 1956 Costello was again convicted, sent to prison, and again released on appeal. By then Vito Genovese had begun his move to take over the Luciano Family by convincing Carlo Gambino, Costello ally Alberto Anastasia's underboss, to switch loyalty.

And so it was that on May 2, 1957, and shortly after his second release from prison, Costello was shot in the lobby of his Manhattan apartment building by Vincent "The Chin" Gigante. Before pulling the trigger Gigante shouted, "This is for you, Frank!" Costello turned his head to see who was taunting him, and the move saved his life. The bullet entered the right side of his scalp, traveled around his skull, and stopped over his left ear, amounting to little more than a serious scalp wound.

After learning that he had failed in his attempt on Costello's life, Gigante hid out for a time and then, hoping that Costello would observe the Mafia code of secrecy—"omerta"—turned himself in to the family. Young Turk though he had once been, Costello's observation of such traditional rules as omerta was rigid, and Gigante was acquitted after a mob trial. Frank Costello and Vito Genovese then made a peace of sorts about the time of the notorious 1957 gangster get-together in upstate New York called the Appalachian Meeting. Costello abdicated as family boss in favor of Genovese, and Genovese let Costello keep all his legitimate businesses, as well as his gambling operations in Florida and Louisiana. Genovese then appointed himself as boss of the Luciano Family, and called a national meeting of the crime group bosses, which officially renamed the Luciano Family, then the largest and wealthiest crime family in the country, the Genovese Family. (Athough nominally demoted to the rank of "soldier" in the family, Frank Costello would rarely be thought of as anything less than the "Boss.")

Vito Genovese still had to deal with Albert Anastasia, an avowed enemy still furious over the Costello assassination attempt. This was resolved on October 25, 1957, when the waterfront boss and former head of Murder, Inc., was shot in the barbershop of the Park Sheraton Hotel by, it is believed, the Gallo brothers, members of the Profaci Family, under orders of friends of Carlo Gambino. (In the *Godfather* movies, it would be Mo Green, the fictional character most resembling Bugsy Siegel, who would be graphically shot "in the eye" in the barbershop.)

Peace, however, was short-lived. A new conspiracy was reportedly hatched by Costello, Luciano, Gambino (changing sides again in the best Mafia tradition), and Meyer Lansky to avenge the Costello and Anastasia hits and to eliminate Genovese. In 1959 the conspirators arranged the framing of Genovese, Vincent Gigante, and future Bonanno Family boss Carmine Galante on a drug charge. Vito Genovese was convicted and sentenced to fifteen years in prison, where he died in 1969. Carmine Galante received twenty years in 1962, was paroled in 1974, and assassinated in 1979.

During his retirement Frank Costello was still known as "the Prime Minister of the Underworld" and retained power within the New York Mafia structure. Old associates and bosses often visited him at his Waldorf Astoria penthouse apartment to seek advice. In 1973 at the age of 82, Frank Costello died of a heart attack, but his influence lived on.

Soon after his release from prison the following year, Carmine Galante announced Costello's lasting influence on the New York crime scene in a unique way that carried an unmistakable message for all Costello (and Galante) rivals. He ordered the bombing of Costello's masoleum at St. Michael's cemetery in Astoria, Queens. The blasting of the heavy bronze doors off the mausoleum was meant to be seen as the return of Costello via Galante and a revenge of a kind on their old enemies.

Clearly, much of the Mafia history related in these pages took place well after the 1920s, the purview of this book. But like many of the dramatic changes that took place in the Twenties and transformed our very lifestyle—as communications has also—it is important to keep in mind the amazing cultural trajectory of the Mafia from small neighborhood crime groups to a national phenomenon, all beginning in the Twenties.

In 1949, *Time* listed New York Mafia boss Charles "Lucky" Luciano (handcuffed, center) among the 20th Century's top twenty most influential Americans. By the mid-1920s, he and his partners were running the biggest bootlegging operation in the city and would soon control most of the rackets from gambling to garbage hauling. Here he is being escorted by two detectives into a courtroom in 1936. He was convicted of controlling the prostitution business—one crime he didn't commit.
Library of Congress

CHAPTER 4

The Rise of the Mafia, Part II

Meyer Lansky and Lucky Luciano

"Don't worry, don't worry. Look at the Astors and the Vanderbilts. They were the worst of thieves—and now look at them. It's just a matter of time."
— *Meyer Lansky*

In 1949 *Time* listed Lucky Luciano as the "criminal mastermind" on its list of the top twenty builders and titans of the twentieth century. Before we get to his story, though, we must mention Meyer Lansky, called "the Mob's Accountant." Not only was he instrumental in the rise of the Luciano Family to being America's most powerful and richest crime organization, but like so many of these people who inspired characters in the *Godfather* films, he also became powerful himself. In *The Godfather, Part II*, Michael Corleone's great rival is Hyman Roth, played in the movie by the legendary late actor Lee Strasberg (who received an Oscar nomination for his work). Although Lansky was always a Luciano Family loyalist and didn't die in an airport shoot-out, as Roth did in the film, he was, as Roth was also portrayed, an important player in opening Cuba and Florida to Mafia gambling operations.

Lansky was born Meyer Suchowljanski in Grodno, Russia, in 1902. While it may appear that he was a kind of sidekick to

Frank Costello and Lucky Luciano, it is important to remember that neither of them might have reached their eminence without the help of Lansky. As a member of the Jewish Mafia, he was anathema to the old, tradition-bound Sicilian Mafia leaders, but he was just the sort of hustler that Luciano believed could help a crime organization to grow.

Meyer Lansky and Charlie Luciano first met in school, where Luciano tried to shake him down for money. Reportedly, a fight followed. There is no information on who won the fight, but Luciano was impressed with Meyer's fighting ability, and the pair became good friends.

Luciano then met Ben "Bugsy" Siegel, who joined him and Lansky in the Five Points Gang. Together they worked throughout much of the decade of the Twenties bootlegging liquor. They stole from other bootleggers and also played both sides by providing protection for alcohol shipments for huge fees.

By 1936 Lansky had set up gambling operations in Florida, Louisiana, and Havana. In the 1950s he was close to Cuba's corrupt president Fulgencio Batista. In fact, he had bribed Cuba's previous president, Carlos Prío Socarrás, with $250,000 in cash to step down and clear the way for Batista (although the story that Prio was deposed by a Batista coup endures). It was also part of the deal mentioned by the character Hyman Roth in *The Godfather, Part II* in which the Cuban government would match, dollar for dollar, any hotel and casino investment over one million dollars in exchange for a 10 percent kickback, a casino license, and an exemption (unlike in Las Vegas) for background checks of investors.

Lansky, who was given the job of unofficial gambling minister by Batista (and a salary of twenty-five thousand dollars), was also instrumental in making Havana's Hotel National a showplace by opening a high rollers' wing in 1955, with Eartha Kitt as the entertainment. Lansky's brother, Jake, was running the place when the Cuban revolution took place in 1959. Just before Castro entered Havana on January 8 of that year, Lansky was celebrating the $3 million he had made in the first year of operation at his other hotel/casino, the Havana Riviera; he was subsequently forced to flee Cuba, first to the Bahamas and then back to Miami. When Castro then nationalized the casinos in October, 1960, Lansky was said to have lost some $7 million and was reduced to living on the income from his Las Vegas interests.

As a Jew Meyer Lansky was particularly incensed by the Nazi sympathizers in the United States and with his gang broke up several Nazi rallies in Yorkville, then Manhattan's Germantown. During World War II he was also part of the secret Mafia/U.S. government partnership to keep saboteurs out of the country and the vulnerable shipbuilding industry.

When the eighty-year-old Meyer Lansky died of lung cancer in 1983, it was reported that he had left nothing to his widow, Yetta, and their three children because he had nothing left to leave. The FBI, however, believed that he left behind more than $300 million in hidden bank accounts, which has never been found. In any event, the year before his death, *Forbes* listed him as one of the four hundred richest people in America, with assets over $100 million.

In *The Godfather, Part II*, the Hyman Roth character tells Michael Corleone that "we're bigger than U.S. Steel." This was actually a direct quote from Lansky, who said the same thing to his wife while watching a news story on the Cosa Nostra.

His life, too, has been mined for film content. In Sergio Leone's *Once Upon a Time in America*, the character Max Bercovicz, played by James Woods, is based on Lansky. Mark Rydell played Lansky in Sydney Pollock's 1990 film *Havana*, and in *Bugsy*, made the following year, Ben Kingsley played him. Because Lansky was still alive at the time, his character was named Michael Lasker in the 1981 NBC miniseries *The Gangster Chronicles*; and in the 1999 TV movie *Lansky*, he was played by Richard Dreyfus.

Perhaps because Charles Luciano won the highly publicized Castellammare War, or perhaps because of his popularized nickname, or that he survived to die an older man in exile in Naples (or perhaps, given the thirst for liquor in the 1920s, because he and his associates ran the biggest bootlegging operation in America), "Lucky" Luciano became the first and, to date, arguably the biggest Mafia celebrity.

In a case of reverse engineering, one could say that Luciano's life story plays like a movie; in fact, the victories, defeats, and compromises (not to speak of the many hits he made and avoided) that highlighted his life and his crime career were mined extensively by Mario Puzo in his 1969 novel *The Godfather*, and in the movies it inspired. And unlike his predecessors Masseria and Maranzano and many of his successors, Luciano has been portrayed on film and television often by familiar actors, among them Telly Savalas (in an episode of the 1960 TV series *The Witness*); Stanley Tucci (in the 1991 film adaptation of E. L. Doctorow's *Billy Bathgate*, the story of mobster Dutch Schultz's last days through the eyes of a young boy he befriends); Joe Dallesandro (in Francis Ford Coppola's 1984 film *The Cotton Club*); Michael Nouri (in the 1981 TV series *The Gangster Chronicles*); Andy Garcia (in 1997's film *Hoodlum*); and Christian Slater, the actor who many say most resembled Luciano (in 1991's *Mobsters*).

Charles Luciano was born in Lercara Friddi, Sicily, some thirty miles southeast of Palermo, on November 24, 1897, the eldest of five children. He emigrated to New York City with his family when he was ten, and by the time he was a teenager, he was making a living through comparatively petty crimes—considering what was to come—such as theft and extortion. When Prohibition came in, he was working for Arnold Rothstein, who, besides "fixing" the 1919 World Series, was a major banker for both legitimate Broadway theater interests and the Mafia.

Luciano, then in his early twenties, realized that sooner or later the various gangs would have to cooperate—after all, with smuggling liquor during Prohibition, there was plenty of money for everyone. Organized crime needed to reduce the all-too-common lethal rivalries and the hijacking of each other's shipments—and the cost of political protection. This cooperation would come about, but it would take a decade. At the beginning of the Great Experiment, Joe Masseria forbade it. By 1921 Lucky had formed a business partnership with Frank Costello and, through their involvement with the Five Points Gang, began a bootlegging operation. Three years later he and his partners were running the largest bootlegging operation in both New York and Philadelphia, importing whisky directly from Scotland, rum from the Caribbean, and more whisky from Canada, and grossing over $12 million a year (some $135 million today) but, as with Polly Adler's highly profitable bordello business (chapter 5), the cost of bribing politicians and police was killing any real profits.

Before betraying both Salvatore Maranzano and Joe Masseria and ending the Castellammare War, Luciano and Maranzano realized Lucky's decade-old plan to reduce rivalries in New York by dividing up the city into territories exclusively controlled by individual members of the Five Families. Fatally, though, Maranzano didn't stop there. At an upstate meeting of the group, he declared himself the Capo di Tutti Capi—the Boss of All Bosses—with all the former rivals paying him. Anger over that move, as we have seen, and thanks to Luciano's betrayal, ended his short-lived rule.

By the late Twenties Luciano was the most famous and most powerful mobster in the country, controlling most of the criminal rackets in New York City: gambling, bookmaking, loan-sharking, bootlegging, and what drug trafficking there was at the time. Through his union influence he also controlled the Manhattan waterfront, garbage hauling, construction, garment-center business, and trucking. Meyer Lansky, a trusted friend whose advice Lucky always followed, became his right-hand man.

In 1935 when Dutch Schultz made an attempt on the life of Manhattan district attorney Thomas Dewey (who would later lose to Harry Truman in the 1948 presidential race), the mobster had directly violated Luciano's orders. Lucky believed killing Dewey would provoke a major crackdown on the family's business, so Schultz was executed, at the Palace Chophouse in Newark, New Jersey. Other positions in what was now known as the Luciano Family were filled by Vito Genovese (who became the sottocapo [underboss]); Frank Costello (consigliere); Joe Adonis (caporegime [captain]), and Bugsy Siegel, who, being Jewish like Lansky, by Mafia rules could only become an unofficial advisor.

Over the objection of Lansky, who felt the organization needed rituals to create a feeling of belonging, Luciano abolished his title of Capo di Tutti Capi because he knew it only increased tension among rival bosses. One tradition that he kept, and in fact stressed, was the oath of silence—the "omerta"—about all his family's underworld activity. Despite giving up the Boss of All Bosses title, at the suggestion of Chicago's Johnny Torrio, he set up a "Commission" of all the Mafia's national leaders, a sort of gangster Supreme Court, which regulated both the crime territories and the approval of a man who was to be a "made man," the Mafia terminology for membership in the organization.

In 1936 Luciano was convicted of controlling New York City's prostitution business and was sentenced to thirty to fifty years in prison. It was an obvious frame-up by Dewey. The Luciano Family, unlike such mobsters as Dutch Schultz, did not deal with prostitution. Lucky continued to run the family from the Clinton Correctional Facility in Dannemora, New York, through Vito Genovese, and when Genovese was forced to flee to Naples the following year to avoid being arrested for an earlier murder, Frank Costello succeeded him as sottocapo. Lucky was treated rather well in prison, with special meals prepared for him in a private kitchen. In return, through his labor union clout, Luciano arranged for the materials to build the only freestanding church in the New York correctional system at Clinton, which also boasted, above the altar, two of the original doors from Ferdinand Magellan's ship *Victoria*.

Luciano's union connections also served him well during World War II, when the U.S. government asked him to provide Mafia assistance in preventing enemy infiltration of the U.S. waterfronts and through Albert Anastasia, who controlled the docks, guaranteeing that no dockworker strikes would occur to impede the shipment of men and materiel to the front. Clearly, despite his being a convicted felon and head of the country's largest crime organization, the American government put scruples aside and turned to Luciano when they felt he had something they needed: Because of his close connections to the Mafia in Sicily as well as throughout the rest of Italy, he provided connections that furnished intelligence for the U.S. forces that invaded the country in 1943. Both during and after the war, the U.S. military and intelligence agencies reputedly also used Luciano's Mafia connections to root out suspected Communist influence in labor groups. In return, Lucky was allowed to run his crime empire from his jail cell, and after the war ended he was paroled.

There was a major string attached to his parole, however. He had to agree to leave America and return to Sicily because the last thing the government wanted was for the deal between the U.S. and the Mafia to become public knowledge. Although Lucky loved Sicily, he loved New York more and was very unhappy about having to leave the country and city he considered his own since arriving at the age of ten. He was also worried about maintaining control over his crime kingdom from such a distance, so he secretly moved to pre-Castro Cuba.

For a while he was able to manage his operations effectively from Havana, and he also ran several casinos there with the permission of Cuban president—and Lansky friend—Fulgencio Batista, who, as with Havana's Lansky-controlled casinos, naturally received a percentage of the take. While Luciano was there, Lansky arranged a gathering of the heads of all the major American Mafia families at his Hotel Nacional de Cuba. To get them there he told the mobsters that it was a junket to hear Frank Sinatra (who flew to Havana with Lansky's friends, the Fischetti brothers) perform at the opening of the hotel's casino.

In reality, Lansky got them together so Luciano could seek an agreement on three matters of serious concern: the heroin trade, Cuban gambling, and whether Bugsy Siegel (who obviously wasn't told of the Havana conference) should be eliminated for defaulting on loans he had received from several Mafia investors to build his Flamingo Hotel in Las Vegas. Before the group, both Lansky and Luciano argued that Siegel should be given a chance to open his resort/casino and pay back his investors. Their argument carried the day, and the hit was postponed, but the pressure on Siegel to deliver was intense—so intense that Siegel opened the Flamingo (named after his girlfriend Virginia Hill's nickname) before the casino wing was even finished. The first audience, on December 16, 1946, was a star-studded one, with patrons that included Clark Gable, Lana Turner, and Joan Crawford.

After two weeks Siegel closed it to finish construction, and a completed hotel and casino finally opened the following March. That month the still unhappy investors met again in Havana to decide if he should be eliminated. Luckily for Bugsy, the casino showed a profit that first month of full operation, and Lansky convinced Luciano, who had basically given up on his old associate, to give him one last chance. But when the place started losing money, Siegel's fate was sealed. According to Luciano later, Lansky was convinced by then that Bugsy had also skimmed some $2.5 million from the building funds, which had been smuggled to Switzerland by Virginia Hill in advance of Bugsy's planned "bugging out." On Lansky's orders he was killed by four shots fired through the living room window of Hill's home at 810 North Linden Drive in Beverly Hills.

Luciano decided that to regain control he should again be declared the Boss of All Bosses. All of his friends and business associates agreed that he deserved it except Vito Genovese, who wanted the title for himself and leaked the news to the U.S. government that Luciano was living secretly in Havana. Uncle Sam decided to play hardball and advised the Cubans that unless Luciano flew to Italy, the shipment of all medical drugs to the island nation would be stopped. Lucky left immediately.

By the early 1960s Luciano must have been getting somewhat paranoid when he decided that his old friend Meyer Lansky was cheating him by sending too little money to Italy from the New York Mafia operations. Although in failing health, he decided to get even by buying an Italian candy company that sold confetti (not the torn paper floating down on Manhattan's ticker-tape parades, but the Italian sugar-coated candies). Clearly, as Interpol and the U.S. government suspected, it was a cover for Luciano to ship heroin into the United States. Nevertheless, when U.S. Customs seized and smashed sixty cases of the confetti, there was no trace of the drug. Perhaps the same government contacts who hired him during the war warned him that the seizure was coming. In any event, the subsequent uproar over this suspected drug smuggling and the rumor that a hit had been ordered on him caused Rome's municipal administration to order Luciano's exile from the city, so the Boss moved to Naples.

Although hardly as colorful as in his earlier life, Lucky Luciano, now in his late fifties, seemed more relaxed and happy in the shadow of Vesuvius. After the hit was called off, he lived in a sixty-room house he bought on the Via Tasso with a picture-postcard view of the Bay of Naples and dined in the best restaurants (his favorite was the Ristorante California, where tourists often recognized and spoke with him). He reportedly loved speaking English on any occasion he could. Lucky also cultivated a philanthropic image, helping many poor Italians before opening a medical supply store as a front for dabbling in illegal business.

After arriving in Italy in 1945, Luciano fell in love with Igea Lissoni, an Italian dancer twenty years younger than he. They were clearly devoted to one another; when they learned of the hit, they went into hiding together, moving from apartment to apartment and hotel to hotel until the contract was canceled and they lived together openly in Naples. She was clearly the center of his new life, and when she died of breast cancer, his love of life seemed to evaporate, and he began to lose control of his business and Mafia operations. It is not known if they married, although for some reason, his marrying was banned in his parole agreement.

Luciano was reportedly told not to promote or participate in films about his life, as it would have attracted unnecessary attention to the mob. Francis Ford Coppola took care of that, but Luciano nearly beat Coppola to the punch. After Igea Lissoni died, he agreed to meet a film producer at Naples Capodichino International Airport, where, on January 26, 1962, he died of a heart attack while awaiting the plane's arrival.

Although he was denied his desire to live in New York City after his release from Dannemora in 1946, in death that desire was granted. His body was returned to New York, where he was buried at St. John's Cemetery in Queens. More than two thousand mourners attended his funeral, where his longtime friend, Carlo Gambino, the only other boss besides Luciano to have complete control over the Commission and thus over every other Mafia family in America, spoke the parting eulogy.

Although Prohibition gave the Mafia its golden age, by

bucking the traditional conservatism of the Mustache Petes and working with non-Italian gangsters, the 1920s upstart Luciano reinvented the Mafia into the most powerful crime syndicate in the country. He is today regarded by many as the most powerful—thus the greatest—Mafia boss of them all.

In the 1920s, Polly Adler was so famous that her business card needed only to show the image of a Polly parrot and a phone number. That was enough to identify the city's most celebrated madame, whose club-like bordellos were popular not only for the girls (who, she said proudly, "gave a man his money's worth"), but as places where many of the city's tastemakers would stop by for a drink and a lively conversation before or after a night on the town.
Author's Collection

CHAPTER 5

America's Most Famous Madam
Polly Adler

A House Is Not a Home
— Title of Polly Adler's autobiography

In her day and for years afterward, she was one of the most famous women in America.

So famous in fact that, in an era when it was rare for a woman to be in business for herself, neither her name nor her address appeared on her business card. The card bore only her telephone number (Lexington 2-1099) and a drawing of a parrot, a pun on her nickname.

Polly Adler, at the height of her renown in the 1920s and '30s, seemed to be an intimate of everyone who was anyone in New York City: politicians, socialites, mobsters, and literary lions. But the fame wasn't derived from being a celebrated chanteuse or the head of a company fueled by the booming stock market. Polly Adler was America's most famous madam.

She once tried to explain why people liked her, despite the opprobrium normally associated with her profession: "I am one of those people who just can't help getting a kick out of life, even when it's a kick in the teeth." She also delivered the goods, once explaining her success this way: "My girls give a man his money's worth [unlike] 'whores in everything but name' . . . women who marry men for money, to escape their relatives or to gain social standing."

But her bordellos, which would later give her best-selling 1953 autobiography its title, *A House Is Not a Home*, were more than just once-notorious markets for sex. Unlike other famous American brothels, such as the Chicken Ranch, or madams such as Heidi Fleiss, Polly Adler ran a business where the women were certainly an attraction but not always the main course. Despite the *New York Daily News*'s assertion in 1928 that "her career has made her name synonymous with sin," Polly's place had always been more than a whorehouse for patrons; it was a clubhouse for many members of what then passed for New York's beautiful people. In fact, "Going to Polly's?" became one of the most popular catch phrases in New York in the '20s (there is evidence that Adler herself, with her fine-tuned instinct for generating publicity, popularized its use). Many patrons came by for drinks, backgammon, and card games as much as for the girls.

Despite admittedly spending half her income on bribes and kickbacks, Adler was forced to move her brothel more than a dozen times during her twenty-three-year career as a madam. All her places of business were located in elegant upper East or West Side rented apartments or brownstones, the most famous of which was probably at the Majestic at 215 West Seventy-Fifth Street. Built in 1924, the building (and her apartment) was perfect for a bordello, replete with secret doorways and hidden stairs. Her largest bordello was a brownstone at 63 West Seventieth Street between Central Park West and Columbus Avenue. In addition to rooms for the girls, the place also housed a bar, a library, and an office for Polly.

All her bordellos were sumptuously decorated, boasting plush carpets, expensive furniture, fine paintings, and walls lined with books. Some people thought it was all a bit tacky, but for many of the members of the famed Algonquin Round Table, the legendary association of (mostly) writers that included many of the most prominent tastemakers of the era, it was just fine. In its time, Polly's place was almost as popular with The Round Table crowd as, well, the Algonquin Hotel itself. George S. Kaufman, a

Round Table member who would co-write (with Moss Hart) two of the most enduring plays of the twentieth century (*The Man Who Came to Dinner* and *You Can't Take It with You*), even had a charge account with Polly.

Bon vivant, actor, humorist (and Round Table member) Robert Benchley was another fan of Polly with a charge account at her place; he and his friend and fellow Round Table member, the iconoclastic poet/writer/critic Dorothy Parker, became close friends of Polly in mid-1924 and would, like many others, often visit her place for a drink or two before beginning a night of parties or after a night at the theater (they also suggested the titles in her book walls in the bordellos). Benchley, in fact, often spent the night there, playing backgammon with Polly in exchange for a girl for that night (who were going for twenty dollars a throw), and Adler claims in her autobiography that he even did some of his magazine writing in the company of prostitutes.

Benchley also kept a black kimono at her brothel, which was laundered and ironed by Polly's personal maid, Lion, who also pressed his suits, washed his socks and underwear, and served him breakfast in bed. Described by Adler as a person who "lighted up my life like the sun," Benchley would also occasionally rent out the bordello for lavish parties for the political and literary crowd. At one party of his, a drunkenly despondent prostitute jumped out an open window; after checking to make sure she was okay, Benchley kept the party rolling. The Benchley/Adler friendship endured. Years later, when both he and Polly had retired to Los Angeles, they would often have drinks together at Chasen's restaurant, then Beverly Hill's famed hangout of the stars.

One reason Polly was so successful was simply that she was in the right place at the right time. Prohibition came into effect in January 1920 and with it the rise of the mobsters and the Mafia. New York City, as noted elsewhere in this book, became a wide-open, nearly lawless town, supervised by the corrupt but immensely popular mayor Jimmy Walker (also a client and friend of Adler). She also catered to sports stars of the era, including Joe

DiMaggio, and probably had no preference for the Yankees or the Dodgers, as long as the customer settled his tab with her.

Besides making money on the girls, Polly brought in lots of cash selling booze under the table, and all-night parties were a regular event at the bordello. Some of the girls also worked outside jobs as call girls. In fact, a valid case could be made that Polly Adler was one of the inventors of what are today often referred to as "escort services." The timing was right again; ordering up call girls, or for that matter, call boys (which Polly didn't do), wasn't generally possible until the telephone (invented in 1876) had come into general use. By 1920 there were more than enough phones in New York City to make such access possible. But as direct dialing was only beginning during the 1920s, you often had to give the number you wanted to an operator instead of dialing it yourself, so discretion was an imperative. The direct-dial innovation gave patrons unassisted access to the madams and encouraged business with a critical jump in technology, allowing Polly and her ilk to keep their business contacts more tightly under wraps.

In 1920 Polly opened her first bordello under the protection of Dutch Schultz, a rich, powerful Jewish numbers racketeer and bootlegger who shook down restaurants and saloons for protection money. In return she protected Schultz for years by letting him hide out in her place whenever he needed to disappear for a time. Until Schultz was shot dead in Newark, New Jersey, in 1935 by hit men ordered up by Meyer Lansky, Polly lived in constant fear that one of Schultz's rivals would find out she was hiding him and kill her.

Despite her celebrity and her chosen profession, Polly lived alone, rarely dated, and never settled down with anyone. She was on the taller side of short, with stringy black hair and prominent Russian features that made her look interesting but not beautiful, and her only real friends were her whores and her customers. But she was never apologetic about her career. "If I was to make my living as a madam, I could not be concerned with either the rightness or wrongness of prostitution," she wrote. "Considered either from a moral or criminological standpoint, I had to look at it simply as a part of life which exists today as it existed yesterday. The operation of any business is contingent on the law of supply and demand. And if there were no customers, there certainly would be no whorehouses. Prostitution exists because men are willing to pay for sexual gratification, and whatever men are willing to pay for, someone will provide."

Pearl "Polly" Adler was born April 16, 1900, in Yanow, Belorussia, the eldest of two daughters and seven sons of Morris Adler, a tailor, and his wife, Gertrude Koval. In the beginning the plan was for her to attend school in Pinsk to complete her education, begun under the Yanow village rabbi. However, when she was thirteen, her father decided to send her to relatives in Holyoke, Massachusetts, as the first of a planned (and eventually successful) emigration of the entire family to the United States. After her move Polly did housework while attending school to learn English. When World War I severed both communications with her family and the monthly stipend they sent to supplement her income as a maid, she moved to Brooklyn to live with cousins and worked in a shirt factory while continuing to attend school.

At seventeen she was raped by a foreman at the factory. When she discovered she was pregnant, she had an abortion and, after an argument with her scandalized relatives, moved to Manhattan, where she found work in a corset factory and shared a Riverside Drive apartment. Her roommate, a showgirl, introduced her to a bootlegger, who offered her the opportunity to go into the business that would make her infamous. She would live in an apartment paid for by the bootlegger, and whenever he and his married girlfriend weren't there, she would procure girls and provide the apartment as a rendezvous site for his friends. Adler soon ended up with her own clientele and received her first arrest for operating a house of prostitution (the first of thirteen arrests; she got off free on all but one, in 1935, for which she served thirty days scrubbing floors in jail). The bootlegger, unidentified in all the biographical material, was clearly Dutch Schultz, as he was credited by her with providing protection for the new business.

In 1922 she ended the arrangement because she had saved enough money to open her own legitimate business (a lingerie store). When it folded the following year, Polly was left broke and, seeing no other options, took up the career of a madam again, opening the first of a series of ever-more-luxurious bordellos. In the late '20s she would also open a branch bordello in Saratoga Springs, New York, then a famous summer retreat for upper-class racehorse aficionados, many of whom were her clients. Polly also took advantage of the influx of visitors for the 1939 World's Fair, since out-of-towners needed her services just as much as native New Yorkers.

As her fame (or infamy) grew, flogged by the newspapers of the day, Adler became the avatar of the classic American madam: feisty, disreputable, but nevertheless a victor over adversity. She would often show up at major nightclub openings surrounded by a bevy of her most beautiful girls, which prompted many in the audience to relate the latest "Polly gossip." She chose her girls carefully. "I always engaged girls with enough experience behind them to make them interesting to my customers," she once said. She was also demanding about their appearance. "I insisted that they use a minimum of makeup and dress quietly," she explained. "The days of the flagrantly dressed, flagrant tarts who tossed down their snorts of rotgut with their little finger well out were long past." Patrons of her bordellos were always formally introduced to the girls, mostly by their real names, since they knew that Adler would never betray them. It was customary for a client to have a drink or two with the ladies available, then nod to the one he chose and suggest, "Let's take a walk. . . ."

In 1931 Adler was called to testify before the Seabury Commission, which was impaneled to investigate corrupt cops and judges but was really out to get the goods on the popular mayor, Jimmy Walker. To avoid testifying she hid out in Florida for a few months until she missed New York (or missed the money from her business) and returned. She was then summoned before Judge Seabury and the district attorney but refused to talk about her business or clients or betray any of her associates. After a major raid in 1935, Polly changed her operation from having girls live on premises to calling them in when she—well, her clients—needed them.

Polly Adler remained in business until 1943 when, realizing that in the World War II–paced New York City, the time had passed for brothels like hers, she closed her doors and retired to Burbank, California, before moving to Hollywood. She completed her high school education and enrolled in L. A. Valley College when she was approaching fifty.

Her fame didn't end after she retired. When *A House Is Not a Home* (ghostwritten by novelist Virginia Faulkner) was published a decade later, it shot right to the top of the *New York Times* best-seller list (ironically, for a time it shared that number-one position with Norman Vincent Peale's *The Power of Positive Thinking*, a subject about which Adler, who claimed that "your heart often knows things before your mind does," was something of an authority).

Surprisingly, the attraction of her memoir was not only its titillating tales of the sexual and political exploits of the rich, the famous, and the infamous. It was a success because she put together a book that provided a fascinating social history of the era: immigrant mobility; prostitution; police dishonesty; the "white slavery" scare; political corruption; and Jewish life in New York in the early part of the twentieth century. Most other accounts of the New York City underworld focus on the lives of men—from Herbert Asbury's *Gangs of New York* through Mario Puzo's *Godfather* books to more recent studies about Jewish and Italian gangsters. Adler's book brought women's lives and problems during a tumultuous period to the forefront. Although suffrage had finally succeeded (in 1920), women were still treated like chattel by many levels of society, and Polly wrote on these issues in a frank, honest, appealing manner. For the 2006 republication of *A House Is*

Not a Home, Elizabeth Ewen, author of *Immigrant Women in the Land of Dollars: Life and Culture on the Lower East Side, 1890–1925*, wrote: ". . . it rescues from oblivion a vibrant and compelling immigrant story, presenting it from a new vantage point and allowing the reader to see the contradictions of the period Polly Adler lived through within a broadly painted historical context."

In 1959 her notoriety led the writer and critic Cleveland Amory to list her in his register of celebrities.

Polly Adler died of cancer on June 9, 1962. Two years later, Embassy Pictures made a film based on her book, starring Shelley Winters as Polly, Robert Taylor as a bootlegger, Cesar Romero as Lucky Luciano, with Broderick Crawford, Kaye Ballard, and, in the role of a call girl, Raquel Welch. Taylor's role of Frank Costigan was obviously inspired by Dutch Schultz, but Hollywood being Hollywood, the handsome actor could never have directly played a person whom Lucky Luciano said looked and dressed "like a pig." As with many films, despite a good cast the movie wasn't nearly as captivating as the book.

The end of Polly's life resembled more the "kick in the teeth" she had joked about earlier than the "kick out of life." Dale Olson, destined to become one of Hollywood's most famous film publicists, met her when he was still covering the nightclub circuit for *Daily Variety*. "She lived in a small apartment in Hollywood and had nothing, no money, nothing," he recalled recently. "She was bitter with what life had dealt her and would never talk about the old days. Her brother, Bob Adler, owned a nightclub in La Cienega Boulevard, Adler's 900, and basically kept her alive.

"(Bob) was very fond of her, and we became friends because he knew I liked her," Olson added. "We met at the opening night of a production of Jean Genet's *The Balcony* at a small theater in Hollywood. A friend of hers, Beatrice Kay, brought her, and we had drinks together at Bob Adler's place afterwards. [Kay was a Gay Nineties–type singer who was the first headliner in Las Vegas and was famous for her song "Mention My Name in Sheboygan," as well as for popularizing "Only a Bird in a Gilded Cage." She made several films, perhaps the most notable being *Billy Rose's Diamond Horseshoe* with Betty Grable.] We became friends but not close friends. . . . I don't think she had any close friends other than some neighbors who didn't know anything about her background.

"She seemed a bit dotty, but then of course Beatrice Kay was a bit dotty, too. Polly Adler just looked old and tired," Olson recalls, "dressed like a JCPenney discard," alone with her memories.

Former chorus girl Mary Louise ("Texas") Guinan initially rode into history as Hollywood's first movie cowgirl but then became a legend as New York's Queen of the Nightclubs. She ran several of the most famous speakeasies in town. Her secret? The best booze, the sexiest chorus girls, and possessing one of the rudest mouths in town with which she would genially insult patrons ranging from society leaders and film stars to gangsters and tourists.

Billy Rose Theatre Division, The New York Public Library for the Performing Arts, Astor, Lenox and Tilden Foundations

CHAPTER 6

QUEEN OF THE NIGHTCLUBS
Texas Guinan

Hello, sucker!
—Texas Guinan's frequent greeting to her nightclub's patrons

Millionaires were made during the Roaring Twenties, both via the stock market and by bootlegging illegal liquor during Prohibition. But no one made money more colorfully than a tough-talking lady from Waco, Texas, who, after a short stint as a wife in Denver, moved to New York in 1906 to break into show business. It took a while, but eventually Mary Louise Cecilia Guinan found a job as a chorus girl. Over the next decade she became popular on the vaudeville circuit and appeared in several musicals, among them *Miss Bob White*, *The Hoyden*, and *The Gay Musician*.

Then in 1917 she was noticed in one of her shows by a scout visiting from the Balboa Studios in Long Beach, California, a film production company that boasted it was the largest independent studio outside Hollywood. He was looking for promising girls to cast as gunslingers in the popular Westerns that were being cranked out (literally, for cranking was how early film cameras were operated) by the hundreds in Hollywood. Reportedly, someone had told him about Mary, who was by then going by the nickname of "Texas," and although it was stretching a point to call her a "girl" (she was thirty-three at the time), it was otherwise a perfect match. Texas Guinan had been raised on a ranch near Waco and not only had learned to ride well, but had also become a highly accomplished roper . . . or so she claimed.

The movie in which she first rode into film history as Hollywood's first cowgirl was *The Wildcat*; unfortunately, America's entry into World War I limited the movie's release. Guinan later claimed that she then took off for Europe to entertain the boys in uniform for a few weeks before returning to the film capital to make more films that would earn her the title of "Queen of the West" and "the female Bill Hart" (after William S. Hart, a popular early film cowboy known as "two-gun Hart" for his shoot-out technique).

Hart claimed that the guns he used in his films were originally owned by Billy the Kid. Who knows? Again, Hollywood being Hollywood, a good story could always be improved upon. So it's not surprising that Texas Guinan became a virtuoso of the tall tale. After she became famous she would claim that as a youth she rode broncos, single-handedly rounded up cattle on a fifty-thousand-acre ranch, and attended an elite East Coast finishing school—but also that she once ran off to join a circus. Her claim about entertaining the troops in France was also pure hokum, as was her added claim (which, like everything she said, most of the press swallowed wholesale) that she had received a medal from French Marshal Joffre.

In fact, Guinan apparently had never left Hollywood, where she worked throughout the war and until 1922, making thirty-six films—mostly hour-long two-reelers—although she would later claim she made three hundred. At least she was consistent in playing a tough Western gunslinger; among her titles were *The Hellcat*, *The She Wolf*, *The Gun Woman* (1918), and *Little Miss Deputy* (1919). Some of her movies were made for her own production company, which she formed in 1921 because her age was catching up with her and producers, then as now, favored younger, more beautiful stars. Nevertheless, she had attracted fans, which, it was said, included President Harding and Edward, the Prince of Wales, later King Edward VIII and then the Duke of Windsor. Edward visited San Diego in 1920, where he almost certainly met Wallis Warfield Simpson, the woman for whom he gave up his throne (she was then married to a naval officer stationed there). And since the visit was highly publicized, Texas, opportunist as she was, probably made a beeline for the reception for the prince at the Del Coronado Hotel.

Be that as it may, by then Prohibition had arrived, and Guinan, tired, as she put it, of "kissing horses in horse operas," sensed an even greater opportunity in New York. She died her brunette hair a brassy blonde and headed back East in 1922. Like her move to Hollywood, it was the right one at the right time, the difference being that this move would make her so famous that, within a generation, several major movies would be made that were about or inspired by her new career—the Queen of the West became the Queen of the Nightclubs.

As Louise Berliner recounts in her book, *Texas Guinan: Queen of the Nightclubs*, one evening Texas showed up at a party at the Beaux Arts Café on West Fortieth Street, where among the guests was operetta composer Sigmund Romberg and Pearl White, star of the popular *Perils of Pauline* film serials. Nevertheless, as Texas recalled years later (perhaps telling the truth for once) the party was so dull that "someone asked me to sing, I didn't need much coaxing, so I sang. First thing you know we were all doing things. Everybody had a great time." Getting people "doing things" was, from that moment on, her life's work (the more inebriated they were, the better, since during Prohibition that was a good way of separating their money from the owners).

Emile Gervasini, the Beaux Arts Café's owner, knowing a good thing when he saw it, hired Texas as his café's "hostess." Although she was the first woman to be an emcee in a club, she didn't stay long. The owner of the King Cole room at the Knickerbocker Hotel on West Forty-Second Street invited Texas to run his club, and she did (the thirty-foot-long painting by Maxfield Parrish titled *Old King Cole and His Fiddlers Three* that gave the room its name now hangs in the St. Regis Hotel). The place became so popular that on a given night you might see Rudolph Valentino and John Barrymore there, as well as a string of society leaders including Mrs. W. K. Vanderbilt, a reigning queen of New York society.

Probably motivated by realizing where the real money was, in 1924 Texas joined forces with a Broadway hustler and mobster named Larry Fey. Via a fleet of taxis he owned, Fey smuggled so much liquor from Canada that, bankrolled by the mob, he decided to open the El Fey Club, the "granddaddy of all speakeasies," as it has since been called, to sell his illegal hooch. Guinan liked the place (a narrow space located at 105 West Forty-Fifth Street, with a dance space so small that barely a dozen people could squeeze onto it), and she soon became the hostess—perhaps "ringmaster" is a better word—backed by a troupe of scantily clad chorus girls and receiving a cut of the profits. She soon made it the hottest "speak" in town, attracting everyone from the top society leaders to mobsters. Writers Dorothy Parker, Robert Benchley, and Damon Runyon were regulars, as were George Raft (then the top Charleston dancer in town and later a wooden actor and "greeter" at Havana's Mafia-owned Capri Hotel and Casino), Mayor Jimmy Walker (chapter 1), and screen cowboy Tom Mix. The place was catnip for gossip writers of the time.

Another reason for the success of the El Fey club was the notoriety engendered by Guinan's legendary rude quips. She famously greeted many customers with "Hello, suckers!" and coined the phrase that defined the entire decade: "Curfew shall not ring tonight." Soon she began calling her rich customers "butter and egg men." How that line came about was also part of the mythology of the era.

One night, so the story goes, a drunk customer started handing out fifty-dollar bills to Guinan's girls. When Texas asked him what business he was in to be able to throw around so much cash ($50 then had the buying power of more than $600 today). "Dairy produce," he answered. Without missing a beat, Texas exhorted her audience: "Give a big hand for the big butter-and-egg man." Playwright George S. Kaufman, a regular patron of the El Fey (as well as Guinan's later clubs) knew a great line when he heard it and lifted her quip as the title for his theatrical send-up of Broadway, *The Butter and Egg Man*.

Eventually, curfew did ring at the El Fey itself, and Guinan moved on. She opened a new "speak" at 151 West Fifty-Fourth Street, which she dubbed the "300 Club," not far from Sherman Billingsley's original site for his famous Stork Club. The operation was similar to that of the El Fey, but now, because the place was bigger, there were forty dancers; as before, she usually served the best and most expensive booze in town (champagne was $25 a bottle, more than $300 today).

Clearly, there was more to Guinan's operations than beautiful chorus girls and expensive, illegal booze. Like Polly Adler's bordellos (chapter 5), the "speaks," the good ones anyway, were places where like-minded people could gather and socialize, clubs in effect where the insiders got together. By reporting the nightly carryings-on at Guinan's place, Walter Winchell, a young reporter and gossip columnist, made his name and career (explored in depth in chapter 7).

The print publicity explains the popularity of the place; people like to see their names in writing, as well as have fun. And at her new place not only did Guinan's old patrons such as Rudolph Valentino and John Barrymore become regulars, so too did millionaires—Walter Chrysler, Harry Payne Whitney, Reggie Vanderbilt—and other film stars—Gloria Swanson, Al Jolson, Pola Negri, John Gilbert, Clara Bow—all happily downing bottles of Moët while George Gershwin played the piano. And it was at the 300 Club that George Raft and Ruby Keeler, two of Guinan's regular dancers, were discovered by Broadway and Hollywood talent scouts.

In 1926 Guinan reportedly made more than $700,000 (the equivalent of over $8.5 million today). A lot of that money had to go out as payoffs; in fact, Texas was able to stay in business only by repeatedly paying bribes and exorbitant fines, then opening a new club after the fines went into some politician's pockets and the place was padlocked anyway. She was occasionally arrested, but her clashes with the law actually brought in more business. "Two Senators See Guinan Club Raided" ran one tabloid headline that said more about her place than any publicity she could have devised herself. "I like your cute little jail," Texas was quoted as remarking after one of her (short) incarcerations. "I don't know when my jewels have seemed so safe."

Finally, in June 1928, 150 Prohibition agents raided fifteen New York speaks. Of all those arrested only Texas Guinan pleaded not guilty ("I never sold any liquor, etc.") to the charges, which automatically meant a trial.

Of course, everyone important knew she was guilty, but as so many of them were also customers, most wanted her to get off. Both agents testifying for the prosecution admitted under tough questioning by Guinan's attorney that they had often patronized her club and had not only used taxpayers' money to buy enough illegal liquor to prove that alcohol was being sold on the premises, but enough—several hundred dollars' worth—to entertain themselves and their friends. In cross examination her gift for fast retorts often confused the prosecuting attorney, especially when she claimed that she had never sold a drink (she said the patrons always brought their own), nor touched a drop of liquor in her life because, as a businesswoman, she needed a clear head to run the club. She also added that her girls were forced to dance closely with the customers because the place was so small. Guinan was found not guilty, and all the publicity from the trial, gleefully reported daily in the press, only increased her business. She was immediately offered jobs from around the country and opened more clubs.

But the Great Depression was affecting everything, even the business in the speakeasies. Texas, who starred in a musical revue called *Glorifying the American Girl* (later an all-star film in which stars and celebrities from Eddie Cantor and Helen Morgan to Mayor Jimmy Walker played themselves), also starred in the aptly named *Padlocks of 1927*. The *Time* review of July 18, 1927, says just about everything about Guinan, her image, and the atmosphere of the age:

> *Mary Louise ("Texas") Guinan, queen-mother of the night clubs, shunted her honkytonk furies into the Shubert Theatre to dispense the usual small attentions with large-scale intimacy. She makes her entrance riding down the aisle on a white Arabian horse. Her locally famed "girlies" rush out among the audience, pelting them with cotton balls. Miss Guinan herself is in the aisles as often as on the stage, shaking hands, bantering wisecracks, kissing bald pates that clearly answer for her rouged caresses. While she is changing costumes,*

> *vaudevillians take the stage. There is a heavy tragic skit in which Texas weeps real tears, thanks the audience with honest sobs for their applause. Intimate glimpses of her night club adventure are revealed. "Hello, Sucker, Whaddaya mean ya been overcharged, lemme see that check. Why, ya poor sap! $124, huh! Sucker, you had two telephone calls. Don't be dumb."*
>
> *It is not a revue at all. It is less clever, more loud, bawdy, vulgar and—to people who like that sort of thing—vastly more entertaining than a Times Square revue could ever be, for the revue is not native while the night club is—even in a theatre. It has the perfection of a weed that grows unashamedly where Nature intended. It has the dignity of a hoyden who scorns the hypocrisy of petticoats. Undoubtedly, it lacks refinement and many another virtue. "Honestly, Tex," says a stage policeman along in the second act, "don't you think virtue pays?" To which the Soul of Candor replies with a tolerant shrug, "Sure, if you got a market for it, sure it pays."*

Like the trial that was turned from a setback into a triumph by Guinan's wit, so too was her 1931 decision to take the girls on a tour of Europe, inspired by the impact that the Depression was having on her New York club business and her success in showing off "her girls" in the *Padlocks of 1927* show. But her reputation had preceded her, and her troupe was not allowed to disembark in England or France. Never one to be discouraged, after returning home Texas laughed it off, made a pun based on a famous line about the French: "It all goes to show that fifty million Frenchman *could* be wrong"; and created a new revue with the girls based on her rejection named *Too Hot for Paris*.

When the tour of *Paris* ended, Guinan became hostess (apparently under gangster pressure) of a Chicago club and eventually ended up in Los Angeles, where she claimed she "got religion" from the famous evangelist Aimee Semple McPherson at her Church of the Foursquare Gospel. The pair had met in New York in 1927, when McPherson made a 3 a.m. visit to the 300 Club. Texas welcomed her by asking for "a hand for the brave little woman" as Guinan, wearing all her jewels, stood arm in arm with the white-gowned, marcelled McPherson. Needless to say, the unlikely friendship was milked for all its publicity value, especially when Texas took all her girls to McPherson's services at her Glad Tidings Tabernacle on West Thirty-Third Street. As cameras clicked, Texas and her gang joined in the prayers and hymns and listened solemnly to the evangelist's sermon.

But Texas was getting tired. She had driven herself every night for a decade in New York and before that successfully competed in the dog-eat-dog world of early Hollywood moviemaking. As New York and the nation sank into the gloom of the Great Depression, Texas decided that the only way she could stay alive professionally was to keep moving on to places where her fame could guarantee a box office. In 1933 one of the destinations on a tour of the Northwest was Vancouver, British Columbia. While there she suffered amoebic dysentery and a perforated bowel and, after unsuccessful surgery, died on November 5, 1933. A month later Prohibition ended.

"The funeral I want is a nightclub wake, a motorcycle escort, and college boys singing songs to the cemetery," Texas once joked. She didn't get the nightclub send-off or the singing college boys, but what she did get would probably have pleased the lady from Waco. More than twelve thousand people, including many of her show-biz friends, filed past her flower-banked casket at Frank Campbell's Funeral Chapel in New York, the same place where thousands had mobbed her former patron Rudolph Valentino's funeral six years before. She was dressed in a sequined gown and large diamonds, which her family removed before closing the casket. Movie cameras recorded it, and the *New York Herald Tribune* editorialized: "She was a master showman, and accomplished psychologist. . . . She had ability too, and would have been successful in any one of a dozen more conventional fields. To New York and the rest of the country Texas was a flaming leader of a period which was a lot of fun while it lasted."

Texas Guinan felt the same way about the city that had given her fame. On her deathbed in Vancouver, she said, "I would rather have a square inch of New York than all the rest of the world." She was only forty-nine when she died.

Before her death, Texas had returned to Hollywood to make three sound films, in each playing somewhat fictionalized versions of herself: *Queen of the Night Clubs* (1929), *Glorifying the American Girl* (also 1929, in which she, like many of her costars, was unidentified), and then *Broadway Through a Keyhole* (1933, written by Winchell). None was successful, although *Glorifying the American Girl*, with its amazing cast and the occasional use of the new technique of Technicolor, is much sought after by film fans.

Mae West based much of her career on being a wisecracking vamp, and much of it, certainly her first such film appearance in 1932's *Night After Night*, was based directly on Guinan. In the film West's leading man was played by Guinan's former dancer George Raft in his first leading-man role. Supposedly, Raft wanted the studio to cast Guinan in the film, but West got it because she was nine years younger.

In the 1939 film *The Roaring Twenties*, the character Panama Smith, played by Gladys George, was based on Guinan and costar James Cagney's part on Larry Fey. In 1984's *The Cotton Club*, the part of Vera (played by Diane Lane) is based on Texas, who also inspired the song "All That Jazz" in the musical *Chicago*. Madonna once planned a Guinan revival but it didn't pan out; however, some of the songs were included in her 2005 album *Confessions on a Dance Floor*. And in *Star Trek: The Next Generation*, the bartender played by Whoopi Goldberg was named Guinan after her.

Sophie Tucker remembered that Guinan "had something that made everyone feel instantly at ease and ready for a good time." Texas herself once said: "Listen, suckers, why take life so seriously? In a hundred years we will all be gone or in some stuffy book. Give me plenty of laughs and you can take all the rest."

In the 1920s, by dishing dirt directly and by innuendo, former vaudevillian Walter Winchell more or less invented the gossip industry as we know it today. At the height of his career, when more than 50 million people read his newspaper column and, in the 1930s, another 20 million tuned in to his radio broadcasts, even the most powerful people in America—among them FBI boss J. Edgar Hoover—would cater to him.

Courtesy of Marc Wanamaker/Bison Archives

CHAPTER 7

The Birth of Gossip Journalism

Walter Winchell

What do you know that I don't know?
—Gossip column pioneer Walter Winchell's usual greeting to people, both acquaintances and strangers, in the 1920s

Gossip has been called the second oldest profession . . . and with good reason. Columnist Liz Smith has said that gossip "is news running ahead of itself in a red satin dress"—in other words, news of who's doing what to whom (and why) in the next cave down the way, confided in an irresistible way. Sometimes the news is flattering, sometimes it's hurtful; nevertheless, most people have always been hooked on gossip, whether they admit it or not. In fact, a recent survey turned up the astonishing fact that people in the early twenty-first century spend up to *two-thirds* of their time gossiping (and gossip is *always* about people), making scuttlebutt the most highly valued social currency there is.

Today it's a major industry, but that wasn't always the case, at least not in its present dimensions. There have long been people who dished the dirt: Daniel Defoe, who, a decade and a half before writing *Robinson Crusoe* in 1719, devised what was apparently the first gossip newspaper. And during the so-called Gay Nineties, New York's high society quailed at the revelations Colonel William d'Alton Mann peddled in the waspish *Town Topics,* which could be considered New York's first gossip rag. But his audience was relatively limited. Mann rarely concerned himself with the carryings-on of those outside the legendary "400," said to be the number of people who could be accommodated in the ballroom of Caroline Astor, Mrs. William Backhouse Astor—*the* Mrs. Astor of the era. The circulation of *Town Topics* rarely topped four thousand.

But with the arrival of the movies in the early years of the twentieth century, matters changed dramatically. No longer was an audience limited to a few hundred; now millions wanted the inside skinny about all those beautiful people up there on the silver screen. People became passionately interested in what the stars did with their spare time, what they liked or disliked—even their favorite food—but most important, people wanted to know who they were dating (unlike today, "dating" in the 1920s meant little more than a movie and a burger), sleeping with, or—bingo!—with whom they were cheating on their spouses.

Enter the syndicated gossip columnist. Supported by the newly arrived professional press agent who, as part of the job, "serviced" gossip—sometimes real, sometimes made up—to the columnists. In the 1930s and '40s, Louella Parsons (whose column was carried in William Randolph Hearst's newspapers) and her archrival Hedda Hopper, who wrote for the Chicago Tribune Syndicate, became so powerful that they terrified publicists and stars alike. When Douglas Fairbanks and Mary Pickford, the reigning "king and queen" of Hollywood, decided to divorce in 1933, Parsons was the first person Mary, beloved by millions of film fans as "America's Sweetheart," telephoned with the news.

The kind of power that came to be wielded by gossip columnists began in the 1920s, when the very concept of a gossip columnist was born. And the person who started it all and who, for more than a generation, remained the most powerful of them all, was a five-foot, seven-inch, ferret-faced New Yorker named Walter Winchell. In his heyday he would write six fast-paced columns each week that were printed in nearly two thousand newspapers and reached an estimated fifty million homes. His Sunday radio broadcasts, begun in the 1930s, reached another twenty million.

What set him apart from everyone else? For one thing, it was his style. On the radio, his breathless, high-pitched voice introducing the show ("Mr. and Mrs. North and South America and all ships at sea: Let's go to press!") would be instantly recognized by a generation of listeners. So, too, would his narration of the news and gossip with machine-gun speed (he was once clocked at one hundred ninety-seven words per minute) while a telegraph key clicked away in the background. In his column he also introduced a shorthand reporting style that was instantly imitated: terse items of news connected by three dots.

Unlike his Hollywood counterparts, who, although tyrants to work with, were relatively gentle in their reporting (even at their toughest they never forgot that the golden goose of Hollywood was providing the golden eggs of their fame and power), Winchell would more often than not go for the jugular, gaining (and keeping) his power and fame by revealing the salacious, mean, and bitchy scandal and gossip. Usually, he did it by innuendo, but in such a way that everyone knew exactly what he was saying. He once admitted, "Gossip is the art of saying nothing in a way that leaves practically nothing unsaid." He, as pointed out in Neal Gabler's brilliant biography, *Winchell: Gossip, Power, and the Culture of Celebrity*, "understood the bitter subtext of gossip; how invading the lives of the famous and revealing their secrets empowered both the purveyor and the audience."

For years Winchell ruled his kingdom from table fifty in the exclusive Cub Room of Sherman Billingsley's Stork Club, which, when starting out, he first made famous as New York's place to be and to be seen (chapter 2). There he would hold court with film stars, politicians, occasionally mobsters and lucky press agents; that is, when they could get past the Cub Room's imperious maitre d'. A mention of a client in Winchell's column could make a press agent's career, as well as that of his or her client. Some "flacks," as press agents were called then (and now), were hired merely because they could "break Winchell" (referring to his column); the going rate to the client was $150 (some $1,800 today) for an "orchid," slang for praise in the column. Of course, to be able to "plant an item" about a client meant that a press agent had to have become a reliable supplier of inside news and especially scoops. Winchell preferred that the "items" be written in his own style so he or his long-time assistant, Rose Bigman, had to do little more than put it in the daily column verbatim.

By the 1930s Winchell's word could make or break a Broadway show. Like his Hollywood counterparts, his announcements of celebrity romances, marriages, and divorces—all couched in his slangy terms—engrossed his readers while still keeping his Stork Club table busy as he reported the local carryings-on of café society. Nightly, he, like the burgeoning crowd of Broadway gossip columnists, including Leonard Lyons, Earl Wilson, Ed Sullivan, and the legendary Cholly Knickerbocker (the pen name of the *Journal American*'s gossip columnist), would visit other clubs and restaurants, such as Jack and Charlie's "21," a speakeasy turned restaurant, and the popular El Morocco, to pick up news. By the 1930s, when his fame and number of enemies had become gigantic, Winchell would often be accompanied by a pair of burly bodyguards when making his rounds of the nightspots; a favorite was Lindy's, a restaurant then frequented by reporters from the nearby *New York Times*, as well as a host of Damon Runyonesque characters.

Even J. Edgar Hoover, the formidable head of the FBI, supplied Walter Winchell with news in the 1930s in return for his support. The Hoover connection started when Winchell, who had become "an intimate friend" of Owney "the Killer" Madden—who was heavily involved in New York's crime world of the '20s, owner of the Cotton Club, and a boxing promoter—began to worry that he might be "rubbed out" for knowing too much. Winchell fled to Los Angeles but soon returned as an outspoken supporter of Hoover, for whom, in 1939, he claimed to have engineered the dramatic surrender of Louis "Lepke" Buchalter, head of Murder, Inc. (although those close to the affair suggest that mobster Frank Costello had more to do with Buchalter's surrender). Whatever the real story, Winchell would later consider Buchalter's surrender his own "real-life movie," although the publicity potential was lessened by the news coverage of the buildup of the Nazi war machine, which would invade Poland one week later.

Winchell, who was Jewish, was one of the first journalists to go after Adolph Hitler and the pro-Nazi organizations in America, especially the German-America Bund, which was headquartered in Manhattan's German community on East Eighty-Sixth Street. Throughout his term as president, FDR enjoyed Winchell's fervid support, and during World War II the highly patriotic columnist often made optimistic predictions to divert his readers and listeners from bad news.

Walter Winschel (the original spelling) was born on April 7, 1897, at 116 East 112th Street, the second child of Jacob Winschel, a shirtmaker, and his wife Jennie. The couple were so poor that they constantly moved from apartment to apartment during Walter's childhood, both to stay ahead of the rent collector and to take advantage of move-in discounts, then as now offered by many landlords. Walter's parents also had a contentious relationship, fueled by Jacob's infidelity and frequent neglect of their children.

When he was nine Walter was making a little money by delivering the Harlem *Home News* and the *Evening Journal* and selling subscriptions to the *Saturday Evening Post* at a news kiosk at 116th and Lenox Avenue (where on rainy days for a nickel he would shelter passengers getting on or off the elevated railroad). He was also teaching himself to tap dance and, with a friend, ushered and sung songs at the Imperial Theater in Harlem (a soon-to-be-added third member of the group, billed as "Little Men With Big Voices," was George Jessel, who would evolve into a multitalented comic entertainer and one day would be known as the "Toastmaster General of the United States" for his frequent role as master of ceremonies at major political and entertainment events).

For several years Winchell made a living—barely—as a vaudevillian, eventually partnering with a dancer named Rita Greene, whom he married in 1919 when he was twenty-two. The following year he began to get off the vaudeville circuit when he got a freelance job as a writer for the newspaper published by impresario Edward Albee's National Vaudeville Artists organization, the *Vaudeville News*. He was soon hired full time, but as Gabler noted in his biography, the decade he spent in vaudeville (instead of going to school) "made Walter an entertainer for life and *in* life. Growing up in vaudeville as he did, he not only absorbed its diversity, its energy, and its nihilism, and then deployed them in his journalism, but [he also] learned how to create his journalism *from* them: journalism as vaudeville."

Rita meanwhile continued as a vaudevillian, and her touring, combined with Winchell's full-time obsession with his job, eventually destroyed their marriage. Meanwhile Winchell had received an offer to work for a new paper, the *Evening Graphic*, a tabloid project of an eccentric health faddist named Bernarr Macfadden, who had made a fortune with the magazine *Physical Culture* and a more sensationalized publication named *True Story*. Macfadden knew what he wanted the *Evening Graphic* to be; a newspaper that delivered entertainment rather than news, with screaming headlines above provocative innuendoes, news of mayhem and disasters, often accompanied by doctored photos (called "composographs"). It would (and did) far out-yellow the notorious yellow journalism of earlier days. Along with the *Chicago Tribune*'s New York baby sister, the *Illustrated Daily News*, and William Randolph Hearst's *Daily Mirror*, both launched only months before, the *Evening Graphic* would be one of America's first tabloids. It eventually became so outrageous that *Time*, then in its infancy (chapter 16), described the *Graphic* as "hardly a newspaper," and the New York Public Library stopped carrying it. One reportedly true story that became a standing joke in New York's journalism world involved a reporter's mother, who suggested that her son leave the *Graphic* and return to his former, more respectable job as a piano player in a whorehouse.

But for Winchell—no longer "Winschel"—whose column "Your Broadway and Mine" first appeared on September 20, 1924, the *Evening Graphic* would be his passport to journalistic legend. He was nervous about competing with the many other columnists in the New York media who basically reported general news about happenings about town, Broadway, and the like, but he had help. Through Sime Silverman, the founder of *Variety* in 1905, he met the speakeasy "queen" Texas Guinan, and from that moment her El Fey Club became his "fort" where he would nightly—usually from midnight until she closed the place around 5 a.m.—get much of the news for his column. In addition, Silverman, who knew New York show business like no one else, provided additional news contacts. Another acquaintance, Mark Hellinger—five years younger than Winchell and soon to be a columnist himself—became his inseparable buddy on Winchell's nightly prowls for news, when his standard greeting to people, whether he knew them or not, was, "What do you know that I don't know?"

Hellinger always spoke in slang, and his speaking style was absorbed so well by Walter that he would later be dubbed "the dictator of contemporary slang" by a New York speech professor. Speakeasies were often referred to in Winchell's column as "hush houses," liquor was "giggle-water," a mistress was a "keptive," and an exotic dancer was a "thigh-grinder." Winchell then soon added a new column on Mondays in which he dished the dirt on people with items separated by the soon-to-be-familiar triple dots, originally planned to give the column a new, up-to-date jazzy look.

His Broadway columns were hardly being neglected as he dug up dirt for the new column. Through his ability to gather news about happenings on the "Main Stem" (slang for Broadway), they became so important that he became known as the "Boswell of Broadway" in an era when the very name "Broadway" was as synonymous with escapism as Hollywood would become with glamor. Broadway (or "the incandescent belt," to use another Winchellism) was a place where gangsters looked like gangsters, showgirls looked like showgirls, and Winchell, with his slouched fedora and rumpled suit, looked like, well, a reporter.

There was more than gossip gathering going on in his life. Although he and Rita were only separated, he had taken up with a vaudevillian named June Aster, and in June 1923, while Winchell was still with the *Vaudeville News*, they had a baby girl. She was probably adopted, although cynics suggested that the child was theirs and had been born out of wedlock. Whatever the truth of the matter, Walter adored the child, whom he and June named Gloria. Four years later Walter and June had another child (no question this time: she was theirs), whom they named Walda, presumably short for "Waldarling," which cynics then insisted was an example of Winchell's fast-growing egomania. They also moved into the Whitby apartments at 325 West Forty-Fifth Street, convenient to Walter's theater district "beat."

June and Walter would never marry. Gloria would die of pneumonia in 1932 at the age of nine, Walda would spend time in psychiatric hospitals, and their son, Walter Jr., born in 1936, would commit suicide in the garage of his Orange County, California, home on Christmas night, 1968, after bouts of mental illness, failing as a minor columnist, and supporting his family with welfare payments of $191 monthly plus what he made as a dishwasher in a restaurant.

In 1929 Winchell was hired by the *New York Daily Mirror*, where his column was first syndicated.

There is a truism that the best way to become successful in life is to do what you really love to do. Walter Winchell loved gossip. Howard Clurman, his ghostwriter for more than twenty-five years, once wrote, "Winchell reacted almost physically to gossip, and seemed to purr with delight when he had a particularly juicy item." And for a generation, by dishing the dirt—true or made up—he would rule equally as kingmaker and destroyer.

After the Second World War, Winchell became as outspoken an enemy of Communism as he was of Nazism, and though understandable, given the Red Scare of the time, it was the beginning of the end of his career. Winchell's support for Senator McCarthy, who used lies and innuendoes in his notorious witch hunts to eradicate "Communists" and "fellow travelers" in government, was vocal and loudly so. As it turned out, McCarthy was never able to prove any of his charges; it was all grandstanding (or drunken fantasizing—McCarthy was an alcoholic who would die of cirrhosis of the liver in 1957). But by the time his fellow senators censured him in 1954, innumerable honorable careers had been destroyed by his accusations. Through his support of McCarthy, Winchell had also painted himself into a philosophical corner, filling his columns and broadcasts with vindictive and largely unsubstantiated accusations and tirades against those he considered America's enemies as well as his own, which resulted in libel lawsuits and the precipitous loss of syndicated outlets.

But he did some good with his power. In 1946, after his friend Damon Runyon died of cancer, Winchell went on the air soliciting funds to fight the disease. The response was so great that he set up the Damon Runyon Cancer Memorial Fund (since renamed the Damon Runyon Cancer Research Foundation), a popular celebrity charity to this day, which Winchell headed until his own death from prostate cancer in 1972.

In 1948, along with political columnist Drew Pearson, Winchell mounted a personal attack on Secretary of Defense James Forrestal over Forrestal's opposition to defense cuts, which was said to have contributed to Forrestal's suicide in 1949. (Winchell also revealed that Forrestal had cut a private deal with the 1948 Republican candidate, Thomas Dewey, to continue as secretary of defense when, it was assumed, Dewey would defeat Harry Truman. This of course backfired when Truman was reelected.)

After the expatriate African-American singer Josephine Baker accused him of hypocrisy in not denouncing the racist policies of his Stork Club hangout, Winchell accused her of being a Communist, thus preventing her from having her visa renewed (the case was so sensational that even such Stork Club regulars as Grace Kelly never set foot in the place again).

The late Lyle Stuart, who worked as a Winchell legman (a person employed to gather news) before deserting him when Winchell became a supporter of McCarthy, wrote in his 1953 expose *The Secret Life of Walter Winchell* that, although there was no documentation, his father, Jacob Winschel, was known as a child molester. Stuart later admitted that the story was as "scurrilous as the stuff [Winchell] does," but it showed that by midcentury, Walter Winchell, after decades of impregnability created by fear of his power, was himself beginning to be as vulnerable to gossip as those he had victimized.

In 1956 Walter made a deal with Desilu Productions (Lucille Ball and her husband Desi Arnaz's company) for a television show to be called *The Walter Winchell File*, sponsored by Revlon. It was narrated by Winchell, and he also appeared in it. But the times were changing, and now that television was in the ascendancy, celebrities no longer had to hang around the Stork Club or El Morocco in New York or Ciro's or Romanoff's in Los Angeles to have a chat with a columnist; they, if they were important enough, could go on air and tell their story their way.

For Hollywood, Walter Winchell's own life story read like a movie script, and in fact it inspired one with dire consequences for the columnist. Audiences attending 1957's *The Sweet Smell of Success* knew very well that Burt Lancaster, who played a destructive gossip monger, was really a stand-in for Walter Winchell in the film. But instead of flopping at the box office as Winchell optimistically predicted, it not only was a huge success but, because of the apparently honest way in which it portrayed the sleazy underbelly of Broadway journalism, also became a cinema classic. As Gabler points out in his book, it was a film "that was to destroy his [Winchell's] reputation for posterity the way his association with [Senator Joseph] McCarthy had destroyed it in the eyes of so many of his contemporaries."

Several years earlier Winchell had run a totally specious item claiming that broadcaster Jack Paar's marriage was in trouble. Paar asked him for a retraction, which Winchell refused. Then, after 1957, when Paar became the host of *The Tonight Show*, he got even. Paar attacked Winchell personally (in one unforgettable episode, suggesting that Winchell's voice was high "because he wears too-tight underwear"). When the nurse attending June in a Phoenix hospital showed her the story, she, according to the columnist, "had a third heart attack."

As PBS's *Pioneers of Television* "Late Night" episode pointed out in 2008, "Paar's feud with newspaper columnist Walter Winchell marked a major turning point in American media power. No one had ever dared criticize Winchell because a few lines in his column could destroy a career, but when Winchell disparaged Paar in print, Paar fought back and mocked Winchell repeatedly on the air. Paar's criticisms effectively ended Winchell's career. The tables had turned, now TV had the power."

Revlon canceled his television show, and he returned to his vaudeville roots for a stint at the Tropicana Hotel in Las Vegas (at a reported thirty-five thousand a week, a far cry from his vaudeville earnings forty years earlier). But he was getting old—and sounding it. Even when he signed on to narrate ABC's new series *The Untouchables*, his signature growl had lost its punch.

By 1962 Winchell's New York column was dying, too. After an extended newspaper strike, the *Mirror* went out of business, and Hearst passed him over to their *Journal-American*, but it was not the same, and Winchell constantly complained about how much he missed the *Mirror*. He retreated to Los Angeles for a time, where his sixty-seventh birthday was celebrated by a full house at the Ambassador Hotel's Cocoanut Grove nightclub, attended by the likes of Jayne Mansfield and Robert Stack, the star of *The Untouchables*. Eventually, Winchell was left with only one outlet, the *Journal-American*, where editors, fearful of libel suits, heavily edited his work, occasionally running only one of six columns submitted weekly.

The gossip column—at least as it was written from the 1920s—essentially died in the mid-1960s, when Louella Parsons gave up hers, and Hedda Hopper died. It would eventually find new, gentler life under the bylines of Liz Smith, whose column was carried by New York papers for thirty-three years (she started her career as Igor Cassini's assistant when he wrote the *Journal-American's* Cholly Knickerbocker column), and Marianne Strong, who wrote for the *New York World-Telegram and Sun* for a decade starting in the mid-1950s before opening her own society-oriented public relations firm. On June 30, 1967, after the last paper to be carrying his column, the hybridized (for economy) *World-Journal-Tribune* folded, a Hearst executive told Winchell that his contract was being canceled. He became desperate, actually running an "I'm available" ad in *Variety* and telling the publisher of *Women's Wear Daily* that he would stand on a corner and sell it if they would carry his column.

Finally, he bowed to the inevitable, announcing his retirement on February 5, 1969, although in fact he really had nothing to retire from. He cited as the reason both his son's suicide and June's delicate health (who died the following year).

Winchell moved back to Los Angeles and lived as a recluse at the Ambassador Hotel, where he died on February 20, 1972, at the age of seventy. Larry King commented: "He was so sad. You know what Winchell was doing at the end? Typing out mimeographed sheets with his column, handing them out on the corner. That's how sad he got. When he died, only one person [his daughter Walda] came to his funeral."

Nevertheless, his obituary appeared on the front page of the *New York Times*. In it the writer commented that Walter Winchell had been "the country's best-known, widely read journalist as well as its most influential."

For years Bob Hope had planned a biopic of Winchell to star himself, but as plans kept intersecting with Winchell's diminishing power and importance, it never really got off the ground. Walter was also slated to star in his own biopic, *Okay, America!* but when it was made in 1932, he had to drop out of the project, in which his character was played by Lew Ayres. He was portrayed on television by Craig T. Nelson in 1991's *The Josephine Baker Story*, by Joseph Bologna in *Citizen Cohn* the following year, and by Stanley Tucci in 1998's *Winchell*.

In the 1920s when Walter Winchell began the gossip column, no one could have predicted how pervasive the business of minding other people's business would become.

For good or bad, that is Walter Winchell's legacy.

Most people of a certain age remember Fanny Brice from her popular 1940s radio persona, a precocious, bratty child named Baby Snooks. Her rise to fame as one of America's most famous comics started in the 1920s after the former follies entertainer had her nose reshaped in possibly the most broadly reported surgical procedure of the era, and embarked on a headline-making relationship with a gambler and con-man named Nick Arnstein. Here, the woman whose life would be famously celebrated on stage and screen as Funny Girl, appears in a rare, post-nose job glamour shot.
Author's Collection

CHAPTER 8

America's Conflicted Queen of Vaudeville and Comedy

Fanny Brice

It's cost me a lot
But there's one thing that I've got
It's my man
He isn't good
He isn't true
He beats me too
What can I do?
Oh, my man I love him so
He'll never know
All my life is just despair
But I don't care
When he takes me in his arms
The world is bright
For whatever my man is, I am his forever more!

— Lyrics to "My Man" as sung by Fanny Brice

Back in the days when, to break into movies, looks (and maybe the casting couch) were more important than acting ability, more than one female star (and a few male stars) resorted to "cosmetic enhancement" to improve their chances. "First we must change your name," one can hear a Hollywood talent agent named Johnny Hyde confiding to his hopeful client, in the 1940s, "and then we must get your nose fixed." That is, of course, how it worked with his famous client Marilyn Monroe, born Norma Jean Mortenson (later Baker). But often trying to improve on Mother Nature backfires, as when plastic surgery or a nose job—rhinoplasty to use the medical term—instead of enhancing a career has helped destroy it.

And so it was when, in 1923, Fanny Brice, then a nationally famous comedienne and songstress (the legendary film director George Cukor hailed her as "one of the great, great clowns of all time"), decided to have a nose job. Brice claimed it was to modify her Jewish image, which she had comically exploited for more than a decade so she could act in serious plays. This is, of course, exactly what Barbra Streisand did—she, who so compellingly played Brice in her first film, MGM's 1968 movie *Funny Girl*. Streisand won her first Oscar for the role, an Oscar she shared with Katharine Hepburn for her performance in *A Lion in Winter*, the only time two Best Actress awards were given.

Unlike actors today, who usually go underground when they have plastic surgery, there was nothing secret about Brice's operation. On August 2 of 1923, despite covering the sudden illness of President Harding, the *New York Times*, and most of the other papers in the country, told its readers that Ms. Brice planned to alter her nose through "facial sculpture." Then nothing more was heard about it until August 15, when the *Times* reported, "Fanny Brice's nose to be scaled down." The reason for the delay? Harding died on August 2, the day the original *Times* story came out, and all the media was occupied with his funeral and the elevation of Calvin Coolidge to the presidency. So Fanny, determined to corner the most publicity possible out of her rhinoplasty, had postponed the operation until the presidential news lessened.

It all was likened to a media carnival by writer Barbara Grossman in *Funny Woman: The Life and Times of Fanny Brice.* On August 16 the *Times* reported that the operation to reduce her nose from "prominent" to "decorative" had taken an hour and forty minutes and was a success. But in the same edition, the paper also editorialized caution over her decision: "Miss Brice, already successful in . . . comedy for which the old nose was an asset, now wants to branch out [where] the old nose might distract attention. It is a perilous undertaking artistically if not surgically."

The editorial was prescient.

Born Fania Borach to a Jewish couple who owned seven saloons at one point (her father was French, her mother Hungarian), Fanny Brice's fame had come from her ethnic comedy skits. She once did a skit of *Romeo and Juliet,* for example, with a Lower East Side Jewish accent and started her career singing what were then called "coon" songs. But her decision was understandable. Building a career on ethnic material probably seemed dangerous to her in a decade which, in New York, began with a "Red Scare" that resulted in the wholesale deportation of aliens and would be the high point of the Ku Klux Klan's terrorizations of minorities in the name of Aryan supremacy. And it may also have been partly due to her realization that her second marriage to a convicted swindler who was also cheating on her was doomed, and she wanted a new look.

Dorothy Parker (chapter 15), a satirist with an eagle eye for human silliness, put it even more sharply than the *New York Times* with a racially offensive (but accurate) quip that Brice "had cut off her nose to spite her *race*."

And that is exactly how most others saw it as well. On Brice's return to the stage, many claimed she wasn't as funny as she used to be. Her previous appearance, which could be turned into a sight gag even when she was doing nothing on stage, was gone. But Brice wanted to branch out into drama; sadly, she would learn that, although she may have done great comedy, plastic surgery doesn't make one a dramatic actress. Eventually she would return to comedy and make it her own again—sans her original nose.

The career of the real Funny Girl started in 1910 when Brice joined the Ziegfeld Follies.

If you lived in New York during the early years of the twentieth century, when radio was in its infancy and television was nonexistent, the most popular escapes from the monotony of a workaday life were to see a silent (until 1928) film, attend a play or a vaudeville performance, or visit the Ziegfeld Follies.

Vaudeville—and its more blue-collar, often raunchy predecessor, burlesque—had been a part of New York life from the early 1880s. But when impresario Florenz Ziegfeld, inspired by Paris's Folies Bergère and prompted by his common-law wife, the actress Anna Held, conceived and mounted his Follies in 1907, he stood the city on its ear. Ziegfeld's productions—new every year and kept fresh by presenting new entertainers with the standbys—were the most elaborate theatrical productions the city had ever seen, lavish revues somewhere between a Disney-produced extravaganza of today and an elaborate, high-class, variety show.

Many of the most famous entertainers of the era (and long afterward) got their start courtesy of Ziegfeld and his producers, the turn-of-the-century theatrical emperors Marcus Klaw and A. L. Erlanger. Among them: the comic who went on to enjoy a famous film career, W. C. Fields; the entertainer Eddie Cantor; the humorist, social commentator, and film star Will Rogers; and the singer Ruth Etting ("Ten Cents a Dance" and "Shine On Harvest Moon" were among her sixty hit recordings).

Also making their first bows on the stage of the Jardin de Paris, a roof garden atop the New York Theater where Ziegfeld mounted his early shows, or later at the New Amsterdam theater where the Ziegfeld Follies performed for fifteen seasons of its twenty-four-year run, were the stage and screen entertainer Ray Bolger (who would achieve film immortality by playing the scarecrow in *The Wizard of Oz* in 1939); the torch singer Helen Morgan; comic Ed Wynn; the dancer Gilda Gray (who popularized the "shimmy" dance in the 1920s); and the immortal actress and singer of comic and risqué songs, Sophie Tucker, known then and in memory as "The Last of the Red Hot Mamas."

And then there was Fanny Brice, who first appeared with the Follies in 1910 as a nineteen-year-old headliner in its fourth season and remained at the top of the bill for nine of its subsequent years (she was one of the few members of the stage show who appeared in the 1936 triple Oscar winner *The Great Ziegfeld*). While with the Follies, she would also appear in Broadway shows, make a few tentative stabs at moviemaking, and launch a radio career that would make her a household name. Along the way she would marry three times (once notoriously, and last, to the great showman Billy Rose), become a top recording star, and inspire a hit Broadway musical.

Born October 29, 1891, on the Lower East Side of Manhattan, she spent most of the first twelve years of her life in Newark, New Jersey, where her parents ran those seven saloons, which a financial panic in the 1890s quickly shrunk back to one. In 1903 her mother, Rose, who had been running the remaining saloon, bought an eight-family tenement on 128th Street in Manhattan and left her husband, Charles, who subsequently dropped out of sight. Later in her career Fanny basically ignored the years in Newark, preferring to romanticize about a childhood in a New York ghetto.

She would also romanticize about a childhood as a newspaper girl, but what she often cited as the turning point in her life occurred when, in 1906 at the age of fourteen, she went onstage as a child singer at Frank Keeney's Fulton Street Theater singing several sentimental ballads, which were popular at the time. Her encore, however, says less about the sentimentality of the era than its racial tenor: Fred Fischer's *If the Man in the Moon Were a Coon*, a song written the previous year and which became so popular that over three million copies of its sheet music were sold. As offensive as such songs would be today, such "coon" songs became a fad around 1890, and one of the sheet-music editions listed forty-eight singers who included such songs in their repertoire, among whom was Fanny Brice. (Soon after the founding of the NAACP in 1909, indignant outcries silenced such songs.) After joining Keeney's troupe and earning plenty of money from her performances, as well as from ushering at a nickelodeon at Eighty-third and Third Avenue, she dropped out of school.

The following year Fanny—still Fania Borach—auditioned for the chorus of George M. Cohan's Broadway musical *The Talk of the Town* but was turned down for, "singing too well and dancing too poorly." Apparently, she wasn't too surprised, as she later admitted that she never learned to dance until the following year when, as an understudy with a burlesque touring company, she replaced the ill star and received a standing, tumultuous ovation. She also changed her name because, as she said, she was tired of being called "borax."

She then bounced from one gig to another, including an audition with a rising songwriter named Irving Berlin that would open her eyes to a talent that she hadn't known she had. The story goes that he rehearsed two songs with her, and one, entitled "Sadie Salome, Go Home," he did in a Yiddish accent. "I had never had any idea of doing a song with a Jewish accent," she said in later years. "I didn't even understand Jewish [she meant Yiddish, somewhat undermining her claim of a ghetto upbringing]. But if that's the way Irving sings it, that's the way I'll sing it." She did so for years; in fact, "Sadie Salome," which mocks a Jewish girl who wants to be an "actress lady," became the inspiration for her theatrical "mask" (as blackface did for many others, including her later colleague Al Jolson) for the first of a series of memorable comic characters she would create. A review in the *New York Clipper*, then a competitor of *Variety*, hailed her as "one of the finds of the season" and predicted that she would soon be "snapped up" by a smart Broadway producer. She was.

Only two years after her debut with Keeney, Fanny received a telegram from Florenz Ziegfeld requesting a meeting, which she first dismissed as a trick until she was told he was serious. They met, she auditioned, and he invited her to join the Follies. Ziegfeld once told an interviewer that the secret of his success was giving the public "girls and laughter." His celebrated chorus of beauties took care of the girls, and he needed Fanny Brice's skits to take care of the laughter.

But she also sang as she had all her career, and it was her vocal talent that began her national fame when, in 1921, in addition to exchanging quips with cast member W. C. Fields, she introduced two songs. The first was the sentimental ballad "Second Hand Rose," a follow-up to her "Rose of Washington Square" song of the previous year. Barbra Streisand also recorded it in 1966. The second song, "My Man," became a big hit, Brice's signature song, and an early best-selling Victor record for which, after her death, Fanny would receive a posthumous Grammy Hall of Fame Award.

Brice's version of "My Man" was actually a sanitized version of a brutal song made famous by the French chanteuse Mistinguett about a woman's inability to suppress an intense physical attraction for a "demon man" who she knew would ruin her. As anyone who followed the gossip of the time knew, it also reflected Fanny's then traumatic personal life with a man she had, literally overnight, begun a torrid love affair with nine years earlier when she was twenty-one.

In February 1910 Fanny impulsively married an Albany, New York, barber named Frank White. Apparently, she regretted it immediately, explaining to those who asked that she did it because she "had nothing else to do." Cynics claimed it was all a publicity stunt, and it may well have been, although Brice later passed it off as a "serious mistake." In any event, after only three days of the marriage, she decided to end it and never saw White again. She first tried to get an annulment, claiming the union was never consummated, but as she was over eighteen, she was legally forced to file for a divorce, which was granted in 1913.

Then, during a 1912 Baltimore run of the musical *The Whirl of Society*, in which she starred as a Jewish maid opposite Al Jolson (who played a butler in his trademark blackface), she met a handsome, thirty-three-year-old man who seemed elegant and sophisticated (she later claimed to have been impressed by his seven toothbrushes and monogrammed silk pajamas in his hotel room). In reality, though, he was a petty gambler and con man born Julius Arndt-Stein, who went by a number of aliases but is remembered in showbiz history as Nick Arnstein.

Fanny fell helplessly and, as it turned out, hopelessly in love. Despite her mother's objections she immediately moved him into her current apartment at Fifty-second and Broadway that she shared with Rose. It was the beginning of a fifteen-year relationship during which Arnstein, more or less totally supported by Brice, treated her like dirt and continually cheated on her—just like the lyrics of her song "My Man," quoted at the top of this chapter. They soon moved to a large apartment at Eighty-Third Street and Central Park West and had a summer place in Huntington, Long Island. "It was the only thing Nick ever bought," she later wrote. "He made some money gambling and paid $14,000 for it." Brice then spent $25,000 (equivalent today to some $550,000) remodeling it and adding mahogany-lined stables for her husband, who fantasized about having a career as a racehorse owner.

Finally, in 1918, after they had been together for six years (two of which he spent in Sing Sing prison on a wiretapping conviction), he divorced his wife and married Brice. They had two children, Frances, born the following year, and William, who was born in 1921 and, using his mother's maiden name, became an accomplished artist. (Frances would marry Ray Stark, who became a famous film producer and in 1968 would make *Funny Girl,* based on the 1964 musical, and in 1975 *Funny Lady,* a sequel that focused on Brice's later marriage to Broadway producer Billy Rose. Both were highly fictionalized.)

In 1920 Arnstein was accused of masterminding a $5 million Wall Street bond robbery. After a long trial he was sentenced to two years in the federal prison at Fort Leavenworth, Kansas, and fined ten thousand dollars (which Brice paid). Despite his conviction Fanny never gave up believing in Nick's innocence. "Mastermind?" she once asked rhetorically. "He couldn't mastermind a lightbulb into its socket."

Soon after his release from prison in 1927, she filed for divorce but even then it was halfhearted. "I didn't believe we were through," she said years later. "I thought Nick would be downstairs to call it off. I had proved my love for Nick every day for fifteen years. Now I wanted him to prove his love for me," she added sadly. Arnstein didn't contest the divorce or the award of custody of their children to her; in fact, he never saw them again.

Later he reminisced about the relationship. "I didn't even go back to the New York house for my clothes," he said in an interview after Fanny's death. "She auctioned them off with her furniture later. I was through." By way of explaining the attraction, Brice herself once wrote "All my life I was afraid I was going to get stuck on some little guy who played the piano in a joint filled with smoke. [Then I met] this tall, handsome guy with the beautiful hands and thin ankles . . . this [was] the guy to have children with."

Her Follies pal Al Jolson had already left for Hollywood and made the immensely popular film *The Jazz Singer*, the first "sound" film (although billed by Warner Brothers as the first full-length "talking picture," only the songs were sound; the rest of the story was silent). Nevertheless, the way people *sounded* was suddenly more important than the way they acted or looked, a fact that opened Hollywood's door for Fanny Brice but would spell finis to the careers of many silent film stars whose voices recorded badly, most famously, that of John Gilbert, Marlene Dietrich and Greta Garbo's lover. In fact, the demand for stage actors who possessed fine voices was so great that Cecil B. DeMille actually built an apartment building to house Hollywood's imports from Broadway.

So armed with a Warner contract (the studio announced the deal with a full-page *Variety* ad declaring that, thanks to Warner Brothers, "added millions . . . [would soon enjoy] the most accomplished comedienne of the legitimate and comedy stages"), Brice had her teeth capped and set out for Hollywood. The movie chosen for her debut was *My Man*, in which the studio promised she would sing "all her old favorites—and many new ones." The songs were well received, but the movie was not. Like *The Jazz Singer*, only the music was in sound, which left a third of the 1928 film silent. Brice had to depend on silent film acting techniques, which she clearly lacked. Religion also played a part in the response to her film, as it did in the anti-Catholic vote that year when Herbert Hoover defeated New York governor Al Smith (who was a Catholic) in the presidential election. As Barbara Grossman points out in her book, "She was seen as 'too New York,' code at the time for 'too Jewish.'"

Apparently, Warner Brothers ended her contract about the time that Earl Carroll, famous for producing risqué musicals, engaged her to star in the operetta *Fioretta*, in which, according to *Variety*, she was miscast. "She just can't get going," they reported. Discouraged, she called in Billy Rose, whom she had married earlier that year (1929) to help; his assessment was that Carroll, instead of using Brice's comedic talents, was "trying to play her straight."

Being short and stocky, Billy Rose was physically the opposite of Arnstein, and although it seemed to be a mismatch to friends, Brice seemed happy enough about the union—at least in the beginning. "She told me once," Rose later recalled, "that she married Frank White, the barber, because he smelled so good, she married Nick Arnstein because he looked so good, and she married me because I thought so good." She later added after they separated, "I was never bored with Billy. Life with him was a different kind of thing, and of course we had that much in common—our work. What I found thrilling with Billy was that I was with a man who was creating all the time. After Nick, who was just talking and never doing anything."

Rose had helped her get a new Hollywood contract, this time with United Artists, but the result of her appearance in *Be Yourself* was a failure, again because she wasn't permitted to be herself. Fanny hadn't improved as a dramatic actress (in the scenes where she plays a nightclub entertainer, at least she was allowed to "be herself" and sing a song and do a couple of comic skits). And although a costar said that she "ain't bad lookin'," that wasn't enough of what people wanted from Hollywood. Brice was simply not pretty enough to play a leading lady or ugly enough to play a character actor like Marie Dressler was, and UA dropped her contract. By then, however, she had signed a three-hour radio deal with Philco and was taking her first steps on the road to the biggest triumph of her life: her own radio show.

The first Philco Hour aired on February 5, 1930, and in it she introduced her Yiddish dialect version of *Romeo and Juliet*, with comic Phil Baker as her Romeo. Repeated live at the Palace Theater three days later, it was, according to the *New York Times*, "absolutely hilarious." Nevertheless, it would be a little longer and a few theatrical failures and radio opportunities later (Billy caused Chevrolet and Chesterfield and Lucky Strike cigarettes to cancel radio projects by demanding that he direct her), before she landed her big show.

Then, on July 9, 1932, the Palace, the last remaining vaudeville house, changed over to being a moving picture theater. Two weeks later, Florenz Ziegfeld died of a heart attack. If anyone doubted that an entertainment era had ended and a new one begun, one only had to walk over to Rockefeller Plaza in Manhattan where the gigantic Radio City Music Hall had opened its doors the previous year and the equally gigantic new RCA building was close to being completed.

In 1934 Brice returned in a posthumous (to Florenz) edition of the Ziegfeld Follies, coproduced by the Schuberts with Ziegfeld's widow and former Follies star (by then also a film star) Billie Burke. Because she was once again in a show where her comic persona was showcased, Fanny was hailed as a supreme talent and would continue to be so until the end of her days. One of her skits in the Ziegfeld Follies of 1934 (in which she would create six characters) was "Soul Saving Sadie," a spoof of the then-celebrated Christian evangelist Aimee Semple McPherson. In another she performed a fan dance spoofing Sally Rand, to audience hysteria (Rand had become an overnight star when she performed her striptease at Chicago's "Century of Progress" exhibition the previous year and was then performing it in various New York venues).

But one skit would be prophetic: It was about a bratty child named Baby Snooks, in which Brice, costumed in a pinafore, ankle socks, and Mary Janes, with a bow in her hair (all of it being a sight gag, as she was then forty-three), employed her entire repertoire of rubber faces and uncoordinated body movements. *Times* critic Brooks Atkinson wrote, "She has never been more enjoyably funny. . . ."

After recording several songs in Hollywood for MGM's Oscar-winning production of *The Great Ziegfeld* (starring William Powell as Ziegfeld, Luise Rainer as his first wife Anna Held, and Myrna Loy as Billie Burke), she returned to triumph again in the Follies of 1936, for which the *Boston Herald* praised her as "America's greatest comic."

Brice first appeared on CBS's Metro–Maxwell House Hour "Good News of 1938" (a cosponsorship between MGM and General Foods) on November 25, 1937, the fourth broadcast of what seemed to be an uninteresting series. On it she performed two skits, one with the child star Freddie Bartholomew and the second as Baby Snooks. The show was a huge hit despite, being radio, the absence of sight gags. Commenting on the radio performance, Atkinson said, "There are comedians and comedians, but none with the unfailing artful resources of Fanny Brice, none with such unfaltering . . . skill in establishing the precisely comic nuance of timing, exaggeration, or distortion." The *Literary Digest*, then the most influential mass-market magazine in America, basically summed up Brice's appeal when it called her "skilled and subtle . . . with an evil talent for sly dissection of all that is fake and preposterous."

By saving the MGM–Maxwell House show, Brice established the radio character that would be hers for fourteen years, until her death in 1951. Fanny decided to move to California, where the show was produced, returning to New York only to sell her apartment and its contents (including, as noted, Nick's clothes). Her marriage with Rose was breaking up, too, apparently for the same reason that many show business unions fail—competitive careers. Rose said, "It's no fun being married to an electric light—our careers clashed. I have to travel a lot, and I want my wife by my side." Rose was being somewhat hypocritical, as he had by then fallen in love with the former Olympic swimmer Eleanor Holm Jarrett, star of his *Aquacade* show. Walter Winchell echoed the media view of Rose's infidelity, which was being headlined across the nation: "Billy Rose may have the nation's headlines, but Fanny Brice has its heart."

Hollywood, which had spurned her as a star, then exploited her career (well, what's new?) with a fictionalized biopic *Rose of Washington Square* starring Tyrone Power as Nick Arnstein and Alice Faye as Fanny, who went so far as to sing "My Man" in the film. Brice filed a $750,000 defamation of character suit against the whole lot of them; it was all settled out of court in 1940 for $30,000. When CBS wanted to cut her salary, she stayed off the air for a year, then returned, but to NBC, where the *Baby Snooks Show* started and remained among the top-rated shows on radio for more than a decade.

On May 24, 1951, Fanny Brice suffered a cerebral hemorrhage and died five days later without regaining consciousness.

Fanny built a long career doing little more than what she did so well in the 1920s. . . . But while she was doing this, radio, a phenomenon that was also born in the 1920s, was becoming universally popular. After she and radio got together in the late 1930s, she would become one of the most famous comedians in America.

Even more lifestyle-changing in the 1920s than the arrival of Prohibition, was the arrival of radio. Seemingly overnight, "listening in" became a national obsession as the new medium brought the world to even the most isolated Americans. The man who made it happen was a Russian emigrant named David Sarnoff, an ex-telegrapher who eventually created not only the giant RCA, but also the NBC network and, before he retired, color television.
Courtesy of Marc Wanamaker/Bison Archives

CHAPTER 9

The Rise of Radio

David Sarnoff

"The wireless music box has no imaginable commercial value. Who would pay for a message sent to no one in particular?"

— The early response by David Sarnoff's associates to his 1920 solicitations for advertisements in radio

Prohibition arrived at the dawn of the 1920s, and it would change the way America lived. Another change occurred in the '20s, one that would have even more dramatic effect on America's lifestyle; it created as great a change as that when the personal computer became generally available in the 1980s, and it seized the imagination of the country just as fast. It was the arrival of radio.

Seemingly overnight, a means of communication that had been limited to a rhythmic tap-tap-tap of the telegraph for a generation suddenly spoke and sang. Oddly, the man who would turn radio from an interesting scientific development into a national obsession started his career with a monumental lie.

David Sarnoff, a twenty-one-year-old Russian immigrant who operated a telegraph station at Wanamaker's department store in Manhattan, was on duty on the night of April 14–15, 1912, when he claimed to have heard the distress call from the "unsinkable" White Star liner RMS *Titanic*. Thereafter, regardless of the fame and honors he amassed in future years, he would always falsely assert that he stayed by his receiver for ninety hours, exclusively receiving the full story of the sinking and the list of survivors. "The *Titanic* disaster brought radio to the front," Sarnoff would say later, "and also me." As the Sarnoff profile done for Manhattan's Museum of Broadcasting points out, however, when the *Titanic* sank, Sarnoff was already out of the telegraph room and into the Marconi (telegraph) company management. In addition, the tragedy occurred on a Sunday, when the store—and its telegraph room—would have been closed.

It was, perhaps, an understandable fib. It was an era of ballyhoo when, as Hollywood would soon understand, fiction is often more compelling than fact. And it was a chance for a young man who had been baited with such taunts as "Jew boy" from an early age to assert his self-worth. In any event, who's to say that if the mythmaking hadn't given Sarnoff the fame that catapulted him into a position where he, more than any other, enabled the radio age, it might never have happened . . . at least not the same way?

In 1917 KDKA, a small radio station atop the Westinghouse office building in Pittsburgh, began broadcasting, if only for an hour every night. They did so to sell their new home "music boxes," which, equipped with the newest superheterodyne vacuum tubes (more about that later), brought talk and music into nearby homes.

But more important was what followed. In 1919 the Radio Corporation of America was organized through a merger of Marconi's company and General Electric. One of their early employees was that selfsame young Marconi telegrapher, David Sarnoff, who had started his career as Guglielmo Marconi's personal messenger. With a speed remarkable even in the Roaring Twenties, he rose to head the company, would make it the leader of the communication industry, and in 1926 found his own National Broadcasting Company. Sarnoff's hustle was part of the reason for his success, but none of it could have happened without his embrace of a technological breakthrough called the vacuum tube.

There are millions today who have never seen a vacuum tube, much less heard what music or voice sounds like when amplified through it. But for many years in the lifetime of millions of others, the tube was literally the backbone of all mass communication: radio, telegraphy, television, and even early computers.

Despite their omnipresence there were (and still are) problems with tubes; sure, they've been used in the flight control computers of Russian MIG jet fighters until fairly recently, but they are somewhat fragile and bulky and put out a massive amount of heat. Then in 1948 the transistor (and later the integrated circuit), which takes up a fraction of the space of a tube but essentially does the same thing, was invented. Seemingly overnight the tube was gone. I say "seemingly" because there are many hardcore audio aficionados who are convinced that the sound put out by a tube-powered amplifier is markedly better than that put out by newer "solid state" amplifiers.

One big change that came about with the miniaturization of electrical circuits through the use of the transistor and its offspring was the computer revolution, which brought to everyone's homes the kind of computing power hitherto available only from tube-driven equipment (which often filled entire rooms).

So what exactly does a vacuum tube do? Simply speaking, the glass tube encloses a vacuum across which a current can flow from an electrically heated, negatively charged filament (the cathode) to the positively charged plate (also in the tube, usually referred to as the "anode"). The flow, called the "thermionic emission," can be used to amplify, switch, modify, or create an electrical signal by changing voltage applied to a grid placed between them. Keeping it simple: The more electrons released and flowing to the anode, the greater the amplification.

Thermionic emission was actually discovered and patented by Thomas Edison and originally called the "Edison effect." He was fiddling with his invention of the lightbulb when he discovered that an electrical current could jump from the hot lightbulb filament to a metal plate at the bottom. In other words, an electrical current didn't need a wire to move; it could flow through a gas or even a vacuum. It was as revolutionary a discovery in its day as was the invention of the transistor, which by the 1960s would wean the world off tube electronics.

Nevertheless, Edison, who was more a tinkerer than a scientist (discovering the "Edison effect" was his only pure science discovery) didn't have a clue about what to do with his new baby. That was left to Lee de Forest, the son of a poor clergyman who would one day hold 180 electronics patents and self-style himself the "Father of Radio." In 1907, by placing a bent piece of wire between the cathode and the anode, allowing the current to be modified along the way, de Forest developed what he called the "Audion." But the Audion wasn't a real vacuum tube. That would be developed at the General Electric laboratory in Schenectady, New York, in 1915, and the road was open for the birth of broadcast radio.

But we're getting a bit ahead of ourselves. Yes, David Sarnoff would become rich and famous as the evangelist of the new medium, but without the pioneering electrical experiments of Nikola Tesla in the late nineteenth century and the work of Lee de Forest; Edwin Howard Armstrong, a reclusive genius who modified the vacuum tube and made it possible to amplify faint signals a thousandfold and send them around the world; and many others, there would probably not have been a radio industry as it evolved.

Around the turn of the century, the invention of the vacuum tube and other "regeneration circuits" made possible wireless telegraphy, the successor to the telegraphy carried over wires or cables, so that even international communications could be exchanged, however faintly, between Europe and powerful stations on the East Coast. Soon ships, too, were using the new technology, at least when it was turned on. The immensity of the tragedy when the *Titanic* sank on April 15, 1912, might have been lessened if the wireless operators on the nearby ships had not turned off their wireless receivers for the night, thus making it impossible for them to hear the CQD, CQD (the predecessor of SOS) signals from the sinking liner. The only ship to hear the signals was the fifty-six-mile-distant RMS *Carpathia*, whose wireless operator was on duty; it rushed to the scene and rescued those passengers who had made it into the lifeboats (those that didn't had long since succumbed to the frigid waters).

David Sarnoff, the eldest son of Abraham and Leah Sarnoff, was born February 27, 1891, in Uzlyany, a small Jewish village near the city of Minsk, the capital of Belarus. At the time and in that place, the only way for a bright but poor Jewish boy to escape poverty was to become a rabbi, and accordingly, until his father emigrated to America to find work so the rest of the family could follow, young David studied and memorized the Torah.

Then in 1900 he, his sister, and his three brothers and their mother came to New York City; Sarnoff remembered later in life that when he arrived in New York he saw more people on a block-long sidewalk in Manhattan than he had seen in his previous lifetime. Since, as the family discovered on their arrival, Abraham Sarnoff had contracted tuberculosis and was essentially unable to work, it was left to David, the eldest, to end his education at the eighth grade and go to work. Like thousands of immigrants before and after, he sold newspapers (and sang in the local synagogue for extra money) to support the family; in fact, he liked it so much that he decided on a career as a journalist.

Young David most admired publisher James Gordon Bennett's *New York Herald*, famed for gathering news faster than any of the city's other dozen or so dailies and weeklies (in 1869 the *Herald* had sent Henry Stanley to Africa to find explorer David Livingstone). So on a Saturday morning in 1906, the fifteen-year-old David Sarnoff set out from the newsstand he now owned to interview for a job at the *Herald*, which, he explained a half century later, was part of his plan to rise above his "ghetto background."

But fate intervened when, after entering the newspaper's building, he went down the wrong corridor and walked into the offices of the Commercial Cable Company, a company that Bennett had formed in 1883 to construct an Atlantic telegraph cable. Sarnoff was immediately hired as a telegraph delivery boy for $5 weekly. It didn't last long; he was fired when he wanted to take three days unpaid time off for Rosh Hashanah and Yom Kippur. But while there he had developed a desire to master the telegraph key, buying one for two dollars to practice on at home.

After being fired, he learned of an opening at the American Marconi Wireless Telegraph Company, which he had known about through stories of Guglielmo Marconi's exploits, many of them in the *Herald*. In 1901 Marconi demonstrated the possibility of wireless telegraphy by miraculously, or so it was considered at the time, transmitting the Morse Code signal for the letter "S"—three dots—through the ether from Ireland to America; the feat is considered a landmark in the history of communication because it freed communications from the bonds of wires or cables. So on September 30, 1906, "Davey" Sarnoff, as he was called, started a job as an office boy sweeping floors and running errands at Marconi's office on William Street in lower Manhattan, the beginning of a six-decade career in electronic communications. His salary was $5.50 a week.

Within months he was promoted from office boy to Marconi's personal messenger (essentially his gofer) and then, just after his sixteenth birthday, to junior wireless operator at $7.50 weekly, enough money to move his family from Hell's Kitchen to a fifth-floor walk-up in the Brownsville part of Brooklyn. All the while he was developing his "fist" for tapping out the messages, both by practicing at home and through serving as a telegrapher at Marconi stations on several ships and land stations, including his post at Wanamaker's. (Really good telegraphers developed a rhythm and swing to their taps—their "fist" as it was called—that was recognizable to other telegraphers. Sarnoff would keep a telegraph key on his desk throughout his career and happily demonstrate his technique for visitors.)

Besides his claim that he was the only telegrapher in the world receiving the distress signals from the *Titanic*, Sarnoff also claimed to have predicted the coming phenomenon of radio and having a "radio music box" in every home as early as 1916. Though this claim was initially discounted, like his *Titanic* vigil story, a memo mentioning a plan to develop and market home receivers has recently been found. In any event, although Westinghouse and other smaller operations may have beaten him to the actual broadcasting punch, Sarnoff's genius for prophecy and later the marketing of radio and the equipment to receive broadcasts would soon make the company he eventually headed the country's radio leader.

Within two years of the sinking of the *Titanic*, Congress passed a law requiring continuous staffing of shipboard radio stations; most of the equipment to do so came from Marconi, boosting their revenues even as David Sarnoff rose in power within the company. The future of broadcasting also came in sight that year when Sarnoff allowed a demonstration of a hydrogen-arc transmitter, a predecessor of the vacuum tube, to broadcast music from the Wanamaker station. The success of this event, as well as his competitor AT&T's 1915 demonstrations of long-distance wireless telephone service, prompted the memo mentioned earlier suggesting the company develop a "radio music box," to be sold for $75 (the equivalent of $1,600 today) for the home enthusiast.

What made Sarnoff's activities different—for, other than the tubes, none of this progress was taking place in a vacuum—was that Sarnoff, alone in the beginning, saw the potential of radio as a point-to-mass-audience rather than a one-person to one-person medium.

The world was changing in Sarnoff's profession by the demand created during World War I for telegraph operators and technicians. When David arrived at Marconi in 1906, he was already beginning to consider himself less a Russian and more an American, despite the viciousness of the "Jew boy" taunts thrown at him. When war arrived, he decided to prove his patriotism by trying to enlist as a private; this was quickly short-circuited when the head of acquisitions for military radio equipment issued an urgent exemption for him—so Sarnoff ended up having it both ways. The Marconi Company sold some $5 million in radio equipment to the government during the war, and he continued his advance within the company.

In 1919 a General Electric Company vice president named Owen Young arranged the merger of American Marconi and turned it into what was essentially a radio-patent monopoly, since it held so many of them; the new company, as noted, was named the Radio Corporation of America. Now all that was needed was to solidify it as the leader in radio communication. RCA began that process by broadcasting the Jack Dempsey/Georges Carpentier boxing match held in Jersey City, New Jersey, on July 2, 1921. It was boxing's first million dollar gate, but more important for RCA, over three hundred thousand people "listened in" (as it was then called), one hundred thousand of whom were gathered around loudspeakers mounted on the *New York Times* building. Fortunately for Sarnoff and everyone else at RCA, Dempsey knocked out Carpentier in the fourth round, just at the moment the transmitter melted into "a molten mass," according to the RCA engineers who examined it. Reliability was also in its infancy, but the demand for Sarnoff's "radio music boxes" exploded.

By 1923 radio had become a full-fledged craze in the country: 556 stations opened (there were only thirty in 1922), and close to a half million households owned radios. By 1926 more than $100 million had been spent buying radios (the equivalent of more than a billion and a quarter dollars today). Everyone was getting into broadcasting, from newspapers to the Nushawg Poultry Farm in New Lebanon, Ohio, which had its own station. Obviously, it was only a matter of time before the first commercial was broadcast. This occurred at 5:00 p.m. on Monday, August 28, 1922, when a Mr. Blackwell of the Queensboro (New York) Corporation paid fifty dollars and stepped up to a microphone at WEAF, New York's first radio station (then owned by AT&T). He urged listeners to leave the congestion of the city for an apartment home in "Hawthorne Court" in, of course, his borough, which paid for the spot. Radio had become a commercial enterprise as well.

In the early days of filmmaking in Hollywood, major filmmakers decided to control distribution of their movies by owning theater chains (eventually broken up by the government's antitrust rulings in the 1940s). So it isn't surprising that Sarnoff, who certainly had his ear to the ground, came up with the idea of a radio *network*, a vast expansion of the point-to-masses concept. In 1926 RCA bought New York City's WEAF from AT&T as part of Sarnoff's launch of the National Broadcasting Company.

The following year Sarnoff was again on top of the biggest news of the day when NBC broadcast President Coolidge's welcome for Charles Lindbergh, and the event provided the opportunity to organize the infant network concept. What NBC did was to link fifty stations in twenty-four states by over twelve thousand miles of AT&T telephone wire for a twelve-hour coverage of the event. How many people listened in across those twenty-four states? No one knows for sure, but what is known is that the four hundred thousand radio sets in households in 1923 had grown by 1927 to more than six million. It was estimated at the time that five people were listening in on each set for at least a portion of the broadcast, which suggests an aggregate audience of thirty million.

Sarnoff, now president of RCA, oversaw the splitting of NBC's single network into two, called the Red and the Blue. The Red network offered commercially sponsored entertainment programming, the Blue carried mostly nonsponsored programs such as news or cultural events. On the West Coast he created the Orange network, which carried the Red's commercial programs, and the Gold, which did the same for the Blue's schedule. The Blue, divested from RCA for antitrust violations in 1942, became the American Broadcasting Company in 1945, after years of efforts to become a stand-alone network.

In the late 1920s David Sarnoff also began a few other projects, one of which would dramatically change the future of communications in America. In 1928 he met with Westinghouse engineer Vladimir Zworykin, who was developing an all-electronic television system in his spare time on his company's premises. When Zworykin told Sarnoff he could build a viable television system in two years with a hundred thousand dollar grant, Sarnoff decided to fund his research. The estimate, as might be guessed, was off by a decade and some $50 million (including $1 million in royalties paid to Philo Farnsworth, who held the patents for RCA's final television system).

But no one else was close to the new technology, and so in 1939, when television finally did arrive in America, it was from NBC. The first television show aired at the New York World's Fair that year and was introduced by Sarnoff himself. It looked like the new invention would take off as quickly as radio, but then World War II stopped everything in its tracks . . . it wasn't until 1950 that television became commercially viable.

In 1929 Sarnoff's RCA bought the Victor Talking Machine Company, the nation's largest manufacturer of records and phonographs, which was, other than radio, the major form of electronic home entertainment at that time. The one innovation in home entertainment that Sarnoff would miss came in 1948 when CBS pioneered the long-playing record. By spinning at 33⅓ rpm, it delivered more than twenty minutes of music per side, compared to four minutes on the old 78 rpm disks, which were the industry standard for the two previous generations.

Movie sound arrived in 1928. And Sarnoff, realizing what this addition would mean to the movies, moved quickly, negotiating a deal with Joseph P. Kennedy, who controlled the Keith-Albee-Orpheum vaudeville theaters, to buy them so he could convert the venues into sound motion picture houses equipped with the new RCA and General Electric sound and film equipment. The name of the new company? Radio-Keith-Orpheum . . . RKO.

Great men tend to want to memorialize their accomplishments, whether by giving a library named in their honor to a university or, say, a cancer wing at a major hospital. David Sarnoff was thinking much bigger than that; much, much bigger in fact. In 1933, the year after RKO built Radio City Music Hall, RCA completed a massive, seventy-story, art deco cathedral to commerce at Rockefeller Center, which is still, today, a destination for tourists and residents alike. The numbers were staggering: It took nearly ten and a half million bricks to build the RCA Building—now renamed the GE Building—enough to build seven hundred houses. It had seventy-five high-speed elevators that could lift a person to the still-elegant Rainbow Room on the sixty-second floor in less than thirty-eight seconds.

From the huge rooftop observatory atop the graceful skyscraper, one could view two other testaments to humankind's optimistic hope for the future, both completed in 1931—as with the RCA Building in the depths of the Great Depression: the transcendentally deco Chrysler Building (see epilogue) and the 102-story Empire State Building, which would remain the tallest building in the world for forty years. The RCA Building, in its day the largest office structure in the world, could house 16,500 workers in a "city within a city," complete with restaurants, beauty salons, and its own post office and subway station.

Among those workers, of course, was David Sarnoff himself, who ruled his electronic empire from a corner office on the fifty-third floor. It was lavishly finished, as one might imagine. One door opened into a room entirely lined in white tile, which boasted a wardrobe, a toilet, a shower, and a barber chair, where his private barber trimmed his graying locks daily. Sarnoff had a special drawer built into his desk, which contained a telegraph key on which he often communicated with an old telegrapher friend, by then head of RCA Communications, headquartered on

Broad Street in downtown Manhattan. And on the mantel over his suite's fake fireplace sat the telegraph key he had used at the Wanamaker Building in 1912 to, as he still stubbornly claimed, communicate the news of the *Titanic*'s sinking. High above his office, on both flanks of the skyscraper, huge red neon signs proclaimed "RCA" for all Manhattan to see, just in case anyone needed to be reminded of how David Sarnoff and RCA had changed the nation in the 1920s.

David Sarnoff would occupy his office for another thirty-seven years, finally retiring at seventy-nine in 1970. During the war years he would be chosen by General Eisenhower to head up his communications staff, during which Sarnoff also beefed up the radio circuits in Europe so NBC could corner news from the invasion of Europe. After the war David restored Radio France, which the departing Germans had destroyed, and set up Radio Free Europe. For all this he received a brigadier general's (Signal Corps) star in December 1945 and thereafter was always called "General Sarnoff." He wore his star proudly and frequently afterward, and it was buried with him.

After the war, when black-and-white television finally got off and running, the next major goal was color television. NBC once again won out because of Sarnoff's tenacity and his company's engineering superiority. As CBS already had an electromechanical system that had been approved by the Federal Communications Commission, Sarnoff pushed his engineers to develop an all-electronic system. A few days after CBS premiered its system in June 1951, RCA demonstrated a fully functional, all-electronic color television system and soon became the leading manufacturer of color television sets in the United States; in December 1953 the FCC approved RCA's system as the new standard in the United States.

Sarnoff was also a family man. On July 4, 1917, he had married Lizette Hermant, the daughter of a French immigrant family who had settled in the Bronx. It was a fifty-four-year marriage, which was said to have been the bedrock of his life. The couple had three sons: Robert W. Sarnoff, who succeeded his father as RCA's chairman in 1971; Edward; and Thomas, who became NBC's West Coast president.

David Sarnoff died in 1971 at the age of eighty. He was interred in a mausoleum in Kensico Cemetery in Valhalla, New York, which has a stained-glass window featuring the image of a vacuum tube.

The most famous dance of the 1920s was certainly the Charleston, but the most culturally important and lasting was the transformation of European-style ballet into an American idiom that reflected the passion, anger, and joy of the human condition. We call it Modern Dance, and the woman who created it was Martha Graham, hailed by *Time* in 1998 as "the dancer of the century." Here, in the late 1920s, she assumes an ecstatic pose wearing, as she did often, a particularly revealing costume.
Library of Congress

CHAPTER 10

DANCE

The Charleston, the Black Bottom, and Martha Graham

There is only a queer divine dissatisfaction, a blessed unrest that keeps us marching and makes us more alive than the others.
—Modern dance creator Martha Graham to Agnes de Mille

Aside from modern dance, which we'll get to shortly, if anything has come to epitomize the Jazz Age in the minds of the public, it is unquestionably the international dance crazes of the 1920s, especially the high-energy, fast-kicking dance known as the Charleston. Most frequently associated with the image of the emancipated white young female of the time known as the flapper—think Mia Farrow as Daisy Buchanan in the 1974 film *The Great Gatsby*; unfortunately, a critical flop in the book-to-movie category—the Charleston was considered immoral and provocative by the bluenoses of the era. Dancing it, often alone or together, it was for these young women—already on a freedom high from finally being given the right to vote—a way of mocking their "dry" elders when Prohibition came in.

One reason the Charleston has remained an icon of the era to succeeding generations is its infectious, rhythmic beat and many theatrical depictions, particularly in films such as the perennial classic *It's a Wonderful Life*, where Jimmy Stewart and Donna Reed perform it in a dance competition. In season nine of *Dancing with the Stars*, a partner Charleston routine was also introduced to the competition.

The Charleston, or what became the dance to bear that name, was developed in the African-American communities in the United States, where it was probably an evolution of the black dance called the juba. When the dance hit Harlem in the early 1920s, the previously relaxed rhythmic twisting of the feet in what was basically a walking step performed in place (with the arms' forward/backward swing opposite to the leg movement) became a fast kicking step, eventually to a high tempo of more than two hundred beats per minute. Whether the arms are swung from the shoulder or, more frequently, with bent elbows, the hands are often held at right angles from the wrist, a characteristic of many African dances. Originally, it was too athletic for most dancers, but it was soon modified into an easier quickstep.

The dance got its name when the song *Charleston* was added to the production of the musical *Runnin' Wild* and the *Ziegfeld Follies of 1923*, and Joan Crawford made it huge when she performed the dance in 1928's *Our Dancing Daughters*. The dance's distinctive beat was said to have first been heard on the Charleston docks in the 'teens, and following its popularity in the 1920s, it would evolve into the Lindy Hop, in which its hot jazz timing was mixed with the swing jazz of the 1930s and '40s.

In its original concept it was a solo dance; in the Twenties and when it is danced today, it is often danced with a partner, although the couple's contact is usually limited to the eyes alone. There are a number of variations, including the often-competitive "Solo 20s Charleston," which usually combines other steps from dances of the era (such as the Black Bottom and the cakewalk) and jazz dance, as well as improvisation and creative variations on familiar dance steps. Sometimes they are done in a jam circle format where individuals take turns stepping out and dancing alone for a phrase or two, to "stroll" or "shine." There is also a variation called "30s and 40s Partner Charleston" in which partners may be facing forward with only their hips touching or tandem, in which one partner stands in front of the other.

Also popular in the Twenties was another dance that originated in the South, in this case New Orleans in the early years of the century. It grew from a dance for which the sheet music, printed in 1907, was called "Jacksonville Rounders' Dance" ("rounder" was a synonym for "pimp"). It was composed by a black pianist, composer, and dancer named Perry Bradford, who later credited his inspiration and the name to a dance he had seen done in Jacksonville, Florida, "way back." "That dance is as old as the hills," said one professional dancer at the time, adding that it, unlike the Charleston, of which there is no trace in the plantation era, was well known among semirural blacks across the South. Its rhythm, however, which is similar to the Charleston's, does suggest a connection at one point.

In 1924 a dance called the Black Bottom made its way to New York, where it was first presented in a musical entitled *Dinah* and then was featured in the *George White Scandals* revue at the Apollo Theater in Harlem during 1926 and '27. Jelly Roll Morton, the early jazz pianist and composer, wrote "Black Bottom Stomp" in 1925; its name, like many of the cultural phenomena originating in Harlem in the 1920s, was said to refer to Detroit's predominantly black neighborhood (although the composition was originally titled "Queen of Spades"). In any event the Black Bottom became a sensation, quickly overtaking the Charleston in popularity and eventually becoming the number-one social dance nationally.

Occasionally, instructions on how to dance the Black Bottom were printed with the sheet music. They offer a delightful look into the jazz argot of the time, as well:

Hop down front, then Doodle back [doodle means slide].
Mooch to your left, then Mooch to the right [mooch meant shuffle forward with both feet; hips go first, then feet].
Hands on your hips and do the Mess Around,
Break a Leg until you're near the ground
[break a leg is a hobbling step].
Now that's the Old Black Bottom Dance.

"Ma Rainey's Black Bottom" is a song about the dance by Harlem's Ma Rainey, who was known as the "Mother of the

Blues" and who mentored Bessie Smith. The same title was used by Pulitzer Prize–winning playwright August Wilson for his 1982 play about the experiences of African-Americans, set in Chicago in the 1920s and dealing with black culture and the exploitation of black recording artists by white producers.

If there is a common denominator to this chapter, it is that the Charleston and the Black Bottom came out of American culture, rather than what was previously fashionable: importing the latest dance craze from Europe.

So too was the dance inspiration of a woman who would in the 1920s transform ballet, hitherto a European import as well, into a transcendent, homegrown art form. Her name was Martha Graham, and her influence on dance has been likened to that of Picasso on art or Frank Lloyd Wright on architecture. In 1976 President Gerald R. Ford hailed her as "a national treasure"; *Time* listed her in 1998 as the "Dancer of the Century."

What Graham did through her shatteringly innovative choreography and brilliant dancing—all beginning in the 1920s—was to bring to dance a new language of movement that no longer dealt with fairy tales (like *Swan Lake*) but was a medium that, frequently moody, has been described as reflecting the passion, anger, and ecstasy of the human condition. She called it "contemporary dance"; posterity calls it "modern dance."

One problem in remembering Martha Graham as a 1920s star is that her career was long—seven decades, in fact—during which she choreographed seemingly hundreds of ballets. Scholars dispute the actual number, and some even disagree on which was the last of her ballets in which she herself danced. To pick out landmarks in a career longer than some lifetimes is a challenge. With a lesser talent any one of them could be considered definitive. In fact, she choreographed and danced a lot in the 1920s, becoming so familiar—or controversial—that comedienne Fanny Brice actually spoofed her modern dance style in a 1927 Ziegfeld Follies skit.

Her signature moodiness continued into the next decade and beyond. In 1936's *Chronicle* dancers performed in dark costumes amid a dark set. The ballet dramatically dealt with the then-serious issues of depression and isolation created by recent events, including the Wall Street crash, the subsequent Great Depression, and the Spanish Civil War. It was a far cry from dance episodes in Broadway musicals and revues and culturally light years away from 1940's Disney film *Fantasia*, presumably aimed at the general audience, where animated fairies, mushrooms, and goldfish dance to Tchaikovsky's classic *Nutcracker* ballet.

Graham's largest-scale dance, the evening-length *Clytemnestra*, would not be created until 1958, and her last ballet, *Maple Leaf Rag*, was created in 1990, two decades after she had stopped dancing at the age of seventy-six and a year before she died.

During her long career she also worked with some of the more renowned composers, including Aaron Copland (whose *Appalachian Spring* ballet was commissioned by Graham), Samuel Barber, the modernist William Schuman, and Gian Carlo Menotti, the Italian-American composer, who was most famous for his operas.

Another problem for posterity was that for most of her life, Graham generally refused to allow her dances to be photographed or filmed, believing that they should exist only as live stage performances. She also burned diaries and notes about the dances to prevent them from being read and used by others. There were a few exceptions, but not many. In the 1930s she worked occasionally with the still photographer Imogen Cunningham and in the 1940s with Barbara Morgan and Philippe Halsman, who took stills of several of her late 1930s and '40s ballets, including *Letter to the World*, *Cave of the Heart*, *Night Journey*, and *Every Soul Is a Circus*. She also considered his photographs of her 1946 ballet *Dark Meadow* as the most complete documentation of any of her dances. In her later years she relented and allowed other choreographers to recreate some of what had been lost.

Martha Graham was born in Pittsburgh, Pennsylvania, on May 11, 1894, into a family considered "social" (her mother, Jane Beers, was a tenth-generation descendant of Miles Standish). Her father, George, was a doctor who was known as an "alienist," a physician who treated mental disorders, and Martha and her two younger sisters were looked after by an Irish maid.

In 1908, in an effort to find relief for Martha's sister Mary's chronic asthma, the family moved to Santa Barbara, California. It would be four years before Dr. Graham would finally close his practice and join them; by then Martha was in high school and later claimed to have discovered the spiritual freedom that would define her life. "My people were strict religionists who felt that dancing was a sin," she told *Dance Magazine* in an early interview. "They frowned on all worldly pleasures. My upbringing led me to fear it myself. But luckily," she added, "we moved to Santa Barbara, California. No child can develop as a real Puritan in a semitropical climate. California swung me in the direction of paganism, though years were to pass before I was fully emancipated."

Despite her family's objection to dancing, on a visit in 1911, Dr. Graham took Martha to Los Angeles to see a concert by Ruth St. Denis, then a famous "exotic" dancer, in which she performed solos from her sensual dance drama *Egypta* (inspired, as a delightful footnote, by a cigarette poster St. Denis had seen on tour in Buffalo). The seventeen-year-old Martha was overwhelmed and decided that, although traditionally too old to become a dancer (dancers usually began training around eight), dance would be her career. Within weeks she made her amateur dance debut as a "geisha girl" in a local production of *The Mikado*.

After attending a junior college in Los Angeles that prided itself on "self-expression," Martha enrolled in a new dancing school that St. Denis and her husband Ted Shawn had recently opened in the city under the name that was also that of their company, Denishawn. Eventually, she would become a member of the company and in June 1920 star in her professional dance debut in a new, exotic dance drama with a pre-Columbian Mexico theme, titled *Xochitl*. After a West Coast tour, the show opened at Grauman's Million Dollar Theater in downtown Los Angeles and, after an eight-week tour in England, was booked into New York's Town Hall for a dozen performances.

In September 1923 Graham opened in *Greenwich Village Follies* with comedian Joe E. Brown and the brother-sister dancing team of Elisa and Eduardo Cansino (Eduardo was Rita Hayworth's father) and rented a studio apartment in the bohemian community. She was finally in the right place, at the right time, with the right talent, given her and the public's fervor for the new and the experimental.

Fate then arrived in the form of music lover George Eastman, the founder of Kodak, who decided to establish his own opera company in his hometown of Rochester, New York. Through its director, who had seen Graham dance in a Denishawn production, she was hired (and would commute from New York City) two days a week to codirect the company's dance department. After teaching at a Manhattan private school for a time, she opened her own Martha Graham Center of Contemporary Dance company in 1926. Today it is the oldest dance organization in America.

Bette Davis, an early student of Graham, claimed that because of her dance training, she gained the flexibility and training to fall down a flight of stairs when cast in a Broadway play early in her acting career. "I worshipped her," Davis once recalled. "Her burning dedication gave her the power of ten men [Graham, slight of build, was only five feet two inches tall]. I had already learned that the body via the dance could send a message. Now I was taught a syntax with which to articulate the subtleties fully. She would, with a single thrust of her weight, convey anguish. Then, in an anchored lift that made her ten feet tall, she became all joy. One after another . . . hatred, ecstasy, age, compassion! There was no end once the body was disciplined. What at first seemed 'grotesque to the eye' developed into a beautiful release for both dancer and beholder."

One of Graham's early students was Bethsabée de Rothschild, who became a good friend. When she moved to Israel in 1965 and opened the Batsheva Dance Company, Martha became its first dancer and created new dances for the company.

But the occasionally perceived "grotesqueness" of her work was not met with universal approval at first. As noted, Fannie

Brice (chapter 8) made fun of Graham and her choreography, on one occasion spoofing Graham's ballet *Revolt* in a Ziegfeld Follies skit, performed in her trademarked baby talk, as *Rewolt.* It was at this time that the term "modern dance" entered the language via *New York Times* critic John Martin. Despite Martin's understanding, Graham would be subject to critical abuse by baffled critics and audiences until her work was finally accepted as both serious and American.

In 1948 Graham married Erick Hawkins, a principal dancer with her company, who was fifteen years her junior and with whom she had lived for eight years at the time. She would choreograph many dances for them together. They divorced in 1953, two years after he founded his own dance company.

By the late 1960s, when she was in her seventies, Graham was still dancing although, because of her declining health, the dances choreographed at the time included roles for herself in which she mostly acted rather than danced, with members of her company dancing around her. Clearly, this was intolerable for a woman who, although she created a body of work that is the bible of modern dance in America, always considered herself a dancer. "I have spent all my life with dance and being a dancer," she once reflected. "It's permitting life to use you in a very intense way. Sometimes it is not pleasant. Sometimes it is fearful. But nevertheless it is inevitable."

Finally, amid a rising chorus of criticism that she was too far past her prime to remain on stage, Graham confronted her own inevitability and left the stage. She was depressed and started drinking heavily, recalling the ordeal in her 1991 autobiography *Blood Memory*:

> *It wasn't until years after I had relinquished ballet that I could bear to watch someone else dance it. I believe in never looking back, never indulging in nostalgia, or reminiscing. How can you avoid it when you look on stage and see a dancer made up to look as you did thirty years*

ago, dancing a ballet you created with someone you were then deeply in love with, your husband? I think that is a circle of hell Dante omitted.

[When I stopped dancing] I had lost my will to live. I stayed home alone, ate very little, and drank too much and brooded. My face was ruined, and people say I looked odd, which I agreed with. Finally my system just gave in. I was in the hospital for a long time, much of it in a coma.

During her lifetime Graham would often use a phrase she picked up in classes with Robert Edmund Jones, a leading scenic and costume designer of the day: "Some of you are doom laden." She was also fond of the phrase "doom eager," borrowed from Ibsen. Perhaps it was such consciousness that enabled the depth and power of her lifework.

"I had a burning desire to be excellent, but no faith that I could be," she recalled in *The Life and Work of Martha Graham* by the dancer Agnes de Mille.

"There is a vitality, a life force, an energy, a quickening that is translated through you into action, and because there is only one of you in all of time, this expression is unique. And if you block it, it will never exist through any other medium and it will be lost. The world will not have it. It is not your business to determine how good it is nor how valuable nor how it compares with other expressions. It is your business to keep it yours clearly and directly, to keep the channel open. You do not even have to believe in yourself or your work. You have to keep yourself open and aware to the urges that motivate you. Keep the channel open. . . . No artist is pleased. [There is] no satisfaction whatever at any time. There is only a queer divine dissatisfaction, a blessed unrest that keeps us marching and makes us more alive than the others."

Martha Graham, who for a lifetime embodied and projected through dance the exhilaration as well as the war weariness of the 1920s, died in 1991 at the age of ninety-six.

It's rare for a classical music star to become as famous as soprano Geraldine Farrar did in the nineteen teens and twenties. She did it through a combination of sheer talent and a flair for self promotion that attracted hundreds of thousands of worshipful female followers known as "Gerryflappers." Scandalous, headline-making affairs with a royal heir, America's leading conductor, and numerous boy-toys (as well as an outstanding film career) only fueled the Farrar fire and fame.

Author's Collection

CHAPTER 11

HIGH CS AND HIGH JINKS: CLASSICAL MUSIC'S BIGGEST SCANDAL

Arturo Toscanini and Geraldine Farrar

Farrar fara ([Geraldine] Farrar will do it).
—Enrico Caruso saluting his frequent singing partner's grit in his native Italian

When you mention grand opera's golden-age soprano Geraldine Farrar to most people today, if they register with the name at all, they think you are talking about Geraldine *Ferraro*, the woman who ran for Vice President with Walter Mondale in his ill-fated 1984 presidential bid.

Sorry, folks; in the history of the twentieth century, for millions—at least millions of classical music lovers in the 1920s—the real Geraldine was once Farrar. In her time she was a living legend, a woman whose life was as dramatic as any of the operas she sang but, happily, not as tragic as many of them. Although she retired from the Metropolitan Opera in 1922 at forty when she said she would, at the beginning of the decade she had become the idol of hundreds of thousands of young female fans, known as "Gerry-flappers," who aped her manner, taste, fashion, and style, and made her one of America's first modern celebrities. According to a *Time* magazine retrospective on December 12, 1934, "(On) that memorable afternoon streamers were hurled from the balconies, flowers and confetti were piled on the stage. A great audience stood and cheered through its tears." And much of that audience was composed of her young fans, who then followed her open car back to her hotel: "She still can sway any kind of audience."

One aspect of Farrar's lifestyle that, presumably, most of her fan base did not copy was that besides being celebrated as a singer and silent movie star, she was notorious for a scandalous love life. Not only was she very publicly involved with the crown prince of Prussia when she was still a teenager, but by the time she retired she had also gone through a number of boy toys and had a very public affair with the very married Arturo Toscanini (whom posterity would dub the greatest conductor of the twentieth century) that was so scandalous he fled the country. Mutual friends claimed she had finally driven him almost crazy with lust.

Born in Melrose, Massachusetts, February 28, 1882, Geraldine was the daughter of Sydney Farrar, a shopkeeper who once played first base for the Philadelphia Phillies, and his wife Henrietta. Possessing a musical talent from an early age, Geraldine began studying instruments at five and singing at eleven. Two years later she was studying voice in New York City; she began giving public recitals when she was fourteen and set off for Europe (on borrowed money, which she soon repaid) when she was seventeen.

Geraldine's talent was first publicly acknowledged when she was offered a starring role at the Berlin Opera when she was eighteen. Five years later she was invited to start at the top in New York when the Metropolitan Opera invited her to debut as Juliet in Gounod's *Romeo and Juliet*. The next year, 1907, she sang the title role in the American premiere of Giacomo Puccini's beloved *Madame Butterfly* at the Met opposite the man then (and to many, still) considered the greatest tenor who ever lived, Enrico Caruso. It is said that Puccini, who was in New York for the premiere, didn't much like her singing but was quickly disarmed—and a bit more, as we shall see—by her charm.

The tabloid side of Farrar's life first became known when she was in Berlin in 1903 and was romantically involved with Friedrich Wilhelm, the eldest son of Kaiser Wilhelm II and crown prince of Prussia (both he and his father, the emperor, would abdicate their succession rights in 1918). When the German press broke the news about her "friendship" with the prince, it created an uproar. Despite feverish efforts by Geraldine's family to quash the rumors (they blamed the press, and her father actually assaulted the editor of the Berlin newspaper who he claimed started the "rumor"), everyone knew that the prince, three months younger than Gerry, had been instantly smitten by her talent and blonde beauty when she debuted in Berlin as Marguerite in *Faust* in 1901; he began an affair with her soon thereafter.

Eventually, due as much to the distance separating them when she returned to New York as anything else, the romance cooled, and Wilhelm married Cecilie of Mecklenburg-Schwerin (after whom the famous German liner of the era, the SS *Kronprinzessin Cecilie,* was named; during World War I the liner was seized and quarantined in Bar Harbor, Maine, and later rechristened the *Mount Vernon*).

All of which is not to say that marriage made the prince especially faithful. He also had an affair with the notorious Dutch exotic dancer and dazzlingly beautiful courtesan who went by the name of Mata Hari. In 1917 she was arrested in Paris, put on trial for spying for her former amour's Germany, and executed by firing squad. (Her story was made into a movie in 1931 starring Greta Garbo.) Years later, after Geraldine Farrar retired to her home in Ridgefield, Connecticut, the prince and princess visited her with their children; reportedly, it was a cordial occasion.

Between 1915 and 1921 Gerry made fifteen silent films (half of them survive), among them *Carmen* in 1915 for Cecil B. DeMille, which, although it sounds improbable as a project for a singer, was a huge success. Albert Innaurato, writing in the *New York Times* in 1997, said that in the film "fully clothed, she is shockingly sexual. [She also] simply shines, like Garbo."

Most of Farrar's other films were also highly successful,

including a 1917 biopic of Joan of Arc, also for DeMille, called *Joan the Woman*. When in Hollywood making her films, Gerry was paid two dollars (that's over $40 today) for every *minute* the sun shone while she was working; in Southern California that can count up pretty fast. She was also provided with a private house on her sets and traveled back and forth across the country in a private railroad car (courtesy of the filmmakers), stocked with, among other personal items, a photograph of another legend-to-be, her inamorato Toscanini in her railroad car's drawing room and the very real presence of a current boy toy in the bedroom.

She met Toscanini in her first season at the Met; it was not exactly a pleasant experience for either, as both possessed feisty personalities that went far beyond the usual "artistic temperament." Shortly before their torrid love affair commenced, she halted a rehearsal of an opera that he was conducting at his signature fast speed and told him that as she was the "star" of the opera, he would have to follow her pace. There are variations on Toscanini's response, the most common being, "The only stars are in the heavens, Signorina," and continued the rehearsal at his own speed.

Their affair eventually became so serious—at least in her mind—that in 1915 she demanded that he choose between her and his family back in Italy. He chose Italy. Years after their passion had cooled and Toscanini had returned to New York (he refused to live in Benito Mussolini's Fascist Italy), he attended a festive dinner party hosted by Farrar. When Toscanini saw that she had served fish, his comment to his tablemate was, "I slept with that woman for seven years, and you'd think she would have remembered that I hate fish."

She later claimed that, despite her indulging in fairly public affairs, she didn't really like being with men (she once told Giacomo Puccini, the composer of several superpopular operas besides *Madame Butterfly*, including *La Bohème* and *Tosca*, that she wouldn't sleep with him because, "although I am no virgin, he looked like a rabbit"). In any event, she could certainly intimidate them; Innaurato added in his *Times* piece that "she was dangerous to know. As a child she was once tripped at a skating rink by a boy named Clarence. She beat [him] with an umbrella until his mother called the police." She and Caruso were great friends as noted (they may have had a short-lived affair as well), but their mutual admiration didn't mean he was invulnerable to her temper. Once, presumably carried away by the passion of singing *Carmen* with the great tenor (or irritated at being upstaged by him), she bit his arm, inflicting a serious wound. Understandably, in future performances when he was paired with Farrar, despite their friendship, he was always cautious around her.

When Geraldine was in Hollywood making *Temptation* in 1915, she met a young actor named Louis Tellegen on an adjoining stage at the Lasky studio, to whom she was immediately attracted, both for his good looks and his romantic aura; they married the following year. Tellegen is an interesting example of the sort of quasi-exotic male stars Hollywood was seeking at the time, which soon would find its apotheosis in the person of Rudolph Valentino.

Born in Holland, Tellegen had a Greek father and a Dutch mother. At the age of fifteen, he ran off with his father's mistress and later was successively a baker's assistant, a trapeze artist, and the model for Auguste Rodin's *Eternal Springtime* sculpture. He studied with Sarah Bernhardt in Paris, with whom he appeared both on stage and in three films, as well as had a brief affair with the legendary actress despite the fact that she was thirty-seven years older.

The Farrar/Tellegen marriage was a disaster, initially because their careers diverged dramatically. In Hollywood Farrar had to be up and on her movie set early in the morning; Tellegen, who was primarily a stage actor and often on tour (where he also cheated on her), could always sleep in.

Because of his stage work, when they were in Hollywood together, he often arrived wherever they were staying (often in her railroad car, post–boy toy) just as she was getting up. They would make one film together, which he followed with several without Farrar that were less than successful, among them the John Ford Western *3 Bad Men* in 1926, in which he played a sheriff (wearing a white hat so you could tell him apart from the bad guys, who wore black hats; it was not a highlight of Ford's Hollywood work). The couple separated in 1920 and divorced in 1923.

After trying (and failing) as a movie director and marrying twice more, Tellegen committed suicide in 1934 in a particularly grisly manner, surrounded by newspaper clippings of his career. As *Time* reported following his death, "Last fortnight the world's eyes were again on Geraldine Farrar. In Los Angeles an impoverished, cancer-ridden man who once had been her husband had gone into a bathroom, stood before a mirror and stabbed himself seven times with a pair of common sewing scissors. Reporters telephoned Miss Farrar at her Ridgefield, Connecticut, home, and asked for comment on Lou Tellegen's death. Her reply was characteristically candid: 'Why should that interest me?' The final Hollywood picture was of a broken, hollow-eyed matinee idol who kept having his face lifted," *Time* added. In a coda Farrar described him as "handsome and stupid . . . (with) the perception of a moron and no morals whatever. May those tormented ashes rest in peace."

Toscanini, whom she would also describe as "handsome" (but hardly stupid) would become as famous as Farrar—far more famous if measured in the length of time one's legend endures—and he was, as might be guessed, as volatile as Farrar.

The family that Toscanini fled to after Farrar demanded he choose between them or her included his wife, Carla, whom he married in 1897, and their children Walter, Wally, and Wanda. Wanda, born in 1906, would later marry the Russian-American pianist Vladimir Horowitz in 1933.

In his lifetime (1867–1957), he would, as a cellist, perform in the world premiere of Giuseppe Verdi's *Otello* at Milan's La Scala opera house in 1887. In the following decade he concentrated more on conducting, including the world premieres of Puccini's

La Bohème and Leoncavallo's *Pagliacci*. It was a talent he discovered in 1886 when, at that time being the assistant chorus master for a run of Verdi's *Aida* in Rio de Janiero, he stepped up and conducted (from memory) a rousing performance of the opera after three previous conductors were booed off the podium. In 1898 he was appointed resident conductor at La Scala, then as now Italy's premier opera house, where he remained until 1908, when he came to New York to conduct at the Metropolitan Opera House.

In 1926 the passions between him and Farrar apparently spent, he returned part time to America as the conductor of the New York Philharmonic Orchestra, a position he held until 1936. Although he had run for the Italian parliament in 1919 as a Fascist, Toscanini swiftly cooled on the party and its leader, Benito Mussolini. Despite Mussolini's opinion of him as "the world's greatest conductor" (an opinion that would soon be shared by millions), he refused to play the Fascist anthem "Giovinezza" at La Scala, raging to a friend, "If I were capable of killing a man, I would kill Mussolini." Eventually, as Toscanini recalled, he was "attacked, injured and repeatedly hit in the face" by a group of the dictator's black-shirted thugs and had his telephone tapped and his passport seized; it was returned only after the outcry over his treatment in his homeland.

In 1937 Toscanini (and his family) returned permanently to the States, where David Sarnoff, head of NBC, offered to create an orchestra for him. The NBC Symphony, a staple of radio broadcasts and recordings made in Studio 8-H in the RCA Building at Rockefeller Center for years, was the result. From 1950 until the end of Toscanini's stewardship of the orchestra, the broadcasts originated from Carnegie Hall. There, during a 1954 broadcast, he had an uncharacteristic memory loss (which may have actually been deliberate, as he had heard rumors that NBC was going to end the broadcasts). The eighty-seven-year-old maestro never conducted again and spent the years remaining to him editing tapes of many NBC Symphony broadcasts, which were released on records by RCA Victor.

He died at age eighty-nine of a stroke at his historic home, Wave Hill, in the Riverdale section of the Bronx, on January 16, 1957, where his wife, Carla, had died five years earlier.

After retirement from the concert stage in 1931, Geraldine Farrar occasionally hosted or appeared as a guest on the intermission broadcasts of the Metropolitan Opera performances and was active in charity work. In 1938 she expanded a 1916 autobiography into a second book, *Such Sweet Compulsion*, in which she adopted the embarrassing technique of alternating her own chapters with those by the spirit of her late mother so she could pay herself compliments and whitewash much of the old gossip.

As with Toscanini, there are dozens of recordings to remember her by. And of course the gossip.

Geraldine Farrar died on March 11, 1967. But her 1920s fame almost certainly affected the cultural life of America for more than two generations to follow.

Although radio pioneer Lee de Forest broadcast two performances from the Metropolitan Opera stage in January 1910, the signal was erratic, and they were heard, if at all, only as far away as Newark, New Jersey. On December 25, 1931, the Met tried again, this time with a broadcast of Humperdinck's *Hänsel und Gretel*. It would be the first of a string of Saturday opera broadcasts that still continues. Sponsorship was spotty at first, but on December 7, 1940, Texaco began what would be a sixty-three-year sponsorship of the Met's Saturday afternoon opera broadcasts, the longest continuous sponsorship in broadcast history.

Supposedly, Texaco became interested because one of its board members was a fan of Geraldine Farrar. Today, eighty years later, there is no way to confirm that. Despite the popularity of Enrico Caruso in the 'teens (his records were among the first big sellers), his fans were mostly opera lovers already. Not so, however, in the case of Geraldine Farrar. With or without a board member's interest in her, Texaco, a company that depended on a mass market of millions, would hardly have sponsored opera broadcasts unless they reached enough potential customers.

Opera fans never approached the numbers of baseball broadcast fans, of course, but there were still enough of them to make it worthwhile. Grand opera was much more of a cultural force in the 1930s and '40s than it is today; nevertheless, largely in part to Farrar's well-remembered, nationally ballyhooed notoriety that had earlier made her a household name, plus the evergreen memories of thousands of "Gerry-flapper" followers, the Met was more than simply a culturally elitist institution. Geraldine Farrar may have brought millions who never even considered attending an opera to an awareness of the Met's importance by largely unintended means, but she had *brought* them, vastly broadening the commercial importance of the institution. The nation knew the Met was something special, and that was a quality no major advertiser could overlook.

That may have been the longest lasting legacy of Geraldine Farrar's 1920s fame.

F. Scott Fitzgerald not only wrote the best book about the 1920s (*The Great Gatsby*), he also coined the term "the Jazz Age," to describe the era. Here, he and his wife Zelda appear in a rare photograph taken on their honeymoon following their marriage April 3, 1920, a week after publication of his first novel *This Side of Paradise*. Tragically, by the end of the decade, jealousy, a lifestyle resembling his novels, alcoholism and, for Zelda, mental instability would destroy the happy self confidence they show here.
Library of Congress

CHAPTER 12

LITERATURE OF THE 1920S, PART I

F. Scott Fitzgerald

It was an age of miracles, it was an age of art, it was an age of excess, and it was an age of satire.

—F. Scott Fitzgerald, describing the 1920s, in "Echoes of the Jazz Age"

Today, just about everyone agrees that F. Scott Fitzgerald, in his 1925 novel *The Great Gatsby,* wrote, if not *the* Great American Novel, certainly the best novel about the 1920s, bringing alive in its pages the excitement, abandon, and cynicism of the era better and more memorably than any other writer.

But when Scott Fitzgerald died on December 21, 1940, in the Hollywood living room of his lover, gossip columnist Sheilah Graham, the man who today is considered one of America's most lyrical and socially and emotionally insightful writers thought of himself as a failure and a forgotten man.

In many ways he was.

Publishers were no longer begging for his work as they had done less than a generation before when, at the age of twenty-three, he wrote the hugely successful novel of the post–World War I generation, *This Side of Paradise*. In his last days Fitzgerald's hopes for recapturing his earlier fame hinged on *The Love of the Last Tycoon*, a novel inspired by MGM's late boy-wonder production chief, Irving Thalberg, who had died in 1936 at the age of thirty-six. But the writing was going at a snail's pace, especially for an author who in his heyday had cranked out seven or eight thousand handwritten words daily.

Nevertheless, he might have pulled it off. A longtime friend, the literary critic Edmund Wilson (with whom Fitzgerald was also feuding at the time of his death) considered *Tycoon*, unfinished when the author died, as potentially his most mature work.

Fitzgerald had also burned his bridges with the Hollywood studios where he had hoped to restore his career as a screenwriter. But in all the time he spent in the film capital—during which he also worked for Thalberg twice—he only received one screenwriting credit, that for the 1938 film *Three Comrades,* based on Erich Maria Remarque's novel. "He took screenwriting very seriously," Fitzgerald scholar Matthew Bruccoli has said, "and it's heartbreaking to see how much effort he put into it." Billy Wilder, a friend and admirer, once explained, "[He was] a great sculptor who is hired to do a plumbing job. [But] he did not know how to connect the pipes so the water could flow." In retrospect Fitzgerald's failure as a screenwriter came from his tendency to novelize scripts, to load them down with too many backstories. By the time he died, despite the one-time celebrity that brought him to Hollywood in the first place, he had become, to paraphrase Jack Warner's famous putdown of screenwriters, just another "jerk with an Underwood."

Meanwhile, Fitzgerald had broken with his agent and confidante, Harold Ober, who had represented him for twenty years. And he had become estranged from his wife Zelda and daughter, Scottie. He quarreled with his close friend Ernest Hemingway, whose climb from being a struggling writer to becoming America's most famous author was the exact reverse of Fitzgerald's fall from fame to failure. Fitzgerald was describing his own disillusionment with what fate and dissipation had dealt him when he wrote, "At eighteen our convictions are hills from which we look; at forty-five they are caves in which we hide."

Compounding his depression his health had failed, a final comeuppance for a lifetime of alcohol abuse and what was called at the time "high living." His fatal heart attack was the third in a month. The first was at Schwab's drugstore near his Hollywood apartment, then a legendary place for actors to hang out. He'd had a dizzy spell there but an EKG the next day showed it was a heart attack, and his doctor prescribed six weeks rest and to refrain from walking up stairs. Accordingly he moved from his third-floor apartment into Graham's house. The second occurred on December 20 after he and Sheilah attended the premiere of *This Thing Called Love*, starring Melvyn Douglas and Rosalind Russell at the Pantages Theater. Again the symptom was dizziness, from which he recovered soon after leaving the theater, and on arriving at Graham's house, he took a sleeping pill and went to bed. The next day at three o'clock in the afternoon, as he finished a chocolate bar while editing an article for the *Princeton Alumni Weekly*, he was stricken by the final heart attack.

"All good writing is swimming under water and holding your breath" was another of Fitzgerald's maxims. But another reason for his dramatic fall from the heights of success and adulation to failure and relative oblivion was much more than an inability to come up for air after a creative outpouring the like of which has rarely been matched in American letters. Time, that ruthless judge and censor, had passed him by.

In fact, time had begun to pass him by early in his career, although he didn't see it happening.

To today's man or woman in the street, the career and life of Francis Scott Fitzgerald (he was named for a distant ancestor, Francis Scott Key, composer of the *Star-Spangled Banner*) is almost totally identified with his novel *The Great Gatsby*. Set in 1922, as the Fitzgerald-named "Jazz Age" was warming up, and published in 1925, unlike his earlier *This Side of Paradise*, which was a best-seller, *Gatsby* was deemed a failure, with initial sales amounting to only 20,870 books.

As years went by, *Gatsby* matters got worse. During the first half of 1940, Fitzgerald's last year, the total sales of the novel were only seven; reportedly, when he wanted to give Graham a copy, they went from bookstore to bookstore looking for his book and found none. It would not be until after the end of World War II, more than twenty years after the book was published and a wartime after the writer's death, that the reading public rediscovered *Gatsby*. And when they discovered it, they discovered it with a vengeance. Sales in the half century since then number in the millions.

Three major films have been made from it. The first, a famous "lost film," starred Warner Baxter, Lois Wilson, and William Powell. From the extant reviews, it may have been the most faithful adaptation. The second was made in 1949 and starred Alan Ladd, Betty Field, and Shelley Winters. In 1974 the most famous (and arguably the worst) version was made from a script by Francis Ford Coppola; it starred Robert Redford as Gatsby, Mia Farrow as Daisy Buchanan, and Sam Waterston as Gatsby's neighbor (and narrator of the novel) Nick Carraway. In 2000 a BBC–TV movie was released starring Paul Rudd, Toby Stephens, and Mira Sorvino.

The reason for the novel's overwhelming modern-day popularity? Matthew J. Bruccoli speculated in a preface to a recent edition of the novel that "great fiction is great social history; [*The Great Gatsby*] has become automatically identified with The Jazz Age, . . . The Roaring Twenties . . . The Boom. The Twenties were not a ten-year binge during which everybody got rich and danced the Charleston in speakeasies while drinking bootleg 'hooch.' They were a time," Bruccoli adds, when World War I "triggered disillusionment, moral reevaluation, social experiment, and hedonism." *Gatsby*, though all too often trivialized today as a literary postcard of a glitzy era, is anything but that, as Broccoli continues: "Fitzgerald wrote in judgment [of] a get-rich-quick decade," which he described in his essay, "Echoes of the Jazz Age." Although Gatsby's sudden riches are never fully explained in the novel, it is clear that he was a bootlegger in an age that, because of Prohibition, brought about a massive growth in the power of crime organizations (chapter 3).

This is not the place to offer a lengthy literary analysis of Fitzgerald's works; with his posthumous elevation as an American literary icon, there are probably thousands of professorial examples and undoubtedly hundreds of thousands of student theses out there doing that. But as *Gatsby* clearly grew out of Fitzgerald's observations of the social fabric of the 1920s, it isn't surprising that the novel's narrator, Nick Carraway, who is involved in the story's events as well as judging them, is essentially a stand-in for Fitzgerald himself. And as much as he borrowed from his own perceptions, it is fascinating to see how much he also borrowed from the real events and people in his own life, including their friends, rivals, and the unscrupulous, as well as his and his wife's experiences and infidelities, all of it filtered through his talent and presented in brilliant, almost poetic, prose.

While writing *Gatsby* in 1924, Fitzgerald wrote that the passage of time, with its related themes of change and loss, is "the whole burden of this novel—the loss of those illusions that give such color to the world so that you don't care if things are true or false as long as they partake of the magical glory." Gatsby does not accept this. "Can't repeat the past? " he asks in the novel. "Why, of course you can." Ironically—or perhaps prophetically—change and loss are exactly the elements that would challenge and overcome Scott Fitzgerald himself.

Like most of Fitzgerald's fiction, *The Great Gatsby* is highly autobiographical, certainly in its viewpoint of 1920s New York society and the characters who populate the book; in fact, there is hardly a person whom he knew who didn't end up in one of his short stories or novels. Certainly, the self-absorption of *Gatsby*'s Daisy and Tom Buchanan parallels that of Scott and Zelda themselves. The witty *This Side of Paradise* was published in 1920, set in the post–World War I decade, during part of which Fitzgerald was at Princeton (he lasted only three years before leaving after catching malaria or to enlist, both excuses meant to whitewash the fact that he was flunking out anyway). The character of Rosalind in the book possesses the impetuous side of his wife-to-be, Zelda Sayre, whom he met while serving in the army in Montgomery, Alabama. And the novel's character of Monsignor Darcy was clearly based on Father Cyril Sigourney Fay, described as a "fin-de-siècle aesthete and dandy" and "a jolly monk" who encouraged the literary ambitions of the sixteen-year-old Fitzgerald while he was attending the Newman (prep) School in his hometown of St. Paul, Minnesota.

In *Gatsby*, as in few of its contemporary works, Fitzgerald captures both the glitter of the Roaring Twenties with its lavish parties, possessions, and abandoned behavior, but also the decadence of a decade populated by machine-gun carrying hijackers, gang wars, bootleggers, and corrupt police and politicians. The financier Meyer Wolfsheim in the novel is based on the career of the Mafia financier Arnold Rothstein, who not only was associated with a neighbor of Scott and Zelda who defrauded his brokerage clients of millions of dollars but was also the man who fixed the notorious 1919 World Series by bribing the Chicago White Sox to lose.

Even locations are from life . . . Scott and Zelda's rented house in Great Neck, Long Island, would star as Ned Carraway's East Egg, Long Island, house in *Gatsby*. Zelda, invoking the title of Sinclair Lewis's best-selling satire of American capitalism, called it "our nifty little Babbitt-house."

Events also played large parts in Fitzgerald's novels. Anthony Patch's anticipated fortune in *The Beautiful and Damned* was inspired by Scott's sudden royalty wealth from *Paradise*, and the screen test episode for the Gloria character in the same novel came from an offer for Scott and Zelda to star in a movie of the book. Zelda, in fact, inspired Gloria's character (if only her worst features), and Gloria's husband and Zelda's real father shared the name of Anthony. "Gloria was a much more trivial and vulgar person than your mother," Scott later explained to the couple's daughter, Scottie (born in 1921). "I naturally used many circumstantial events of our early married life. We had a much better time than Anthony and Gloria had." One of their Great Neck neighbors was an enormously wealthy war hero named Tommy Hitchcock, whose urbane nature mixed with ruthlessness enabled him, in Fitzgerald's words, to become "the greatest polo player in the world." He and his combination of attributes—particularly his brutality—would inspire the pivotal character of Daisy's husband Tom Buchanan in *Gatsby* as well as Tommy Barban in Scott's later book *Tender Is the Night*.

In May 1924 Scott, Zelda, and Scottie sailed to France, where, he decided, he would write *The Great Gatsby* while living on the Riviera, which was then, apparently—for this was their reason for going—a more economical place to live than Great Neck. Nevertheless, it would cost something, so Fitzgerald actually went on the wagon and wrote "twelve hours a day for five weeks to rise from abject poverty back into the middle class," turning out the popular short stories that were always his main source of income (in 1929 his fee from the *Saturday Evening Post* was $4,000 a story, the equivalent of more than $51,000 today).

When ensconced on the Riviera, the Fitzgeralds became part of the social circle of the Gerald Murphys, among the first international travelers to make the South of France the fashionable destination that it has remained since. Theirs was an unlikely friendship. The Murphys were tremendously wealthy, while Scott and Zelda were relatively poor; Gerald's father owned New York's exclusive Mark Cross leather goods shop, which he would inherit in 1931. The Murphys also led highly organized lives, planning their frequent parties down to the last detail, while Scott and Zelda's lives were, at best, chaotic. Both couples enjoyed each other's children; in fact Scott named the child in his short story "Babylon Revisited," first published in the *Saturday Evening Post* in 1931 (and which has many parallels with his own life) after the Murphy's daughter Honoria. And the Murphys shared Zelda's new passion for the recently popular avocation of sunbathing.

The Murphys' social circle couldn't help but be an attraction to the Fitzgeralds. Many of them, even if they were ex-patriots, identified with the New York lifestyle of the Twenties, if only culturally. Among the American ex-pats that summer of 1924 were the Pulitzer Prize–winning poet Archibald MacLeish, Cole Porter, and the writer John Dos Passos. European friends included the modernist painters Juan Gris, Joan Miró, Georges Braque, and Pablo Picasso, some of whose early drawings the Fitzgeralds bought out of their limited funds.

This didn't mean that all went swimmingly between the Murphys and the Fitzgeralds. Scott's drinking and boorish behavior infuriated Gerald, especially on one occasion when Fitzgerald, drunk as usual, threw three of Sara Murphy's gold-trimmed Venetian wine glasses over the wall of the Murphys' luxurious Villa

America before Gerald stopped him and banned him from their home for three weeks. During his exile Scott dumped a can of garbage on their patio while the Murphys were dining.

Gerald Murphy later considered Scott's friend Ernest Hemingway a better writer. "I suppose it was because Ernest's work seemed contemporary and new, and Scott's didn't," he once remarked. But it was Scott who actually influenced Gerald Murphy more than Hemingway and in a remarkable way. Murphy was mesmerized by the unforgettable literary image of the giant eyes of oculist Doctor T. J. Eckleburg brooding omnisciently from a huge advertisement over *Gatsby*'s "Valley of Ashes" slum neighborhood, halfway between the lovely, bucolic West Egg home of the Buchanans and the elegance of Manhattan; he would later use a giant human eye in a 1928 painting of his own as well as on the flag of his yacht, *Weatherbird.*

So, one wonders, how in the midst of all these carryings-on did *The Great Gatsby* get written? Who knows? Especially as during its writing that tumultuous summer, Zelda became so bored that she had an affair with Edouard Jozan, a handsome French naval aviator she met on the beach. Marital matters, rarely calm between the pair, exploded when, on July 13, she told Scott that she loved Jozan and wanted a divorce. The last thing, however, that Jozan wanted was a wife, and, in September after he was transferred to another navy assignment, she tried to commit suicide with sleeping pills. "I knew something had happened that could never be repaired," Scott later wrote sadly of the marriage. (Jozan went on to command France's Far Eastern fleet and was decorated with the Legion of Honor.)

To repair their relationship, both knew they had to leave the Riviera. As soon as he completed *Gatsby* and mailed it off to Maxwell Perkins, his editor at Scribner, they moved to Rome where he would, as with all his works, spend weeks revising it. Perkins, like Gerald Murphy, was also struck by the powerful image of Eckleburg's eyes. "In the eyes of Dr. Eckleburg readers will see different significances," he wrote, "but their presence gives a superb touch to the whole thing; great unblinking eyes, expressionless, looking down on the human scene. It's magnificent!"

Like Hemingway, Thomas Mann, and D. H. Lawrence before and after, Scott and Zelda found life in Fascist Italy depressing and expensive. During the winter, as Scott related in his short story "The High Cost of Macaroni," they skimped on food to economize. Then during a rare cold spell, Zelda contracted an ovarian infection, and after an altercation with a taxi driver, Fitzgerald (who couldn't speak Italian any better than he could French) was arrested and beaten in the police station. "I hate Italians," he told his actress friend Carmel Myers: "They live in tenements and don't have bathtubs!" When his literary agent, Harold Ober, suggested he write a piece on Italy for the *Saturday Evening Post* to bring in some much needed cash, Fitzgerald, who had given up his Catholic faith in 1917, snapped that he would if it could be "about Pope Syphilis the Sixth and his Morons."

In February 1925 the pair left Rome for Capri but were as unhappy with the atmosphere there, although it had less to do with the Italians than with the ex-patriots whom he found superficial. (Somerset Maugham superficial? Perhaps it was because Maugham was gay; that was always a problem for Fitzgerald.)

Another writer who was not dazzled by Capri was Joseph Conrad, and the influence of the author of *Heart of Darkness* and *Lord Jim* is everywhere in *Gatsby*, from the symbolism of the green light at the end of Daisy's dock in East Egg to the use of a narrator—Nick Carraway—allowing Fitzgerald to give the story credibility by telling it from the point of view of a character in the story. Carraway, both sympathetic and disapproving of Gatsby, is Fitzgerald's way of telling his own envy of his rich acquaintances' sophisticated lifestyle—which he would never really be part of—as well as his disillusionment over their often brutal actions. "They were careless people, Tom and Daisy," Nick comments in *Gatsby*, "they smashed up things and creatures and then retreated back into their money." The powerful ending of *Gatsby* with its water metaphor—"So we beat on, boats against the current, borne back ceaselessly into the past" (which is carved on Scott and Zelda's common gravestone in Rockville, Maryland)—is clearly related to the conclusion of Conrad's *Heart of Darkness:* "The tranquil waterway [the Congo] leading to the uttermost ends of the earth flowed somber under an overcast sky—seemed to lead into the heart of an immense darkness."

So who was Daisy's character drawn from? Most scholars agree that she was partially based on the Chicago debutante Ginevra King, with whom Scott had an affair while at Princeton, as well as on Zelda. In fiction and in real life, *Gatsby*'s Tom Buchanan and Scott lose their wives to other men (Gatsby and Jozan), and just as Tom reclaimed Daisy, so too did Scott reclaim Zelda.

The following April Scott and Zelda left Capri and joined the thirty thousand American ex-pats living in Paris, staying until the end of the year in a grandiose apartment near the Arc de Triomphe. And it was there that he would soon meet Ernest Hemingway in the Dingo Bar in Montparnasse; it would become the most important friendship of his life.

The appeal was understandable. Both came from Midwestern backgrounds, both were married and had one small child, and both were members of the new generation of writers. Hemingway, however, was more of a bohemian and hadn't yet published anything, while Fitzgerald was writing regularly for the *Saturday Evening Post*, with its three million readers and big fees. Eventually, Hemingway would join Scribner, and both would share the same editor.

Hemingway, athletic, six inches taller, and forty pounds heavier than Scott was, to quote Jeffrey Meyers in his brilliant biography of Fitzgerald, "the literary version of the bloodied and bandaged football heroes Scott had worshipped in college." Oddly, at least in Fitzgerald's case, both were fascinated by war. Hemingway, who had been seriously wounded while serving in Italy, seemed to take pleasure in writing about grisly wounds (in 1932's short story "The Natural History of the Dead," for example) and collected pictures of corpses left in the wake of a Florida hurricane, and Fitzgerald, who never left America during his army service, had a huge collection of photographs of horribly mutilated soldiers, burned flyers, and executions. They would also critique one another's work.

Hemingway was also attracted to Zelda, whose beauty he praised in *A Moveable Feast*, but he also believed that she was insanely jealous of Scott's writing success and encouraged him to drink whenever he wanted to write. Still, Hemingway was also conscious of her growing madness (beginning in the early 1930s and until her death in a sanatorium fire in 1948, Zelda would be in and out of mental institutions). For her part Zelda was jealous of Scott's enthusiasm for Hemingway, calling him a "phony," a "professional he-man," and perhaps most woundingly, "a pansy with hair on his chest." Eventually, as Zelda and Scott's marriage worsened, she would accuse both of being homosexuals.

For the rest of 1925, and all of the following year, Scott and Zelda basically bounced around Europe, with the Riviera as their base of operations, before returning to America. In January 1927 they went to Hollywood after United Artists had offered him a job writing a "modern flapper story" for Constance Talmadge. They were lionized by much of Hollywood's establishment, including actor Carmel Myers, the novelist Carl Van Vechten, and the hard-drinking John Barrymore, who told Scott after reading *The Great Gatsby*, "I had not expected that you could write so well."

It was during their Hollywood stay that Scott met and fell in love with an eighteen-year-old actress named Lois Moran, who would be the inspiration for Rosemary in *Tender Is the Night*. She had been a professional ballerina with the Paris Opera Ballet when she was thirteen and after coming to Hollywood would make four films for Fox before she was twenty. Zelda was furious, complaining that Scott never took her out on the town because he "was in flagrantly sentimental relations with a child." Scott would later tell Zelda's psychiatrist that his affair with Moran was "a sort of revenge" for Zelda's fling with Edouard Jozan two years earlier. He later revealed much about his lack of self-respect at the time, echoing his reason for drinking when he explained that he would "do anything to be liked, to be reassured not that I was a man of a little genius, but that I was a great man of the world. Anybody

[who] could make me believe that, like Lois Moran did, was precious to me."

When they left Hollywood, Scott, who feared that the social whirl in New York would divert him from working on *Tender Is the Night*, followed the suggestion of Max Perkins and settled into Ellerslie, a huge Greek Revival house in Wilmington, Delaware. But again, as in much of the time on the Riviera, it was time wasted, spent hosting an endless parade of guests (Lois Moran, of all people, was one). The following spring they returned to Paris, where they were to live near the Luxembourg Gardens and around the corner from their (and Hemingway's) friend and admirer, Gertrude Stein.

Through another friend, Sylvia Beach, he met James Joyce, whose *Ulysses* Beach had earlier published and sold at her Left Bank bookstore, Shakespeare & Company. Scott worshipped Joyce, and *Ulysses* had also influenced *The Great Gatsby*. But as with Hemingway, Zelda didn't like Joyce at all, probably for the same jealous reason. She even began writing on her own, and her novel *Save Me the Waltz,* published by Scribner in 1932, recalled the couple's earlier days on the Riviera and in Paris. She clearly was deliberately plagiarizing Daisy Buchanan's line in *Gatsby* (and probably reflecting her own state of mind at the time) when she has her main female character, Alabama, ask her husband, "What'll we *do*, David . . . with ourselves?" Zelda loved to dance, so Alabama was a dancer (Zelda wanted to join Diaghilev's Ballet Russe de Monte Carlo but was only invited to become a shimmy dancer with the Folies Bergère). Alabama's illness also reflected Zelda's growing consciousness of her mental instability. And as in Scott's novels, Zelda drew upon events in her life, including her affair with Jozan, her reckless lifestyle, and the disillusion of their marriage.

The decade was drawing to a close, and in September 1928 the Fitzgeralds returned to Ellerslie, where there were several more months to run on their lease. The parade of guests returned, this time including Ernest Hemingway. Soon Zelda began her spasmodic but irreversible progress through mental institutions, while Scott would continue to write short stories and his penultimate novel, 1934's *Tender Is the Night*. Although he did nothing to control his alcoholism until the last year of his life, he ruthlessly observed it in *Tender Is the Night*. "Drink made past happy things contemporary . . . as if they were still going on; contemporary even with the future as if they were about to happen again." He added in a later short story, "I found that with a few drinks I got expressive and somehow had the ability to please people and the idea turned my head."

Before his death Fitzgerald, who could also be honest about his own problems, told Sheilah Graham, "Zelda and I never should have married. We were wrong for each other. She would have been happier married to almost anyone else. She was beautiful and talented. It was her tragedy that she could not bear to be overshadowed by the attention I received from my early books. For instance, she hated it when Gertrude Stein talked only to me, while her companion, Alice B. Toklas, talked to her. She had a compulsion to compete with me. She could not [do so] as a writer so she decided to be a famous ballerina and studied with the Russian ballet in Paris. But it was too late for her. And when she realized this, instead of accepting the fact and bending with it, she broke."

Scott Fitzgerald's *The Great Gatsby* has, for millions, become the open door to a seemingly miraculous time when anything was possible if you wanted it enough, all of which came crashing down at the end of the decade. In many ways, his own life and that of his wife were, as well, a real-life metaphor for the boom-to-bust decade. Although he would publish *Tender Is the Night* in 1934 and live for another six years after that, nothing—certainly not during the era of the Great Depression—would or could be the same again. Nor would it be for Zelda, whose mind torturously sank farther and farther away from reality.

Their story really ended with the decade of the 1920s. It was all downhill after that.

The 1920s produced some of America's greatest writers working at the height of their talent. And first among them—at least in retrospect—was Eugene O'Neill, often referred to as "America's Shakespeare." Here, with his second wife, writer Agnes Boulton, and their son Shane, he picnics on a Cape Cod beach near Provincetown, Massachusetts, where many of his early plays were first performed.
Library of Congress

CHAPTER 13

LITERATURE OF THE 1920S, PART II
Edith Wharton, Anita Loos, and Eugene O'Neill

By the end of the Twenties [American literature] had achieved the social depth and complexity whose absence [Henry] James had [earlier] mourned. . . . There was a new ferment working, and at last there was an audience quite unconvinced that American literature must be forever inferior or imitative. . . . O'Neill's *Mourning Becomes Electra* sold out even its [top priced] $6 seats.
***—Paul Johnson,* Modern Times**

If any decade was a golden age for American literature, it was the 1920s. Aside from F. Scott Fitzgerald's *The Great Gatsby*, which has become the avatar of the entire Jazz Age and is treated in chapter 12, influential writers included Sinclair Lewis, Edith Wharton, Theodore Dreiser, Thomas Wolfe, Thornton Wilder, and, of course, the man many consider America's Shakespeare, Eugene O'Neill. And then there was Anita Loos, who in 1925 wrote a book that the conservative Edith Wharton declared "The Great American Novel" over such contenders as Sinclair Lewis's *Babbitt* and *Main Street*, Theodore Dreiser's *An American Tragedy*, Thomas Wolfe's *Look Homeward, Angel*, Thornton Wilder's *The Bridge of San Luis Rey*, and her own *The Age of Innocence.* Considering the competition, Loos's work was an unlikely candidate, a small novel entitled *Gentlemen Prefer Blondes*.

Although not all of these literary figures lived or wrote in New York, Manhattan publishing houses were responsible for their fame by bringing work to the reading public. Two of them, however, were born in New York and represent near-polar opposites of the great social and cultural changes that would change America forever in the 1920s. A third lived in New York during much of an amazing career, so it might as well have been her home.

Holding on to the old world, so to speak, was Edith Wharton, whose name and work is invoked over and over again for her detailed descriptions of the New York aristocratic lifestyle that was lost—or became at best irrelevant in the roaring maelstrom of social and cultural upheavals following World War I that produced the new, devil-may-care world of the 1920s.

It's not surprising that she was also the oldest of our trio of writers, having been born in New York City in 1862. It was the year before the city was torn apart by the Civil War draft riots that began only twenty blocks north of her father's brownstone at 14 East Twenty-Third Street. She had an uncanny eye for detail, and many of that brownstone's Victorian details (and staff) would occasionally find their way into her defining novels, 1905's *The House of Mirth* and, most famous, *The Age of Innocence*, which was published in 1920 and for which she became the first woman to win the Pulitzer Prize for literature. In fact, Wharton's early life, complicated by her mother's rigidly Victorian code of manners and the family's financial situation, more vulnerable and not nearly as vast as the nouveau riche Harrimans and Rockefellers, could have been the basis of one of her novels.

Her theme may have been the past, but her writing style was modern for its time; *The House of Mirth* is considered an early example of literary naturalism, a movement that began in the 1880s and that used realistic social conditions, heredity, and environment to create believable characters and story lines unlike, for example, nineteenth-century romanticism.

It helps to know what you are writing about, and Edith Wharton certainly did. Her mother was Lucretia Stevens Rhinelander, a member of New York's iconic, extended Knickerbocker family. Her father, George Frederic Jones, was just as socially impressive (the term "keeping up with the Joneses" was a reference to his family); his mother was Elizabeth Schermerhorn, an equally formidable society name of the time. A friend was the equally aristocratic Theodore Roosevelt, who was four years her elder.

In 1885, when she was twenty-three, Edith married a Boston socialite named Edward (Teddy) Robbins Wharton, who shared her love of travel but little else, and they divorced in 1913. A decade earlier she had built a home in Lenox, Massachusetts, named "The Mount"—which is still there—where she wrote *The House of Mirth* and also entertained many of the literary lions of the day, including Henry James, with whom much of her work has been compared.

In 1911, with her marriage falling apart, she moved permanently to Paris, initially living in an apartment at 58 Rue de Varenne rented from George Washington Vanderbilt II, a friend who had earlier built what still remains America's largest home, the 250-room, French chateau–styled mansion in Asheville, North Carolina, which he named Biltmore.

After World War I Edith was awarded the French Legion of Honor for her relief work and spent much of her time in Provence, where she wrote *The Age of Innocence*. Appropriate to her upbringing, she was politically conservative—in fact was a committed French imperialist—until her death in 1937 at an eighteenth-century mansion she owned near today's Charles de Gaulle Airport outside Paris.

It is nearly impossible to write about Eugene O'Neill except in superlatives. In his career, he would transform America's theater tradition from a dusty library of Victorian romantic conventionalism to a dynamic arena of dramatic realism. His plays were among the very first in which the characters spoke in the American vernacular and lived on the edges of society. There they would struggle to achieve their dreams but, ultimately, become disillusioned. O'Neill would, in fact, write only one comedy, 1933's *Ah, Wilderness*, about a childhood as he might have wished it to have been.

O'Neill would be rewarded with three Pulitzer Prizes for plays written in the 1920s: *Beyond the Horizon*, *Anna Christie*, and *Strange Interlude.* He would win a fourth for *Long Day's Journey into Night*, written in 1941 but not produced until 1956. And he became the only American playwright to win, in 1936, the Nobel Prize. In 1960 his eleven landmark plays were, according to Arthur and Barbara Gelb's monumental biography *O'Neill*, the most widely read, produced, translated, and taught in the world, with the exception of Shakespeare's and possibly George Bernard Shaw's. In his time O'Neill would not only be recognized as America's greatest playwright, he would also be known as the "king" of Greenwich Village, then in its second decade as America's bohemian paradise and center of contemporary anarchist activity.

But as pointed out by the Gelbs, his own life was more turbulent and bizarre than any of his plays.

Eugene Gladstone O'Neill, the son of an Irish actor named James O'Neill and his wife Ella Quinlan, was born October 16, 1888, in a room of a Times Square hotel called the Barrett Hotel (it is long gone; in its place at 1500 Broadway—at the northeast corner of Forty-Third Street—is, at least at the present writing, a Starbucks coffee shop).

His was a troubled childhood; among other conflicts his mother was a drug addict. After spending nine months at Princeton, he and the university (then headed by Woodrow Wilson) parted ways; he because he had come to the conclusion that it offered little intellectual stimulation, and the school because, among other things, he was considered "lawless," cutting classes and not bothering to take exams. He continued educating himself, aided by discovering a bookshop run by an anarchist who, memorably, when O'Neill was eighteen, introduced him to Friedrich Nietzsche's *Thus Spoke Zarathustra*, the German philosopher's devastating criticism of Christianity and its tenets. In later life O'Neill wrote that the book, of which he had memorized long excerpts, "influenced me more than any book I've ever read."

He then spent several years as an ordinary seaman. The sea gave him a sense of near-religious ecstasy, which he tried to put into words in an early poem called "Free." But his seafaring days were also marked by depression and the alcoholism that was to plague him all his life. For most of his life, he would live near the sea and used it as a prominent theme in most of his plays, several of which are set on ships like the ones on which he worked.

For a time in the early 'teens, O'Neill worked as a reporter for the *New London Telegraph* in Connecticut. Then he contracted tuberculosis, and while recovering in a sanatorium during 1912 and 1913, O'Neill decided to devote his life to writing. After recovery he became very much part of the Greenwich Village literary and political scene at the height of its bohemian lifestyle. He became acquainted with Communist Labor Party founder John Reed, the only American buried in the Kremlin wall, who had a small part in the writer's early one-act play, *Bound East for Cardiff*, when it was first produced. He also had a brief affair with Reed's wife, Louise Bryant (much of this story was well told in the 1981 movie *Reds*, in which O'Neill was played by Jack Nicholson, Bryant by Diane Keaton, and Reed by Warren Beatty, who also directed the film).

Writing, however, was O'Neill's passion. He became involved with Cape Cod's Provincetown Players in the summer of 1916, where he arrived with "a trunk full of plays" according to one biographer; by then he had already written a dozen one-act plays.

It was apparently in the living room of a Provincetown home adjacent to the wharf that the Players used as a theater that the first reading of an O'Neill play took place. The play was the previously mentioned *Bound East for Cardiff*, the first of his four *Glencairn* one-acts, written in 1914 and named for the fictional ship on which they take place (they were filmed together in 1940 as *The Long Voyage Home*, which starred John Wayne). The Provincetown Players would go on to perform many of O'Neill's plays, both on Cape Cod and at a theater on MacDougal Street in Greenwich Village.

O'Neill's first published play, *Beyond the Horizon*, a tragedy about two brothers, opened at the Morosco Theatre on Broadway on February 3, 1920, with his seventy-four-year-old father James and his sixty-three-year-old mother Ella (who had cured herself of her drug addiction) in the audience. Alexander Woollcott, then drama critic for the *New York Times*, wrote that the New York theater season "was immeasurably richer and more substantial" because of the play, which he added was an "absorbing, significant, and memorable tragedy, so full of meat that it makes most of the remaining fare seem like the merest meringue." It was, as the Gelbs say, something that had never been attempted in the Broadway theater: dramatic literature, written rather than contrived, and proof that commercial theater could express such serious material rather than simply serve up amusement. It also won the Pulitzer Prize for drama, quite an honor for a writer's first Broadway foray.

He was clearly on his way. Two years later he won the Pulitzer again for *Anna Christie*. In 1924 came *Desire Under the Elms* and in 1928 another Pulitzer, this for *Strange Interlude.*

O'Neill was married to Kathleen Jenkins from October 2, 1909, to 1912, during which time they had one son, Eugene Jr., who committed suicide at the age of forty in 1950.

In 1917 O'Neill met a successful fiction writer named Agnes Boulton, whom he married on April 12, 1918. They had two children: Shane (who became a heroin addict and committed suicide at the age of fifty-nine in 1977) and a daughter, Oona (the Irish name for Agnes), whom O'Neill disinherited when, at eighteen, she married the fifty-four-year-old Charlie Chaplin in 1943. Eugene and Agnes divorced in 1929, after O'Neill abandoned her and the children and subsequently married the actress Carlotta Monterey.

That same year, 1929, O'Neill and Monterey moved to France, where they lived in the Loire Valley for several years before returning to America and settling in Sea Island, Georgia. In 1937 they moved to Danville, California, and lived in Tao House, described by Monterey as a pseudo-Chinese home (the name meaning, in Chinese, "the right way of life"). It is now the Eugene O'Neill National Historic Site.

By 1943 a Parkinson's-like disease had developed that made it impossible for O'Neill to write any longer (he tried but was unable to dictate plays during the remaining decade of his life). In their first years together, Monterey organized O'Neill's life, enabling him to devote himself to writing. She later became addicted to the sedative potassium bromide, and the marriage deteriorated, exacerbating O'Neill's depression and alcoholism. Although they separated several times, they never divorced.

O'Neill died in Room 401 of the Sheraton Hotel on Bay State Road in Boston—now a Boston University dormitory—on November 27, 1953, at the age of sixty-five. As he was dying, he spoke his last words, in a barely audible whisper: "I knew it. I knew it. Born in a hotel room, and God damn it, died in a hotel room."

Like Wharton, who wrote about New York society, so too, in a rather unlikely literary association, did an aspiring young California writer launch her own career and eventually produce the best-seller that earned Wharton's over-the-top praise as being the Great American Novel. Along with Scott Fitzgerald's *The Great Gatsby*, it probably reflected the era more than any of our other literary immortals' work: *Gentlemen Prefer Blondes: The Intimate Diary of a Professional Lady* (the book's original name). After graduating from high school, the author, Anita Loos, began cobbling together portions of published reports of New York social life and mailing them to a friend in Manhattan who would submit them for publication in San Diego, where Loos lived at the time.

Born in 1888, Loos had wanted to be a writer from the time she was six and naturally gravitated to the equally young film industry, where she would write screenplays—"scenarios" in the beginning when the movies were silent—for such legends as D. W. Griffith (his epic *Intolerance* among them), for whom she was the first staff writer at seventy-five dollars weekly. Her first screen credit was for a silent adaptation of *Macbeth* in which her billing came right after Shakespeare's.

Her first visit to New York was in 1916 to attend the premiere of *Intolerance.* She then returned to California and joined the director (and her future husband) John Emerson in writing five films for Douglas Fairbanks that made the future "king of Hollywood" famous. In 1918 when Famous Players–Lasky, the production company that Fairbanks had joined (bringing Loos and Emerson along with him), offered the pair a contract for four pictures to be made in New York, they took it.

The following year found them making a film for William Randolph Hearst's mistress Marion Davies, followed by two films for Constance Talmadge, produced in a New York warehouse by her sister Norma's husband Joseph Schenck. At the time Loos and Emerson were living at the Algonquin Hotel, where Loos later recalled that she liked many of the members of The Round Table (chapter 14) as individuals but found them overwhelming as a group. In the summer of 1919, Talmadge and the Schencks invited Loos to join them for a vacation in Paris.

After Paris Loos and Emerson lived first in Murray Hill and then in Gramercy Park while making more films in New York. Emerson convinced Loos that he needed a night out weekly with younger women, and an understandably unhappy Loos took refuge with a group of "Tuesday widows" that included Marion Davies and Adele Astaire. It was with this group that she first visited Harlem (chapter 18), where she developed a lifelong love of African-American culture. Occasionally, she would take a break from the "Tuesday widows" group and join her friend H. L. Mencken's circle, which included Sinclair Lewis, Theodore Dreiser, Sherwood Anderson, and theater critic George Jean Nathan. It was on a train to Hollywood in 1925 that Loos began writing a sketch of Mencken and his lady friends, which, combined with her memories of the 1919 Paris vacation, would become *Gentlemen Prefer Blondes.*

It began as a series of short stories in *Harper's Bazaar*, known as the "Lorelei" stories from the name of the protagonist, Lorelei Lee, a flapper of loose morals and high self-esteem who was far more interested in collecting expensive gifts from admirers than marriage licenses. It was a combination of crass cash and culture that New Yorkers in the 1920s well understood, and the magazine's circulation quadrupled overnight. The critical reception for the little book that was soon published was unenthusiastic, but word of mouth, augmented by raves from fellow authors William Faulkner, Aldous Huxley, and Wharton, sent it through three more printings in 1925, eighty-five in the next decade, translations into fourteen languages, and eventually a Broadway musical and a hit film.

Loos was often asked whom she based her characters on but would admit only that the toothless Sir Francis Beekman was modeled in part after producer Jesse Lasky, Dorothy Shaw was modeled after herself and Constance Talmadge, and Lorelei Lee most closely resembled an acquisitive Ziegfeld showgirl named Lillian Lorraine (same initials anyway). In 1926 Loos wrote a stage adaptation that ran on Broadway, then went to London, both to get away from a jealous Emerson (who first tried to suppress the book before they eventually made up) and to write the sequel, *But Gentlemen Marry Brunettes,* which *Harper's* was begging for. There her circle included John Gielgud, Noël Coward, and George Bernard Shaw.

The first film version of *Gentlemen Prefer Blondes*, now lost, was made in 1928 and starred Ruth Taylor as Lorelei Lee.

The stock market crash cost Loos much of the money she had earned from *Blondes*, and in 1931 she accepted an offer from MGM's Irving Thalberg to write scripts for $1,000 weekly ($14,000 today). The first project he assigned was a rewrite of F. Scott Fitzgerald's failed work on *Red-Headed Woman*, to star Jean Harlow. When made and released the following year, the movie made Harlow a major star and reestablished Loos in the front rank of Hollywood screenwriters, where she soon became famous for her innuendoes and double entendres that got around the film capital's then-notorious censorship code. Aside from a couple of visits to New York, Loos remained in Hollywood until 1946, when she came back to Manhattan to work on *Happy Birthday*, a play for Helen Hayes, which after a shaky out-of-town opening, ran for six hundred performances.

In 1949 a musical version of *Blondes* starring Carol Channing opened on Broadway and broke records, with a ninety-week run that also made Channing a star. And in 1953 a film of the musical version was made starring Jane Russell and Marilyn Monroe. Loos had nothing to do with the production but thought that Monroe was "inspired casting."

And so it went. Loos worked on her books (including 1974's *Kiss Hollywood Goodbye* and a biography of the Talmadge sisters), continued to work on adaptations, and traveled. Meanwhile, her work ran in *Vanity Fair*, the *New Yorker*, and *Harper's Bazaar*. She became as much of a New York institution as Greta

Garbo, but, as she was frequently seen at fashion shows, movie events, and galas, hardly as reclusive.

She died on August 17, 1981, at the age of ninety-three. At her memorial service her friend, the songwriter Jule Styne, played, among others, the hit song from the musical version of *Gentlemen Prefer Blondes*, “Diamonds Are a Girl’s Best Friend.”

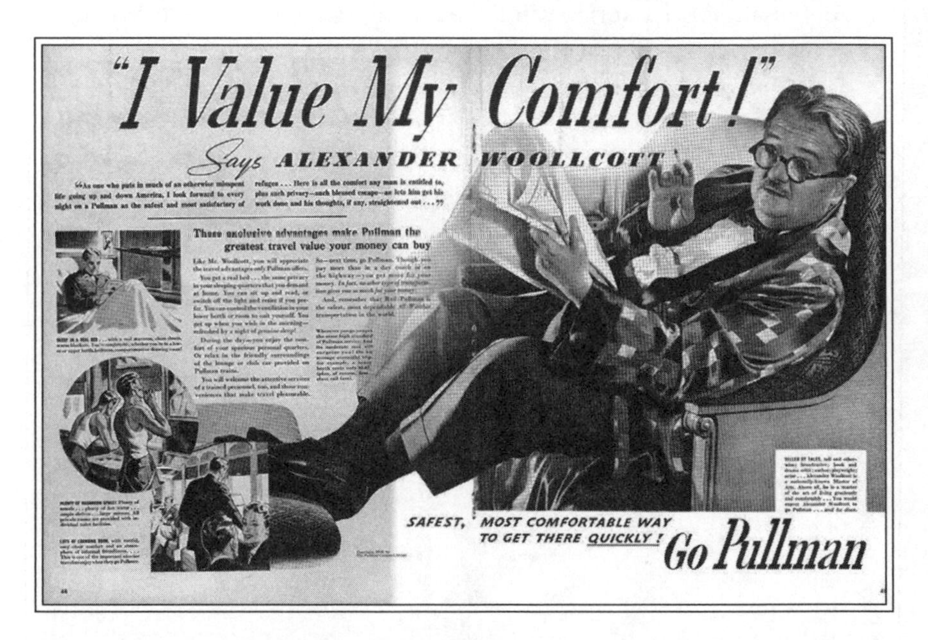

New York set a tone of irreverence for America in the 1920s, and a group of quick-witted members of an informal luncheon club called The Round Table, largely set the tone for New York. Their ranks included the humorist Robert Benchley, *New Yorker* founder/editor Harold Ross, and the acerbic critic Dorothy Parker. The gathering started in 1919 when a press agent, angry with the *New York Times*'s curmudgeonly theater critic Alexander Woollcott for not mentioning a client, organized a lunch to publicly taunt and embarrass him. Woollcott, however, loved the joke, and it started a regular, decade-long lunchtime gathering of the city's wittiest personalities. Here Woollcott appears in a magazine endorsement ad from the 1930s.

Author's Collection

CHAPTER 14

THE ROUND TABLE

Alexander Woollcott, Robert Benchley, Robert Sherwood, Franklin P. Adams, Marc Connelly, Harold Ross, and Dorothy Parker

"Damnit, it was the twenties and we had to be smarty."

—Dorothy Parker on The Round Table

Legends abound about life in New York City in the 1920s . . . the speakeasies, the crime, the exciting sports and music, the art, and, of course, the Mafia. But few legends about the era are as colorful and enduring as that of The Round Table at the Hotel Algonquin.

The reason the scene at the Algonquin became famous was not the food that was served, nor the alcohol that was flagrantly imbibed during the Prohibition years of its fame, but the people who regularly gathered for lunch at a round table. They were an informal club of many of the most influential writers, critics, pundits, and wits New York City had ever seen before or, certainly in our more journalistic homogenized age, since. The Round Table became famous—the group was celebrated even in its own time—through the dissemination of the wisecracks, witticisms, and wordplay exchanged between its members and not only to New York readers but to thousands across the country in newspaper and magazine columns written by its members. Seeing each other on a more or less daily basis created a kind of creative synergism between regular members of The Round Table, as ideas, gossip, and quips were elaborated upon as they bounced from one to another.

It all started in June 1919 when members of a group that initially called itself "The Board" (soon succeeded by "The Vicious Circle") began lunching together at the Algonquin Hotel, conveniently located at 59 West Forty-Fourth Street, near the area where much of the era's journalism was centered. Apparently, the gathering began as a practical joke. It seems that a theatrical press agent named John Peter Toohey became angry with the rotund, curmudgeonly Alexander Woollcott, then the drama critic of the *New York Times,* for refusing to mention one of Toohey's clients in his column. So Toohey organized a lunch at the Algonquin, supposedly to welcome Woollcott back from his World War I service in France, where he, like the *New Yorker*'s Harold Ross, Ross's wife, and Franklin Pierce Adams, had written for *Stars and Stripes*, the independent military newspaper. In reality Toohey used the occasion to poke vicious fun at Woollcott. It backfired, though. Woollcott actually enjoyed the joke so much that he suggested the group meet every day for lunch.

The group's first luncheon area was a long rectangular table in the hotel's Oak Room. When the group grew too large for it, Frank Case, the hotel's manager, moved them to a more substantial round table in the Rose Room. Case, who would be an occasional visitor at the group's lunches, had already earned the everlasting respect of such regulars as Dorothy Parker, who lived in the Algonquin, by overlooking the frequent arrival of illegal hooch to her room, her often uproarious parties, and the tardy payment of her bill. The informal "Round Table" name for the group came when Edmund Duffy, later the Pulitzer Prize–winning editorial cartoonist of the *Baltimore Sun*, caricatured them seated in the Rose Room—all wearing armor to deflect the sharp dialogue.

The original members of The Round Table included the powerful columnist Franklin Pierce Adams, who, under his "FPA" initials, wrote a daily column for the *New York Tribune*;

the humorist and actor Robert Benchley, then managing editor of *Vanity Fair*; the sportswriter and columnist Heywood Broun; and the playwrights Marc Connelly and George S. Kaufman. Among his many hit plays, Kaufman would write 1939's *The Man Who Came to Dinner* with Moss Hart, in which the main character, Sheldon Whiteside, was inspired by Alexander Woollcott. In 1940 Woollcott would actually tour with the play, playing himself. The acidly witty critic, short story writer, and later screenwriter Dorothy Parker (then *Vanity Fair*'s theater critic) was also a member of the group (chapter 15), as was the author and playwright Robert Sherwood (then also writing for *Vanity Fair*). Filling out the regular roster was the man who would eventually found the *New Yorker*, Harold Ross, and, of course, Toohey.

Friends of the group's members were always dropping by, some of whom (like Woollcott's close friend Harpo Marx) became more or less regular members of the table in its maturity. Other occasional members joining in the group's banter were the author and playwright Edna Ferber; Ross's wife Jane Grant; Broun's wife, the feminist Ruth Hale; Kaufman's wife, a playwright herself and an editor, Beatrice Kaufman; *Vanity Fair* editor Frank Crowninshield; actor Tallulah Bankhead; and actors Alfred Lunt and Lynn Fontanne, who married in 1922.

All of The Round Table theater took place more than eighty years ago; inevitably, many of those in attendance are less familiar names now than they were at the time when, as a group, they encapsulated much of New York's and the nation's literary culture. So it is appropriate to take a look at what many of them brought, quite literally, to the table. Alexander Woollcott, subject of the group's original practical joke and initiator of the regular gatherings, first gained notoriety as a *New York Times* drama critic. While employed there, he became celebrated as the curmudgeon of the time and later as a *New Yorker* columnist, and a radio show host. As the *Times*'s drama critic, he wrote the shortest theatrical notice in history; reviewing a show named *Wham!*, he simply wrote "Ouch." His caustic wit was passionately adored and passionately loathed; there was little middle ground about Alexander Woollcott.

While working with Harold Ross and his wife at *Stars and Stripes* in Paris during the war, Woollcott got along so famously with them that afterward he even shared a Manhattan apartment with the pair. Eventually, he became so annoying to live with that the Rosses asked that he leave, and he found his own place on East Fifty-Second Street. It was an event that motivated his fellow Round Table members to try to coin a name for his new home; the winning offering was Dorothy Parker's "wits-end."

In 1916, while he was the drama critic of the *New York Times*, Woollcott was banned by the Shubert theatrical organization for panning shows mounted in their Manhattan theaters. Nothing new about this; critics in similar situations have since taken the easy road and simply bought tickets to the shows they needed to review. But Woollcott went a bit further; he sued the Schuberts, claiming discrimination under the provisions of the New York Civil Rights Act. The case made headlines, but in the end he lost when the state's supreme court ruled that only with regard to race, creed, or color was discrimination unlawful.

From 1929 to 1934 Woollcott wrote a column called "Shouts and Murmurs" for the *New Yorker*. Wolcott Gibbs, his editor, once said that it was "about the strangest copy I ever edited. You could take every other sentence out without changing the sense a particle. I guess he was one of the most dreadful writers who ever existed." Nevertheless, Woollcott's 1934 book, *While Rome Burns*, was picked by the *Chicago Tribune*'s "Books Alive" columnist Vincent Starrett in 1954 as one of the "Best Loved Books of the Twentieth Century."

Woollcott's fame went national when in 1929 he was hired by CBS Radio to review books; the show was billed first as *The Early Bookworm* and after 1933 as *The Town Crier*, which lasted until 1938. Besides promoting and damning books (his promotion of his own *While Rome Burns* made it a best seller), his acidic asides, quips, and anecdotes made him one of the most quoted people in

America; among his most famous quips, often incorrectly attributed to Dorothy Parker, was his description of Los Angeles as "seven suburbs in search of a city." He trashed the popular entertainer Oscar Levant by saying: "There is absolutely nothing wrong with [him] that a miracle can't fix," and described his *New Yorker* boss, Harold Ross (chapter 16), by saying "He looks like a dishonest Abe Lincoln."

Woollcott was born on January 19, 1877, in a ramshackle, eighty-five-room building near Red Bank, New Jersey. The place had been taken over by his maternal grandparents when a commune it originally housed broke up in the mid-nineteenth century. His father drifted through various jobs, and poverty was always near for the young Aleck, as he was then called and would be nicknamed for most of his life. As a child he developed a love of reading, especially the works of Charles Dickens. He graduated from Hamilton College in Clinton, New York, where, despite being unpopular with his fellow students (their nickname for him was "putrid"), Woollcott managed to found a drama group, edit a literary magazine, and join a fraternity before moving to Manhattan and his life's work.

James Thurber, in his memoir of his *New Yorker* days, *The Years with Ross*, claimed that Woollcott, perhaps recognizing that he was basically a storyteller of gossip and anecdotes instead of an original writer, once described himself as "the best writer in America" but with nothing much to say. And despite his reputation his personal letters reveal Woollcott as a warm person who made—and kept—many friends within his theatrical and literary world, prominent among them the actress Katharine Cornell and her husband Guthrie McClintic.

Alexander Woollcott suffered a heart attack during a January 1943 radio broadcast of a panel discussion of Adolf Hitler's Germany. He died, at the age of fifty-six, at Roosevelt Hospital only hours later. He was buried at Hamilton College, where his ashes, having been first missent to Hamilton, New York, were delivered to the college by the post office with sixty-seven cents' postage due.

He always claimed that the popular 1920s cocktail, the Brandy Alexander, was named for him and would often quip, "All the things I really like are immoral, illegal, or fattening." Such a sentiment could in a large part also describe the decade itself.

~

As creative as The Round Table members were, they only collaborated once on a project. It was a revue called *No, Sirree!*, which would be instrumental in launching the Hollywood career of Round Table member Robert Benchley. His part in the revue, titled "The Treasurer's Report," featured Benchley as a nervous, disorganized man attempting to summarize an organization's yearly expenses. His performance received the biggest laughs and applause in the highly successful production.

Robert Charles Benchley was born September 15, 1889, in Worcester, Massachusetts, to Charles and Maria Benchley. Throughout his life, he would be celebrated for his unique brand of deadpan humor, from his early days writing for the *Harvard Lampoon* through his years in New York writing for the original *Vanity Fair* and the *New Yorker* and his later short films made after he moved to Hollywood (his short, *How to Sleep*, won the Best Short Subject award at the 1935 Academy Awards).

His style would long survive him as well, influencing writers and actors from his contemporary, James Thurber, to Groucho Marx, and on to Woody Allen, Bob Newhart and Steve Martin. He was also a committed pacifist, a personal philosophy he credited to the death of his older brother, Edmund, in the Spanish-American War in 1898, when Robert was just nine years old. While he was still in high school, Robert later started an affair with the deceased Edmund's former fiancée; she paid for his attending the expensive Phillips Exeter Academy for his final high school year, as well as provided financial help when he entered Harvard in 1908.

While he was in high school, he met a fellow student, Gertrude Darling, to whom he became engaged while a senior at Harvard and married in 1914. Together they started quite a dynasty; their first son Nathaniel became a successful writer, and his son, Peter, was the author of the best seller *Jaws* (made into a famous thriller film in 1975, directed by Stephen Spielberg), and Peter's brother, Nat, wrote and performed in a one-man play based on his grandfather's life.

While Benchley was at Harvard, several professors had suggested that his future lay in either writing or acting, but instead he left school without completing the "scholarly paper" necessary for receiving a degree and went to work with the civil service in Philadelphia. The pattern for his career as a humorist was apparent, however, when he finally turned in the missing thesis. It was an analysis of the U.S.–Canadian fisheries dispute of the time, written from the point of view of a *codfish*.

After receiving his degree Benchley worked for a time at Curtis Publishing (publisher of the then massive-circulation *Saturday Evening Post*, among other celebrated periodicals of the age) before becoming a freelance writer. His first sale as a freelancer was to *Vanity Fair* in 1914; it was called "Hints on Writing a Book" and was a parody of self-help pieces that were popular at the time. He then joined the staff of the *New York Tribune*, writing reviews as well as features about whatever he wanted.

It was all very successful until the newspaper management became unhappy over Benchley's pacifist views and irreverence expressed in the *Tribune*'s Sunday magazine, which he was by then editing. When they shut it down in 1917, he was out of a job again. After bouncing from one position to another (including the highly unlikely job of publicity director of the government's Aircraft Board, a short-lived return to the *Tribune*, and a stint as a publicist for the government's Liberty Loan program), he was offered the job of managing editor of *Vanity Fair*.

Finally, Robert Benchley had found a place where his kind of humor was welcomed, and he discovered two colleagues who would become close friends: a fellow *Harvard Lampoon* alumnus named Robert Sherwood and Dorothy Parker, who had been hired by *Vanity Fair* earlier to replace P. G. Wodehouse as the magazine's theater critic. Eventually, their collective irreverence even caused problems with that magazine's management, which tried to discipline them by forbidding the trio to discuss their salaries (they responded by wearing placards stating their income) and issuing "tardy slips" to the perennially late writers (Benchley responded to one of his tardy slips by writing an excuse explaining he had been delayed by a herd of elephants on Forty-Fourth Street).

The first to go was Parker, who was dismissed because of complaints from producers whose plays she had panned. When told of her firing, Benchley also quit, only to be deluged with freelance offers, including a thrice-weekly book review offer from the *New York World*, which he accepted. It ran for a year and paid him the same salary he had received as editor of *Vanity Fair*. Soon after the founding of *Life*, he became its theater critic, eventually running the theater department (fellow humorist James Thurber once claimed that Benchley's column was the only reason that the magazine was read at all—which may have been a bit of contradictory humor since *Life*, as noted elsewhere (chapter 16), was a picture-driven rather than a word-driven periodical.

Because of his performance in *No, Sirree!*, Benchley was offered $500 weekly from Hollywood producer Jesse Lasky to write screenplays for six weeks. Though Benchley was being paid the current equivalent of close to $38,600 for his work, the gig resulted in little more than a credit for writing title cards for a silent film. While in Hollywood, though, Benchley made a ten-minute short of "The Treasurer's Report" for Fox. It was one of the first sound films, made only four months after Warner's groundbreaking *Jazz Singer* in 1928. Despite Benchley's feelings that the short wasn't very good, it became a huge financial and critical success, prompting Fox to make two more successful short films with him that year, *The Sex Life of the Polyp*, and another, *The Spellbinder*, starring but not written by him.

The following year he resigned from *Life* and became the film critic for the *New Yorker.* Two years later he returned to Hollywood to make a short film for RKO and then, in 1932, his first feature film, *The Sport Parade*, costarring with Joel McCrea. It was a success, and the studio offered him a one-year contract for far more money than he was making at the *New Yorker;* it was a career-changing event.

Benchley subsequently made a number of movies; perhaps the best was *Rafter Romance*, which got him an offer from MGM to make another series of shorts. At the same time Hearst offered him a syndicated newspaper column. Since the shorts (and of course the column) could be made in New York, he headed back East, but not before making *Dancing Lady* in 1933 with Joan Crawford, Clark Gable, Fred Astaire, and the Three Stooges.

By now it seemed as if everyone wanted Robert Benchley. He returned to Hollywood where, among a couple of other films, he costarred as a drunk in MGM's big-budget *China Seas* with Clark Gable, Jean Harlow, Wallace Beery, and Rosalind Russell. MGM was so happy with his work that they invited him to make a short based on a Mellon Institute study on sleep. The result, *How to Sleep*, his best known short, was made in two days and won him an Oscar in 1935, as well as commitments for several additional shorts. In 1937 he was cast in the film revue *Broadway Melody of 1938* and in his largest film role, *Live, Love and Learn* (which was not a success), as well as another MGM short, *A Night at the Movies*, which became his greatest success after *How to Sleep*.

Then things began to sour a bit, primarily because Benchley was spread too thin. A prospective radio show was canceled; the *New Yorker* replaced him as a movie critic because they felt (with good reason) that his film career was taking precedence over his work for them; and in Hollywood he was more or less tossed around among the studios. A couple of fine films did come out of the turmoil however—*You'll Never Get Rich* (1941) and 1943's *The Sky's the Limit*, both with Fred Astaire. In '43, he also signed a new contract with Paramount and resigned himself to giving up writing after the publication of two books of his *New Yorker* columns. Aside from providing financial security, Paramount didn't handle him well, at one point casting him in the Bob Hope–Bing Crosby comedy *The Road to Utopia* simply to explain an idiotic story line.

Like his friend Dorothy Parker, Benchley had a serious alcoholism problem, which, true to form, he made fun of. Among his most quoted lines was the one uttered while he was living at the legendary Garden of Allah on Sunset Boulevard during one of his long Hollywood stays (it was in Benchley's Hollywood bungalow where Ernest Hemingway met Gary Cooper, the man who would star in the film version of the writer's semiautobiographical novel *For Whom the Bell Tolls*). One afternoon, so the story goes, after a nude Tallulah Bankhead got out of the hotel's swimming pool and wrapped herself in a robe, Benchley approached with an outstretched cocktail glass and inquired, "Why don't you get out of those wet clothes and into a dry martini?" But all the joking about drinking couldn't prevent its toll, and after being diagnosed with cirrhosis of the liver, he died in New York on November 21, 1945.

Marc Connelly is hardly remembered today, which is a pity. He was a superb writer and a marvelous wit who moved from a newspaper job in Pittsburgh to New York, where he became one of the original members of The Round Table. In 1921 he began a four-year writing partnership with fellow Round Table member George S. Kaufman, and together they wrote five comedies, including 1922's popular *Merton of the Movies* and 1924's *Beggar on Horseback*. Outside the partnership he also wrote the books for other musical comedies and contributed articles and poems to *Life* and other magazines.

In 1930 he won the Pulitzer Prize for Drama for *The Green Pastures*, a groundbreaking retelling of parts of the Old Testament that boasted Broadway's first all-black cast.

And then there was Robert Emmet Sherwood. Born in New Rochelle, New York, in 1896, he could number among his ancestors numerous famous painters, as well as the Irish nationalist Robert Emmet, who was executed for high treason by the British in 1803. Sherwood fought in World War I with the Canadian Black Watch and afterward began writing movie criticism for the *New Yorker*, where, as noted, he became close friends with Dorothy Parker and Robert Benchley.

He would stand out in any crowd. At six feet eight inches tall, he towered over his friends. Robert Benchley was once asked how long he had known Sherwood. He stood on a chair, raised his hand to the ceiling, and said, "I knew Bob Sherwood back when he was only this tall."

But Sherwood also stood out—even among New York's most creative writers—for his talent. During his lifetime he would win three Pulitzer Prizes for Drama (1936's *Idiot's Delight*, *Abe Lincoln in Illinois* in 1938, and 1940's *There Shall Be No Night*). Of his fourteen major plays, ten were made into movies; one of them, *Waterloo Bridge*, was made into a movie twice, first in 1931 and then in 1940, starring Vivien Leigh and Robert Taylor. He also wrote a number of screenplays, among them 1946's *The Best Years of Our Lives*, for which he won the Best Screenplay Oscar.

And it didn't stop there. During World War II he worked as a speech writer for President Roosevelt and coined the "arsenal of democracy" phrase that President Roosevelt used in many of his wartime speeches. His memoirs of the period, *Roosevelt and Hopkins*, won him another Pulitzer Prize, as well as Columbia University's Bancroft (history) Prize in 1949.

That Sherwood's career would be spectacular was probably apparent to his fellow members of The Round Table. Unlike the experience of most neophyte playwrights, his first play, 1927's *The Road to Rome* was a success. Perhaps one reason for the play's warm reception was that, although the bad memories of World War I were fast receding, the comedy concerning Hannibal's botched invasion of Rome, was read—as he intended it to be—as a demonstration of the stupidity of war. It would be a theme he would repeat, especially in *Idiot's Delight.* "The trouble with me," he admitted to the writer Lucius Beebe, "is that I start with a big message and end up with nothing but good entertainment." Which, of course, is exactly why his plays and writings were so popular.

The mid-twenties also saw him in Hollywood, where he began writing dialogue cards for silent films in 1926 before easily segueing into sound pictures. He would eventually work adaptations of several of his plays for film, as well as team up with Alfred Hitchcock and cowrite (with Hitchcock's assistant Joan Harrison) the screenplay for 1940's *Rebecca.* Apparently through Sherwood, Robert Benchley and Dorothy Parker also became involved with Hitchcock; Benchley appeared in (and wrote his own lines for) Hitch's *Foreign Correspondent*, and Dorothy Parker was the screenwriter for 1942's *Saboteur.*

Gossip has been called "the second oldest profession." And a recent survey turned up the astonishing fact that much of the human race spends most of its time trading gossip. The reason? Probably that gossip is always about people, and people are what most of us seem to talk about. On the other hand, nothing goes stale quicker than gossip (other than, of course, yesterday's unused theater or sports event ticket). Gossip columnists, too . . . rarely has there been a journalistic fall swifter and greater than that of Walter Winchell—the man who actually invented the gossip column in the 1920s (chapter 7). One day he was the most powerful person in media, with fifty million readers (and twenty million radio listeners), and seemingly overnight, he was peddling mimeographed copies of his column to passersby on Los Angeles street corners.

So, too, the fate of Round Table member Franklin Pierce Adams, whose newspaper column "The Conning Tower" (published under the pseudonym FPA) for the *New York Tribune* was among the biggest things going in the New York media world of the Twenties. Although not strictly a gossip column as we have come to know them, which would have needed Winchell's brashness to have been successful, it still dealt with news about people, albeit more highbrow types such as Edna St. Vincent Millay, George Kaufman, Moss Hart, and Edna Ferber. Like Winchell's column it became a cultural lodestone of an entire generation ("The Conning Tower" lasted for nearly thirty years), and a mention in it was enough to launch a career.

Such was the case for both James Thurber and Dorothy Parker, who acknowledged Adams's power when she quipped, "He raised me from a couplet." It was in "The Conning Tower" where Parker's most famous quip first appeared: "Men seldom make passes at girls who wear glasses."

Much later the writer E. B. White also acknowledged Adams's power when he reminisced, "I used to walk quickly past the house in West Thirteenth Street between Sixth and Seventh where FPA lived, and the block seemed to tremble under my feet—the way Park Avenue trembles when a train leaves Grand Central." From 1938 until 1948 Adams also appeared as a regular panelist on the popular radio show *Information Please.* And then he was gone and forgotten, just like more recent newspaper columnists Earl Wilson, Ed Sullivan (everyone knows the television show, but who remembers the newspaper column?), Leonard Lyons, and Cholly Knickerbocker (a copyrighted name used by several people over the years, including Oleg Cassini and Charles van Rensselaer).

Fate, however, would be far kinder to Dorothy Parker—at least for a while—despite a lifetime's determined effort to mock it.

Today, the best remembered member of The Round Table is the critic and writer Dorothy Parker, then as now famed for her cynical wit and quips including "Men seldom make passes at girls who wear glasses." But she was much more than a facile word-crafter. Despite severe alcoholism and a turbulent personal life, she managed a successful (and extremely profitable) Hollywood screenwriting career for which she was rewarded with two Oscar nominations and published volume after volume of poetry that still reads as freshly as it did eighty years ago. Here she is photographed boarding a train for one of her many trips between New York and Los Angeles.

Courtesy of Marc Wanamaker/Bison Archives

CHAPTER 15

THE WITTY CRITIC

Dorothy Parker

Drink and dance and laugh and lie,
Love, the reeling midnight through,
For tomorrow we shall die!
(But, alas, we never do.)
— *Dorothy Parker*

Today much of the wit and occasional wisdom of The Algonquin Round Table has largely evaporated in the seismic cultural changes that have taken place during the last eight decades. The writings of such tastemakers as Alexander Woollcott have mostly disappeared, the newspaper columns of Franklin Pierce Adams have decayed into dust, and even the talent of a playwright like George S. Kaufman has become somewhat dated. But the wit and writings of one member of the group has endured; that of the outspoken poet, journalist, and satirist Dorothy Parker. In fact, of the dozens of "Portable" books published by Viking for service men and women during World War II, one of the few revamped and republished by Viking's parent company, Penguin, is *The Portable Dorothy Parker*.

It's hard to say why the creative output of some artists, massively popular in their own times, fails to endure. But in the case of Dorothy Parker, the reason for her longevity is clear; she had a unique ability to spot timeless human foibles—even her own—and express them in rhymes, quips, or anecdotes that stick in the mind like glue. Everyone remembers the one quoted in the previous chapter, which she personally disliked: "Men seldom make passes at girls who wear glasses" (Parker wore glasses and never had a problem getting passes).

And then about herself: "Ducking for apples—change one letter, and it's the story of my life." Another reason for her popularity could be that, unlike most other members of The Round Table (Robert Benchley excluded), she remained newsworthy and made headlines throughout most of her life, albeit not always the most flattering. Her friend Alexander Woollcott once called her ". . . a combination of Little Nell and Lady Macbeth."

After moving to Hollywood when The Round Table broke up in 1929, Parker's popularity not only continued but grew, capped by winning two Oscar nominations for screenplays. When she was placed on the Hollywood blacklist because of her suspected involvement in Communism in the late 1940s—essentially making her unemployable in the film capital—she made headlines (the FBI compiled a thousand-page dossier on her). Other incidents of her life that the media were drawn to like a cat to catnip included her several suicide attempts, prompting a bitter poem:

Razors pain you,
Rivers are damp,
Acids stain you,
And drugs cause cramp.
Guns aren't lawful,
Nooses give,
Gas smells awful.
You might as well live.

Her three marriages, two of them to the same man, also kept her in the news. And like her friend F. Scott Fitzgerald, whose funeral she attended in 1944 (memorably commenting—as did a visitor attending Gatsby's funeral in Fitzgerald's *Great Gatsby*—"the poor son-of-a-bitch"), she shared a serious addiction to alcohol.

Born on August 22, 1893, in the Long Branch, New Jersey, summer beach house of her parents, Jacob Rothschild, a wealthy garment manufacturer (whose heritage was German-Jewish and who was no relation to the banking family), and his wife Eliza Anne, of Scottish descent, she was the last of their four children. Immediately after Labor Day they took the infant Dottie back to their Upper West Side Manhattan apartment at 214 West Seventy-Second Street so she would always be considered a native New Yorker rather than a New Jersey-ite. Her mother died in 1898, just before Dorothy's fifth birthday, and her father remarried two years later. Dorothy loathed her father and stepmother, Eleanor. She accused her father, probably unjustly, of abusing her and called her stepmother "the housekeeper" instead of "Mother."

Her anger carried over to school when, somewhat oddly, considering the fact that her father was Jewish and her stepmother Protestant, she was enrolled in the Roman Catholic school of the Convent of the Blessed Sacrament located on West Seventy-First Street. In retrospect one should have known that it couldn't work, and it didn't; Dorothy was thrown out after referring to the Immaculate Conception as "spontaneous combustion." She was then sent to a finishing school in New Jersey, but it was hopeless, and her formal education ended in 1906, when she was thirteen. By then her hated stepmother was dead, and her father followed in 1913. Dorothy, despite having three older siblings, was more or less on her own and played the piano for a dancing school while she indulged a passion for writing limericks and poems.

She sold her first poem to *Vanity Fair* in 1914 and was soon hired as an editorial assistant for the magazine's sister publication, *Vogue*. Two years later she was moved to *Vanity Fair* as a staff writer, where, in 1918 and, now married to Edwin Parker, Dorothy Parker would replace the vacationing P. G. Wodehouse as the magazine's theater critic. It was then that fate entered in. At *Vanity Fair* she became friends with Robert Benchley, then managing editor of the magazine, and writer Robert Sherwood. (Sherwood, as noted previously, was six feet eight inches tall,

Benchley six feet, and Dorothy a diminutive five feet four inches. When they walked down the sidewalk together, Parker quipped that they resembled "a walking pipe organ.")

And they walked down the sidewalk together on a near-daily basis, at least at lunchtime, when they wended their way to the nearby Hotel Algonquin, where they were joined by friends, among them Alexander Woollcott and Franklin Pierce Adams. By reprinting Parker's lunchtime witticisms and short poems in their writings, her fellow Round Tablers launched Parker's national reputation as a popular wit. That wit had a downside, however, particularly with several Broadway producers whose shows she panned. Because of their pressure on Condé Nast, her publisher, she was fired from *Vanity Fair* in 1920. In protest Benchley and Sherwood resigned as well.

Dorothy Parker's poems were celebrated because, by reflecting her sardonic wit, they were a refreshing antidote to the often highly sentimental product of the era. Although she had written poetry since she was a child, she started writing it seriously in 1914, and by the 1920s, when her output hit overdrive, she had turned out more than three hundred poems and free verse works. Many of them were collected in her first book of poetry, 1926's *Enough Rope*, which, fueled by great reviews, sold 47,000 copies. The *New York World* reviewer called her "one of the most sparkling wits who express themselves through light verse," and the *Nation* reviewed her work as "caked with a salty humor, rough with splinters of disillusion, and tarred with a bright black authenticity." She clearly knew what she was about, once writing: "There's a hell of a distance between wise-cracking and wit. Wit has truth in it; wise-cracking is simply calisthenics with words."

She would subsequently publish two more volumes of verse, *Sunset Gun* in 1928 and *Death and Taxes* three years later. She also published several short story collections, including *Laments for the Living* in 1930 and *After Such Pleasures* (1933). *Not So Deep as a Well* (1936) collected much of the material previously published in *Rope*, *Gun* and *Death* and she re-released the fiction with a few new pieces in 1939 under the title *Here Lies*. If you've spotted the black humor predicted in these titles, you'd be correct; an incurably pessimistic view of life always played a part in her creative and personal outlook; as she said, especially when she commented on the arrival of a new challenge during a particularly trying Depression year, "What fresh hell is this?" (The quote has been used by many since, including in the TV show *Frasier* and the movie *To Wong Foo, Thanks for Everything, Julie Newmar*.)

Parker also collaborated on two plays in the 1920s, one, *Business Is Business*, with her Round Table lunch companion George S. Kaufman, and the other, *Close Harmony*, with Elmer Rice.

Harold Ross knew her acerbic look at life would appeal to much of his target audience at the *New Yorker* and unleashed her on them in the form of book reviews under the byline of the "Constant Reader." One of Parker's most memorable reviews was her take on A. A. Milne's soon-to-be-beloved *House at Pooh Corner*: "Tonstant Weader fwowed up." (In 1933 she famously commented on Katharine Hepburn's performance in *The Lake* as, "She runs the gamut of emotions from A to B." Parker later admitted that she was making a joke and really admired the actress.) Of her short stories, most defined by a combination of sparkling wit mixed with the emotionally touching bittersweet, the most famous is "Big Blonde," which received the prestigious O. Henry Award as the Best Short Story of 1929.

Perhaps it was inevitable that she would turn her caustic wit on those closest to her. After she separated from her first husband, a Wall Street broker named Edwin Parker II, she had a torrid relationship with Charles MacArthur, who would gain theatrical fame as the coauthor (with Ben Hecht) of *The Front Page* and would marry actress Helen Hayes in 1928. After Dorothy became pregnant by MacArthur (ended by an abortion), she attempted suicide for the first time. She later remarked ruefully, "How like me, to put all my eggs into one bastard."

She and Edwin finally divorced in 1928 (in the strongly anti-Semitic 1920s, Dorothy was defensive about being half Jewish and often joked that she married Parker to escape her name). By then she was also beginning her leftist political activities and was photographed being arrested at a Boston march on August 20, 1927, protesting the coming executions of the anarchists Ferdinando Sacco and Bartolemeo Vanzetti, controversially convicted of murdering two men. She pleaded guilty to the charge of "loitering and sauntering" and paid a five-dollar fine.

Just as work in Hollywood would prove rewarding for fellow Round Table members Robert Benchley and Robert Sherwood, so, too, would it be a bonanza, at least for a time, for Parker and the actor and screenwriter wannabe Alan Campbell, whom she married in 1934. She would later accuse Campbell of being "as queer as a billy goat." Dale Olson, later to be one of Hollywood's legendary press agents, was at the time the young nightclub reviewer for *Daily Variety*. He recalls that whenever he would visit the pair at their bungalow on Norma Place in West Hollywood, Campbell "would chase me around the sofa" whenever Dorothy left the room.

Based on her reputation, after moving to Hollywood Dorothy and Alan quickly got a ten-week screenwriting contract with Paramount. Parker received $1,000 weekly and Campbell, who also wanted to act, $250 weekly. Her income was soon boosted to $2,000 weekly, and after the couple switched to freelance status, they brought in some $4,000 weekly, the equivalent of $65,000 today.

Separately and together, they worked on fifteen films, among them (with Robert Carson) the screenplay for the first version of *A Star is Born*, filmed in 1937 with Janet Gaynor and Fredric March for which they received a Best Writing Oscar nomination. Separately, Parker wrote additional dialogue for 1941's *The Little Foxes* and received another Oscar writing nomination for cowriting the script for 1947's *Smash-Up: The Story of a Woman*, which starred Susan Hayward.

During the 1930s and '40s, Parker was becoming more and more of a vocal supporter of left-wing causes. At the instigation of a covert Soviet Comintern member, she helped found the Hollywood Anti-Nazi League in 1936, which, eventually, had some four thousand members, who didn't suspect that the organization was feeding money to the Communist Party. In 1937 Parker was reporting on the Loyalist cause in the Spanish Civil War for New York's by then avowedly Communist *New Masses* magazine. She also chaired the Joint Anti-Fascist Rescue Committee, organized Project Rescue Ship to transport Loyalist veterans from Spain to Mexico, headed Spanish Children's Relief, and lent her name to many other left-wing causes and organizations.

In 1932 she met the witty screenwriter S. J. Perelman, who would remain a friend for thirty-five years, despite a start that Perelman described as "a scarifying ordeal." In fact, Perelman and his wife Laura helped Dorothy and Alan buy a farm near their (and George S. Kaufman's) country place in Pennsylvania's Bucks County—then as now an escape for many members of New York's writing establishment. It was because, as Dorothy complained to her husband, "we haven't any roots, Alan."

The marriage was always in trouble, not only due to Campbell's bisexuality, and his relationship with another woman when he was stationed in France during the First World War, but also because of their mutual increasing alcoholism. They divorced in 1947, only to remarry three years later and remain married until Campbell died in Hollywood in 1963 (although from 1952, when Parker moved back to New York, until 1961, they lived apart).

Her last Hollywood screenplay was 1949's *The Fan*, based on Oscar Wilde's *Lady Windermere's Fan* and directed by Otto Preminger. Back in New York she lived in a two-room apartment at the Volney (for which she paid $275 a month, $2,500 today), located just off Central Park at 23 East Seventy-Fourth Street. It would be the setting for *Ladies of the Corridor*, a play she cowrote in 1953 with Arnaud d'Usseau, which opened in October 1953 but ran only six weeks.

In 1957, and for five years thereafter, she wrote book reviews for *Esquire*, but it was not an easy relationship because of her increasing alcohol-induced unreliability.

In 1961 she returned to Hollywood and reconciled with Campbell, with whom she worked on a number of unproduced projects, including a film for Marilyn Monroe that was tabled after her death. In June 1963 Dorothy discovered Alan dead of a drug overdose in their West Hollywood home. To her that meant the end of her Hollywood life, and she soon returned to New York and the Volney. She spent her last years very much alone, in and out of the hospital, and denigrating her former Round Table colleagues, most of whom were now dead, as "just a bunch of loudmouths showing off."

Dorothy died of a heart attack in her eighth-floor apartment at the Volney on June 7, 1967, at the age of seventy-three. In her will she left her estate to Dr. Martin Luther King's foundation. When he was assassinated the following year, her estate passed to the National Association for the Advancement of Colored People (NAACP), over the passionate objections of Parker's executrix, Lillian Hellman.

She was cremated, but her ashes went unclaimed, residing in a filing cabinet drawer in the office of her attorney, Paul O'Dwyer, for seventeen years. Finally, the NAACP claimed the ashes and placed them in a memorial garden outside their headquarters in Baltimore.

Dorothy Parker wrote in *Vanity Fair* in 1925 that she wanted her epitaph to read "Excuse my dust." Instead of that (yet still acknowledging her wishes), the plaque in Baltimore reads: "Here lie the ashes of Dorothy Parker (1893–1967) humorist, writer, critic. Defender of human and civil rights. For her epitaph she suggested, 'Excuse my dust.' This memorial garden is dedicated to her noble spirit which celebrated the oneness of humankind and to the bonds of everlasting friendship between black and Jewish people. Dedicated by the National Association for the Advancement of Colored People. October 28, 1988."

One rather prefers another epitaph she suggested: "What would be a good thing for them to cut on my tombstone: Wherever she went, including here, it was against her better judgment." And yet another poem, entitled "Swan Song," where, as was her genius, she combines her pessimism with biting humor: First you are hot, / Then you are cold; / And the best you have got / Is the fact you are old.

Harold Ross, photographed here during his service in World War I, was born in a Colorado miner's shack. He would famously found the *New Yorker* magazine, and, as its editor for 1,399 issues, guide it to success as the tastemaker of record for millions of sophisticated Americans.
Author's Collection

CHAPTER 16

THE MAGAZINES

Henry Luce and Briton Hadden and Time, *and Harold Ross and the* New Yorker

"If you can't be funny, be interesting."
— *Harold Ross, founder of the* New Yorker

One could make a good case that the 1920s were the golden age of magazines in America. In the absence of television, and with radio only in its infancy, there was a clear demand for periodicals offering a less parochial perspective than local daily and weekly newspapers, as well as feature-length articles. And because of the "anything goes" spirit of the times, the crop of periodicals founded during the decade represented an astonishingly broad journalistic spectrum, from revolutionary manifestos to right-wing jeremiads, from journals designed to make a wife and mother's task easier, to bibles of high fashion. Many were often larded with the irreverent wit that has become identified with the era, and some offered near-seditious writing.

So it is not surprising to see successful radical magazines arrive such as the *New Republic* (then a mainstream liberal magazine), the *American Mercury,* and the socialist monthly *Liberator,* a successor to *Masses*, which boasted as a reporter the avowed Communist John Reed, and which after 1922 was an organ of the Communist Party. In a lighter vein was *Vanity Fair*, a fashion magazine founded by Condé Nast in 1913. (Today's uberglamorous *Vanity Fair,* which many believe descended from the original, does so only in spirit; the first *Vanity Fair* was a victim of the Great Depression and was folded into the publisher's *Vogue* in 1935; the new *Vanity Fair* began publishing in 1983.)

Of these periodicals one of the longest-lived was the *American Mercury*. Founded in 1924 by the Baltimore journalist H. L Mencken and the drama critic George Jean Nathan, it would feature writing by some of the most important writers in America during the 1920s and '30s, among them: Eugene O'Neill, William Faulkner, Sinclair Lewis, F. Scott Fitzgerald, Sherwood Anderson, and William Saroyan. Named for a Revolutionary era journal, it was planned to be, as Mencken explained to his writer friend, Theodore Dreiser, "a serious review, the gaudiest and damnedest ever seen in the Republic. What we need is something that looks highly respectable outwardly. The *American Mercury* is almost perfect for that purpose. What will go on inside the tent is another story."

At least until Mencken resigned in 1933, the magazine provided precisely what he promised: elegantly irreverent observations of America aimed at skeptical, sophisticated readers. Unfortunately, until it folded in 1981, the last decades of the once-important journalistic innovation sank into controversy over its conservative tilt and perceived anti-Semitism.

When it was founded, it was something really new: a sophisticated periodical that was perfectly suited for New Yorkers. The really big magazines of the time, such as *Collier's*, *McCall's*, and the *Saturday Evening Post* were simply too generalist (or—let's say it—often too lowbrow) to be of much interest to many New Yorkers.

But of all the hundreds of magazines that were successful during the decade, only a few, such as *National Geographic* and the *New Republic*, are still with us. Two magazines founded in the boom years of the 1920s also were unique and adaptable enough to survive eight decades of cultural changes as America passed through wars, depression, social unrest, and boom times: *Time* and the *New Yorker.*

Following its birth, *Time* found a large audience nearly overnight by essentially dumbing down the news to make it a quick read (the criticism over the magazine's unique writing style would arrive quickly; the controversy over its policy of editorializing the news would come a little later). The *New Yorker*, ironically, succeeded by idiosyncratically ignoring the temptation to become a big-circulation journal and focusing tightly on a relatively small target audience, a technique known today as "niche publishing," then in its infancy.

Time was founded in 1923 by a pair of twenty-five-year-old Yalies named Briton Hadden and Henry Luce, both former members of the school's exclusive Skull and Bones society, who had also worked together editing the *Yale Daily News*, the nation's oldest college daily. As the *New Yorker*'s founders would do two years later, they decided, with the unbounded optimism of all journalistic entrepreneurs, to focus on an unusual kind of niche audience with the $100,000 start-up money they raised from rich Yale alumni. Unlike the small target audience usually implied by the term "niche," their niche would include millions; they would start a weekly magazine, unlike any available at the time, designed to keep "busy men" informed of what was going on in the world. To do so economically, they decided not to originate reportage but to lift news from other media sources and package it by category in relatively short takes.

According to W. A. Swanberg in his definitive *Luce and His Empire*, *Time*, from its very first issue of March 2, 1923, bearing the cover image of Speaker of the U.S. House of Representatives Joseph G. Cannon, was "not for people who really wanted to be informed. It was for people willing to spend a half hour to avoid being entirely uninformed." It is a formula that has worked circulation miracles for many magazines since, including several subsequent Time, Inc. publications, such as the soon-to-follow, photograph-filled *Life* (the first nonlinear magazine that could be "read" by browsing the images and their captions) and the still vigorous *People*.

In the fifteenth-anniversary issue of *Time* in 1938, the editors reminisced that "[when] the first issue went to press, the entire full-time staff got into a taxicab carrying the [magazine's] entire editorial reference library (*Who's Who*, *World Almanac*, *The Congressional Directory*) and drove to the printers on Manhattan's 11th Avenue" from their tiny office in a former brewery at 236 East Thirty-Ninth Street. It would take a while, but eventually, *Time* would be forced to move into increasingly larger office space, set up its own news bureaus, and report and write news instead of lifting it from other sources. But Luce and Hadden's formula of condensing news for a fast read, albeit often biased, continued and would help build what is today claimed to be the biggest-circulation news magazine in the world.

Which is not to say that their formula was universally accepted. Their style and the intrusion of an editorial point of view on the news caused both mirth and fury among colleagues, competitors, and readers over the years. Many thought the magazine was too frivolous through its policy of telling the news not from an events standpoint, but by focusing on people. Hadden, who clearly respected the seriousness of the project, also saw it as being "fun." And it *was* people driven; for many years *Time*'s signature red-bordered cover carried the image of a single person. Many of them, thanks to the rise of the movies in the 'teens and '20s, were also early manifestations of "celebrities." In retrospect, however, this was not as much a matter of shrewd thinking on the part of Hadden and Luce as might be implied; all they had to do was to take notice of what features in New York's big-circulation newspapers their readers were devouring: sensationalized news, yes, but especially the newly invented (by Walter Winchell) gossip column, providing the inside skinny about what people in the public eye were doing.

Hadden and Luce, although close colleagues from their prep school days, were not close friends; fueled by Luce's egomania and autocratic management style (traits that would land him in controversy throughout his lifetime), their personalities often clashed. Briton Hadden was, as were most of his fellow Yale undergraduates, carefree, sophisticated, and provided with plenty of spending money by his rich parents (he came from a banking family).

Luce, however, born in China in 1898 to a pair of Presbyterian missionaries "intoxicated by God," came from relatively humble origins and was financially strapped. His defensiveness about his background showed throughout his life, even after he was making more than $2 million a year in dividend income from his *Time* stock and possessed enough notoriety to satisfy the ambitions of anyone. Tellingly, he rarely smiled; in fact, photographs of him smiling are "as rare," as the old saying goes, "as hen's teeth." Not surprisingly, he was kidded mercilessly by Hadden, both in school and throughout their professional association.

It would be a while before *Time* was caught up in controversy over its conservative editorializing—that would come some time after Hadden's premature death at thirty-one in 1929 (from septicemia), when Henry Luce became editor-in-chief of the magazine and began to believe that, because he had the power, he also was omniscient. But from the beginning the magazine's literary style was famous (or notorious, depending on one's point of view): a mutant journalistic style filled with double adjectives (such as "flabby-chinned") and sentences seemingly written backwards, called "Timestyle" (or more familiarly, "Time-ese").

Actually, it was all a trick, presumably to simplify a writing style yet still attract notice. "You're writing for straphangers," a former professor of theirs advised them. "You've got to write staccato." And the model for Time-ese had been around for more than two thousand years. Hadden and Luce, both Greek scholars at Yale, actually adapted it from Homer, especially the *Iliad.* They copied such Homeric shorthand as the famous "wine-dark sea" description, which is, obviously, more memorable than "a sea as dark as wine."

But things got out of hand when such familiar terms as "in the nick of time" were shorthanded as "in time's nick." Even reportage assumed proportions more suitable to a Homeric epic than an event such as William Jennings Bryan's death following his defense in the famous Scopes trial. It was reported as ". . . having striven manfully in single combat, a high-helmed champion is stricken by Jove's bolt and the two snarling armies stand at sudden gaze, astonished and bereft a moment of their rancor."

Like Walter Winchell, Hadden also liked to coin words. He imported such familiar terms as "kudos," "pundit," and "tycoon" and invented compounds such as "news-magazine." But perhaps most infamously he invented the inverted phrase and sentence; for example, "famed poet William Shakespeare" (a concerned reader asked if he would next read something like "onetime evangelist Jesus Christ"?), and their common obituary lead: "Death, as it must to all men, came last week to . . ." The formula worked. Within two years the magazine was breaking even and on its way to soaring circulation.

One downside to the million-or-more circulation magazines was that, unless one wanted to sell such nationally distributed products as automobiles, liquor, or breakfast cereals, advertising in them was wasteful and costly for localized marketing. For Macy's to reach a New York buyer, overwhelmingly its target customer, they would have to throw away thousands of dollars for an ad in a nationally sold periodical that probably boasted only a small percentage of New York City readers. The New York newspapers weren't much help, either, certainly not for middle- and high-end merchants; for example, Fifth Avenue's Mark Cross, a purveyor of relatively expensive leather goods. Most of the readers of newspapers, which were priced for only pennies, were generally thought of as being too low income for relatively high-end merchants such as Cross and department stores such as Peck & Peck and Bonwit Teller.

It was for an unlikely high school dropout born in a Colorado miner's shack to buck such commonly accepted wisdom by coming up with the answer. After a year or so of disappointments and challenges that, at one point, momentarily convinced him to give up the project entirely, this man created one of the greatest triumphs in publishing history: the *New Yorker.* His name was Harold Ross, and at thirty-three when he founded the magazine, he was perhaps the unlikeliest looking (and seeming) candidate for the job that could be imagined: Lincolnesque-gangly, with overlong arms, a gap-tooth smile, and a thatch of hair styled to rise straight up from his forehead like some sort of privet hedge, he also lacked, and would always lack (which he readily admitted), the sophistication possessed by a large percentage of his target audience.

Harold Wallace Ross first saw the light of day on a snowy Sunday, November 6, 1892, in the then-tiny, hard-rock silver-mining village of Aspen, Colorado. He was the son of an Irish immigrant named George Ross and his schoolteacher wife, Ida. When Harold was eight, the family left Aspen because of the collapse in the price of silver and moved to Salt Lake City, Utah, after short stops seeking work in Redcliff and Silverton, Colorado. In Salt Lake the preteen Harold got the first taste of his career to come by working on his high school newspaper and acting as a student stringer for the city's largest newspaper. When he was only thirteen, he ran away to Denver, where he worked for the *Denver Post* before returning to Salt Lake and getting a real job at the *Salt Lake Telegram.*

During the next decade, while bouncing from coast to coast, he sharpened his journalistic teeth at seven newspapers (maybe more; no one knows for sure), among them the *Sacramento Union*, the *New Orleans Item*, the *Atlanta Journal* (where he covered the famous 1915 murder trial of Leo Frank and his subsequent lynching), the *Brooklyn Eagle*, and the *San Francisco Call.*

With the arrival of World War I, Ross enlisted in the Army Eighteenth Engineers Railway Regiment and was shipped off to France, where he edited the regimental journal before joining the staff of the independent military newspaper *Stars and Stripes* in

February 1918. Colleagues on the publication included, as noted elsewhere, the curmudgeonly Alexander Woollcott, the columnist Franklin P. Adams, and Janet Cook, who would become the first of his three wives and his partner in the founding of the *New Yorker*.

After the war Ross returned to New York, where he was hired as the editor of a veteran's magazine that was absorbed by the *American Legion Weekly*, before leaving for a job with a humor magazine called *Judge*. While at *Judge* he planned and worked toward his dream for the sophisticated New York reader. Even though he was neither as well off nor as worldly as his target audience, Ross somehow figured out what he believed would attract both the advertisers who didn't want to throw away their promotional dollars in a national magazine and the sophisticated, comfortably well-off readers they wanted to reach. In retrospect it seems obvious, but at the time, when most publishers thought only bigger was better, it was a revolutionary idea.

He and Janet, then a *New York Times* reporter, put their savings and some money she got from her family on the line to prove it. They planned to invest twenty-five thousand dollars in the project, but as they figured that would be only half of the money needed to launch the magazine even on a shoestring budget, they had to find the balance from outside investors. To do so, Ross laid out his plan for what the magazine would be and what it wouldn't be, in what has been called the most famous magazine prospectus in history:

"*The New Yorker* will be a reflection in word and picture of metropolitan life," it commenced. "Its general tenor will be one of gaiety, wit and satire, but it will be more than a jester. It will be what is commonly called sophisticated, in that it will assume a reasonable degree of enlightenment on the part of its readers.

"As compared to the newspaper, [it] will be interpretive rather than stenographic. It will print facts that it will have to go behind the scenes to get, but it will not deal in scandal for the sake of scandal nor sensation for the sake of sensation." Then, after explaining what the magazine would feature (contemporary events, people of interest, cartoons and caricatures, amusements and the arts, new "books of consequence," what was going on in the "smart gathering places," and the "comings, goings and doings in the village of New York") came the clincher: "*The New Yorker* will be the magazine which is not edited for the old lady in Dubuque."

Today, eighty-five years after the *New Yorker*'s founding, even the "old lady in Dubuque," as well as readers from San Francisco to Shanghai revel in the publication's often irreverent, frequently witty, brilliantly written take on happenings in its hometown, now as then still categorized under such familiar headings as *Talk of the Town* and *Fiction*. But that would take a while, and for the first few decades, the magazine's core circulation was, as Ross planned it, essentially within the city limits of New York. For the magazine's popularity to reach beyond Ross's original concept would take a social evolution that transformed America from the still largely rural nation of the 1920s to an urban and suburban culture.

Finding that start-up money wasn't easy either, until a scion of the famous yeast company, Raoul Fleischmann, became interested in the project and provided the additional twenty-five thousand in start-up money. What Fleischmann didn't know—but the Rosses were beginning to suspect—is that it would cost much, much more than the initial estimate of fifty thousand dollars to get the magazine off the ground. Then, and even more challenging, it would cost thousands more to keep it running until circulation and ad revenues caught up with the costs. Sheer survival was actually a close call; the initial circulation of twenty-five thousand of the first issue on February 21, 1925, would sink to three thousand during the summer before the *New Yorker* began to catch on.

Unlike *Time*, whose first cover was political, the *New Yorker*'s debut cover was fanciful, bearing the image of a Georgian-era dandy examining a butterfly through his monocle. Today that same image of the fictional Eustace Tilley appears every February on the magazine's anniversary. Despite the sinking circulation during that first summer, Ross convinced Fleischmann to keep it afloat by pouring more and more money into it, either as a loan or by buying more of the essentially worthless stock from Ross (who as editor always believed he shouldn't own any of the stock in the magazine and, indeed, when he retired, owned none).

Eventually, Fleischmann, the R(oss)-F(leischmann) Publishing Company's major stockholder, would go through much of his million-dollar fortune propping up the fledgling periodical. But as Ross predicted, the magazine caught on with its audience relatively quickly. The circulation rose to more than a hundred thousand with speed, and when the magazine's circulation, along with ad revenues, continued soaring, Fleischmann would reap a new fortune.

After spotting his target audience, Ross then had to deliver the goods, and he eventually did so, largely due to the talent he was pulling in. How he did it, at least in retrospect, seems simple. All he needed to do was tap the friends he lunched with often at a round table in the dining room of the Hotel Algonquin near his office. But at the time that Ross and Fleischmann started the magazine, the talent that would later make The Round Table gathering legendary and, to many, actually define much of the culture of the era (chapter 14) was still young and more notorious for their uproarious lifestyle and capacity for alcohol than their talent.

So he had to try out many writers before the magazine's masthead settled down; in fact, during the first ten months of publication, Ross went through 282 contributors before he managed to separate the journalistic wheat from the chaff and, for the most part, surround himself with the writers, editors, and friends who would make the magazine famous.

In addition, when the *New Yorker* was first published, not only did Ross and his associates have to put in sixteen-hour workdays, find contributors (and edit what they wrote for a consistent style), search for juicy news items and stories that would titillate their readers, and solve the manifold headaches of launching what is, at best, still a difficult and highly uncertain project, they had to deal with a rival that was determined to kill them off. Ironically, the two-year-old *Time*—the "enemy," as Ross himself categorized it—was by then housed in the same building where the *New Yorker* was edited, at 25 West Forty-Fifth Street, but the two publications were about as far apart in concept, style, and philosophy as any two magazines could be. Its editors, Hadden and Luce, immediately attacked the newcomer in a way that, for sheer chutzpah, could have been conceived by Ross himself.

On *Time*'s March 2, 1925, cover, they put a photograph of the bespectacled, grandmotherly looking, fifty-one-year-old poet Amy Lowell, her gray hair done up in a bun and sitting in an old chair, reading. Inside, the caption read: "In Dubuque, Iowa, there lives, doubtless, an old lady. Her existence is recognized only because certain middle-aged people in Manhattan began some weeks ago to think about her. She came frequently into their conversation and, at each allusion, a leer passed around the company. All spoke in derisive terms of her taste, though the kinder-hearted merely pitied her for being a victim of an unfortunate environment."

Time claimed to have mailed this old lady from Dubuque a copy of the first issue of the *New Yorker* and received a telegram back reading, "The editors of the periodical you forwarded to me are, I understand, members of a literary clique. They should learn that there is no provincialism so blatant as that of a metropolitan who lacks urbanity." Ross was less furious than he appeared at the time, demanding to know who at *Time* had written the piece; when he found out he offered him a job at the *New Yorker.*

Otherwise, Harold Ross was more than irritated with *Time*; he actually loathed the publication. But it wasn't for its threat, for they clearly served two different constituencies, an opinion with which Luce and his partner Hadden would certainly have agreed. What Ross, the self-admitted unsophisticated kid born in a prospector's cabin in Colorado, hated most was the "Time-ese" writing style, which he felt degraded the journalism business itself. It took more than a decade, but when Ross had a chance to get even for *Time*'s "little old lady from Dubuque" cover and what he considered was oversimplification of the news, he landed a killer blow.

In 1936 Luce was starting up a new magazine—*Life*—and Ross knew that because of the precariousness inherent in the launch of a new publication, Luce would probably agree to a profile in the *New Yorker.* Luce did, but what the *Time* editor didn't know was that it would be written (by Wolcott Gibbs, a senior editor) in a style brutally parodying Time-ese (as well as Luce's pretentiousness).

Titled "Time . . . Fortune . . . Life . . . Luce": "Backward ran sentences until reeled the mind." Gibbs skewered the contents of Luce's *Fortune* magazine—"how to live in Chicago on $25,000 a year" (the equivalent today of nearly $400,000). And he skewered the contents of the new *Life*—"Russian peasants in the nude," and "The love life of the Black Widow spider." Twisting the *Time*-ese dagger, he described Luce as the "ambitious, gimlet-eyed, Baby Tycoon Henry Robinson Luce," his childhood in a monastery in China as "very unlike the novels of Pearl Buck were his early days," and his ego "Before some important body he makes now at least one speech a year." He even went after the fifty-one–year-old Luce's home: "Described too modestly by him to Newyorkereporter as 'smallest apartment in River House,' Luce duplex at 435 East 52nd Street contains 15 rooms, 5 baths, a lavatory."

Gibbs wrote of the net profits of Time Inc. as "Sitting pretty are the boys." He closed the long profile with, "Certainly to be taken with seriousness is Luce, his fellowman already informed up to his ears, the shadow of his enterprises long across the land, his future plans impossible to imagine, staggering to contemplate. Where it will all end, knows God!"

As agreed, Ross sent Luce a proof, and they met at Ross's apartment, along with St. Clair McKelway (who was the ostensible reporter of the profile whose interview notes were then passed on to Gibbs to write the profile). Luce, understandably, was not happy and complained, "There's not a single kind word about me in the whole Profile . . . Goddamn it, Ross, this whole goddamned piece is malicious, and you know it!" Ross paused. "You've put your finger on it, Luce. I believe in malice."

There is in all affairs of humankind the right time and place for dreams to be realized. Certainly, because of the wealth of writing talent available as well as the need for a journal that would reflect the excitement, the social changes, and the unique creative environment of the era, New York in the 1920s was the perfect place for Harold Ross to launch the *New Yorker.* And because of the cultural changes of the era and the lack of any other world-news-based periodical, probably there was no better time or place for Briton Hadden and Henry Luce to launch *Time*. Posterity has confirmed the daring of these journalistic entrepreneurs.

Henry Luce died February 28, 1967, a force (for evil, many said) to his last days. Harold Ross died earlier; December 6, 1951. Before retiring he personally edited 1,399 issues of his magazine.

If *Time*'s "Little old lady from Dubuque" objected to the *New Yorker*'s dismissal of her lifestyle, it was nothing to what she may have felt about a powerful New York subculture that in its time was largely unknown to Americans—lesbianism. Eventually, mainstream New Yorkers' awareness of lesbians living among them would come; acceptance would take longer, at least in middle America.

Nevertheless, in the 1920s much of what defined New York's cultural life was already heavily influenced by homosexuals (as was, of course, Hollywood's entertainment product).

In the mid-Twenties, the *New York Times* hailed Elsie de Wolfe, then and now largely credited with founding the interior decorating industry as "one of the most widely known women in New York social life." Historian Henry James hailed her success and that of her lesbian lover, the pioneering Broadway agent Elizabeth Marbury, as paving the way for women to defy society's traditional rules by creating their trailblazing independent careers and personal financial freedom.
Author's Collection

CHAPTER 17

NEW YORK'S LESBIAN SUBCULTURE

Interior Design Pioneer Elsie de Wolfe

It's hard to tell 'em apart today! Hey, hey!
Girls were girls and boys were boys when I was a tot,
Now we don't know who is who, or even what's what!
Knickers and trousers, baggy and wide,
Nobody knows who's walking inside,
Those masculine women and feminine men . . .
—Lyrics of a popular 1920s song

Lord Alfred Douglas, the young man with whom Oscar Wilde was infatuated and who got him into so much trouble, famously described homosexual relationships in his 1894 poem "Two Loves," as "the love that dare not speak its name."

Despite the emancipated lifestyle of New York in the 1920s, the same head-in-the-sand attitude was also generally observed, officially anyway. In reality, homosexuality was so commonly accepted in New York City that, in 1927 when Mae West wrote a play called *The Drag*, it was a big hit.

It was one thing to be accepting of homosexuality; it was quite another, however, to have it publicly on display. So at least until the Stonewall riots in 1969 flung open the closet doors, most gay men and lesbian women kept their sexual preferences very private. Some even went so far as to mask their true nature by getting married (then, of course, to a member of the opposite sex), to present a "normal" public image. Such masquerades were even more commonplace in Hollywood, which was even more accepting of homosexuality but where the studios were terrified that if the millions of ticket buyers discovered that their favorite stars preferred partners of their own sex, the almighty box office would suffer. Thus, when in 1936 MGM ordered two of its rising stars, Cary Grant and Randolph Scott, then living in what everyone in the film capital considered a lovers' relationship, to get married, they quickly complied. (Nevertheless, the pair lived as neighbors thereafter, even sharing the same Santa Monica beach house when Grant was married to Barbara Hutton).

As with the film industry, certain New York–centered professions, such as interior design, theater, and fashion, have always boasted a higher percentage of homosexuals than less creatively flamboyant occupations. And so it was with interior design and Elsie de Wolfe, the woman who claimed to have founded the profession, today of course a major industry. Her claim was not entirely accurate, as there were people in the 1920s, albeit only a few, offering independent interior design help, which hitherto had always been a secondary service of upholsterers, furniture dealers, and architects. Nevertheless, the *New Yorker* once affirmed that "Interior Design as a profession was invented by Elsie de Wolfe." One suspects that de Wolfe's reputation as an industry pioneer was due less to timing than to her ability to make news about herself. In 1926, when she would ostensibly dump her lesbian lover for a titled Englishman, the *New York Times* hailed her as "one of the most widely known women in New York social life."

Unlike thousands of New York homosexuals who hid their sexual preference at the time, de Wolfe's lesbian relationship and friends were known to the public—or at least a kindred section of the public. But it didn't make any difference; her talent trumped any gossip. And although she certainly had gay clients for her interior design business, the majority would eventually include such paragons of straight culture as the Duke and Duchess of Windsor and Henry Clay Frick.

Ella Anderson de Wolfe was born on December 20, 1865 (or so she said; as with stars of the film and television industry, birth dates were considered "flexible" even then), the only child of a Canadian-born doctor and his wife. In her autobiography (written in the third person, a style that was then common), she claims to have had a visceral reaction to her surroundings from a very early age. Returning to her home from school one day, she discovered that her parents had redecorated their drawing room. As she told the story (in the third person):

> *She (Ella/Elsie) ran [in] . . . and looked at the walls, which had been papered in a design of gray palm-leaves and splotches of bright red and green on a background of dull tan. Something terrible that cut like a knife came up inside her. She threw herself on the floor, kicking with stiffened legs, as she beat her hands on the carpet . . . she cried out, over and over: "It's so ugly! It's so ugly."*

Hutton Wilkinson, president of the Elsie de Wolfe Foundation, explains that she simply didn't like the then-fashionable Victorian style, with its overdecorated rooms often overcrowded with overstuffed furniture and dark cabinetry, "and banished it from her design vocabulary." She was, in her own words, a "rebel in an ugly world."

De Wolfe began her professional career in 1891 at the age of twenty-six (if her birth date is to be believed), not as a designer, but as an actress in Sardou's play *Thermidor*, performing opposite the actor J. Forbes-Robertson. In 1894 she joined producer Charles Frohman's Empire Stock Company and seven years later, on her own, produced Congreve's *The Way of the World*, in which she starred and toured throughout the country. Despite an acting career that would last more than twenty years, apparently, de Wolfe was only an average actor who was once reviewed as being "the leading exponent of . . . the peculiar art of wearing good clothes well." Then in 1903 she launched her interior design career because, according to biographical material, she had become interested in the business as a result of staging plays.

Like many such biographical notes, this is probably true as far as it goes, but it only skims the surface.

What was really going on was probably far more complex. In 1892 de Wolfe had begun living openly with a theatrical agent named Elisabeth Marbury (known to all her friends as "Bessie") in what everyone who knew them accepted as a lesbian relationship. In 1926, after more than thirty years with Marbury, de Wolfe married Lord Charles Mendl, a British diplomat. The *New York Times* headlined the story on its front page, commenting, "The intended marriage comes as a great surprise to her friends," and adding, "When in New York, she makes her home with Miss Elizabeth Marbury at 13 Sutton Place." According to biographers, the marriage was platonic (understandable, as Charles Mendl was also gay), with the couple maintaining separate apartments in Paris and appearing together only at social functions.

Marbury and de Wolfe were pioneers. In fact, Marbury's friend, the historian (and descendant of two American presidents) Henry Adams, went so far as to assert that the pair personified the American tradition of self-reinvention by defying society's rules for women. They were, he added, paving the way for the "weaker sex" to have both independent careers and financial independence, Marbury by making it acceptable for women to become theater professionals and de Wolfe by establishing an entire industry.

In 1892 when their relationship began, Bessie Marbury had already established herself as one of the first Broadway agents, numbering among her clients the playwrights Oscar Wilde, George Bernard Shaw, Georges Feydeau, and Edmond Rostand. In 1913 she brought the dance team of Vernon and Irene Castle (whom she had discovered on one of her many trips to Paris) to New York. She also helped them set up a dance school that was the springboard for a successful American dance career and that would be the inspiration for the later celebrated dance team of Fred Astaire and Ginger Rogers. She also represented James M. Barrie, whom she persuaded to write *The Little Minister* for another client, the beloved actor and original theatrical personification of Barrie's Peter Pan (1905), Maude Adams.

In the beginning of their relationship, Marbury, the daughter of a prosperous New York lawyer and a descendant of a founder of Rhode Island, supported their lifestyle which, according to one observer "[cut] a wide path through Manhattan society." Friends called the couple "the bachelors," and they were described by the same commentator as "the willowy De Wolfe and the masculine Marbury." Besides monetary support, it is also clear that Marbury had as great an influence on de Wolfe's two-decade theatrical career; among her clients at the time of de Wolfe's theater debut was also Victorien Sardou, author of the play in which de Wolfe debuted.

Two years after de Wolfe started her decorating business, Stanford White, a friend and then New York's most famous architect, helped give her the boost that would soon make her famous. White had designed the Colony Club, soon to be Manhattan's most prestigious women's club. Also numbered among the club's founders were de Wolfe's friends Anne Tracy Morgan (the youngest child of the legendary financier J. P. Morgan), Anne Vanderbilt, and Marbury. Together with White, they got de Wolfe the interior design commission for the club (then located at Madison Avenue and Thirtieth Street, it is now housed on East Sixty-Second, and its original Stanford White building now houses, appropriately enough considering de Wolfe's theatrical career, the American Academy of Dramatic Arts). That same year, 1903, Marbury, with de Wolfe, of course, also restored a mansion in Versailles, which they named the Villa Trianon and where, with Anne Morgan, they entertained extensively, gaining a reputation as generous hostesses known as "the Versailles Triumvirate."

In the early 1920s the threesome (plus Anne Vanderbilt) would move into what was then a squalid neighborhood bordering the East River known as Sutton Place. By their presence it was soon transformed into one of the most desirable of Manhattan addresses (nevertheless, the gossip columns of the time sniped that they had created an "Amazon enclave"). Today Anne Morgan's four-story home at 3 Sutton Place (near the corner of Sutton Place and East Fifty-Seventh Street), built in 1921, is the official residence of the Secretary General of the United Nations.

Morgan became the first woman to be awarded the French Legion of Honor, bestowed for her work helping civilians whose lives were damaged by the war through her American Friends of France organization, which employed hundreds and was largely supported by her private funds. Elsie de Wolfe also received the Legion of Honor for her wartime work with the Ambrine Mission for Burn Victims. Marbury, meanwhile received awards from both France and Belgium for her war work, but never the Legion of Honor, a slight, she felt, about which she often complained.

De Wolfe's popular design innovation was to offer a fresh look for homes traditionally crowded with dark, Victorian excesses, by featuring light colors in rooms filled with both original and reproductions of eighteenth-century furniture. Outlined for posterity in her 1913 book *The House in Good Taste,* several restored examples can still be found in Manhattan.

Another reason for her prominence was clearly her flamboyance . . . not only her blue hair but her clear talent for making news. One of the color schemes she popularized was the inspiration for Cole Porter's song "That Black and White Baby of Mine" whose lyrics include the lines: "All she thinks black and white/She even drinks black and white" (a popular brand of Scotch whisky).

When she first visited Athens and saw the Parthenon, de Wolfe remarked, "It's beige; my color!" Shortly after her marriage, she scandalized French diplomatic society when, with her husband, she attended a fancy-dress ball dressed as a Moulin Rouge dancer and made her entrance turning handsprings. A guest chided, "Elsie, it is wonderful to be able to turn handsprings at your age [she was in her early sixties]. After all, you are Charlie's wife, and do you think it is in perfect taste for the wife of a diplomat to perform acrobatics in a ballroom?" The story became so famous that it inspired Cole Porter to use it in his popular song "Anything

Goes" whose lyrics run: "When you hear that Lady Mendl, standing up/Now turns a handspring landing up/On her toes/Anything goes!" And the *American Decades* series wrote that de Wolfe "was probably the first woman to dye her hair blue, to perform handstands to impress her friends, and to cover eighteenth-century footstools in leopard-skin chintzes."

Even the exercises by which she kept her "willowy" profile for most of her life made news. In her 1935 autobiography de Wolfe wrote that her daily regimen at age seventy included yoga, standing on her head, and walking on her hands. In 1935 Paris fashion authorities named her the best-dressed woman in the world, noting that she wore what suited her best, regardless of fashion.

Besides her social and theatrical connections, Elisabeth Marbury was, at least after women gained the right to vote in 1920, an outspoken Democrat and a close friend of Governor Al Smith. Working closely with friends Cole Porter and Jerome Kern, she is also credited with helping develop the so-called "book" musical (as opposed to the then-popular revue), first seen in Porter's musical *See America First* (composed in 1915 and produced by Anne Morgan and Marbury) and Kern's contemporary musicals *Nobody Home*, *Very Good Eddie*, and *Love o' Mike*. The innovation would define the Broadway musical throughout much of the twentieth century and beyond. Marbury's interest in theater management started when she was twenty-three and was hired as her agent by Frances Hodgson Burnett to represent the stage version of her best-selling novel *Little Lord Fauntleroy*. Her success was immediate, especially among French writers, for whom she arranged English translations of their works and secured full royalties on performances of such now-classics as the previously mentioned *Thermidor* by Sardou.

When Elisabeth Marbury died in 1933, her funeral at St. Patrick's Cathedral was packed with friends, admirers, and theater people. But de Wolfe wasn't there. There have been speculations about why she wasn't, but there are no clear answers. All that is known for sure was that she was the primary beneficiary of

Marbury's will. In both her New York and Paris homes, de Wolfe had taffeta pillows embroidered with a saying "Never complain, never explain."

De Wolfe and Marbury never really hid their lesbianism, and neither did another famous member of New York's theater community at the time: Eva Le Gallienne. Born in London in 1899, she was quite a bit younger than de Wolfe and Marbury (in fact, she died in 1991). After making her stage debut at fifteen in Maurice Maeterlinck's *Monna Vanna,* she visited New York, Arizona, and California, where she established friendships with a number of lesbian silent film stars who were already or on their way to becoming famous (or notorious, depending on one's viewpoint).

Perhaps "notorious" is too strong a word, since at the time, unlike male homosexuality, which was known and somewhat accepted in Hollywood, the very existence of lesbianism was completely unknown to a vast number of Americans. It is estimated that before the relative freedom of the 1920s opened many closet doors, only one in a thousand people knew that such relationships could even exist. Many of course were hidden behind the doors of a marriage of convenience (called "lavender" marriages in Hollywood); such was clearly the case of the marriage of the gay (or opportunistically bisexual) Rudolph Valentino to the openly lesbian Natacha Rambova in 1921 (despite her Russian-sounding name, Rambova, de Wolfe's stepniece and frequent guest at her Villa Trianon, was actually an American, born in Salt Lake City in January 1897 and christened Winifred Kimball Shaughnessy). Rambova was a film set and costume designer whose close friend, Alla Nazimova, got her the assignment to design the costumes for 1921's *Camille*, in which Nazimova starred with Valentino. A very small world, indeed. (How small may be judged from the fact that the lesbian Nazimova was godmother to the very straight Nancy Davis Reagan.)

In 1918 while in Hollywood, Le Gallienne began an affair with Nazimova, who, at the height of her power, introduced the nineteen-year-old to many important lesbian actors with whom

Le Gallienne had affairs including Tallulah Bankhead, Beatrice Lillie, and Laurette Taylor. (Le Gallienne, Bankhead, and actors Estelle Winwood and Blythe Daley were dubbed "The Four Horsemen of the Algonquin" in the early Twenties, referring both to the Algonquin Round Table [chapter 14], which they occasionally joined, and Rudolph Valentino's famous 1921 film, *The Four Horsemen of the Apocalypse*.)

Around 1920 Le Gallienne began a five-year relationship with the poet and writer Mercedes de Acosta, who would later have a long relationship with Greta Garbo. During their affair de Acosta wrote two plays for Le Gallienne, *Sandro Botticelli* and *Jehanne de Arc*. Neither was successful, and it is said that the financial losses combined with de Acosta's possessive jealousy ended the relationship.

Le Gallienne wasted little time in moving on to another lesbian relationship, but it was one that landed her in a lot of scandal. Although a lesbian, Josephine Hutchinson was, like many, married, and as soon as her husband discovered the affair, he started a divorce action, naming Le Gallienne as the correspondent. According to some biographers, despite her promiscuity, Eva Le Gallienne was uncomfortable with it and, barraged by the scandal of the Hutchinson divorce, began drinking heavily. On one winter night she reportedly wandered over to a female neighbor's house and told her, "If you have any thoughts about being a lesbian, don't do it. Your life will be nothing but tragedy." She was, however, understandably conflicted over her actions, later telling a straight friend that love between women was "the most beautiful thing in the world."

In November 1928 Le Gallienne starred in a revival of *Peter Pan* that, thanks to advances in stagecraft, allowed her (as Peter) to fly over the audience for the first time. The critics loved her performance, comparing her to Maude Adams, and in 1929, just after the stock market crash on October 29, *Time* put her picture on its cover. "LeG," as she was shorthanded, was famous. During the Great Depression, President Roosevelt offered her the directorship of the National Theater Division of the Works Progress Administration, which she turned down, saying she preferred to work with established talent rather than nourishing it in struggling actors. Nevertheless, she helped Uta Hagen establish her own acting career by casting her as Ophelia in a production of *Hamlet* in which Le Gallienne, who, like Sarah Bernhardt and other famous women actors before and since, occasionally played the melancholy Dane.

In the 1930s she began a long-time relationship with the theater director Margaret Webster, with whom she and producer Cheryl Crawford founded the American Repertory Theater in 1946. In the late 1950s she had a huge success in an off-Broadway production of Friedrich Schiller's classic play *Mary Stuart*. Then in 1960 Mercedes de Acosta published *Here Lies the Heart*, in which she documented details of her many lesbian affairs, including those with Le Gallienne, Garbo, Marlene Dietrich, and the modern dance diva Isadora Duncan. Like most "tell all" books, it immediately made her persona non grata, especially within the Hollywood establishment, which always protects its own. Le Gallienne was understandably angry and threw away anything she had left of their relationship, which had ended some thirty-five years before.

In recognition of her fiftieth year in show business and her work with the National Repertory Theatre, Eva Le Gallienne was given a special Tony Award in 1964. She won an Emmy in 1976 for her performance in a television version of George Kaufman and Edna Ferber's play about the Barrymores, *The Royal Family*, having played in the Broadway revival earlier that year. Four years later, at the age of eighty, she received an Oscar nomination for her work in the film *Resurrection*.

On June 3, 1991, she died at her home in Connecticut at the age of ninety-two.

If Elsie de Wolfe, Elisabeth Marbury, and Eva Le Gallienne were fairly open about their lesbianism, a Pulitzer Prize–winning writer living in Manhattan at the time, despite her mannish appearance and manner of dress, was far more closeted. Willa Cather, who was (and still is) noted for her predominantly Western-themed novels, spent most of her writing career in New York City, where most of her companions and friends were women and where she lived with an editor named Edith Lewis from 1912 until her death in 1947. Cather also virtually worshipped the Metropolitan Opera soprano Olive Fremstad, whom she memorialized under the name of Thea Kronborg in her 1915 novel *The Song of the Lark.*

Was she a lesbian? Within today's more open society, the answer seems obvious. Yet there are those who passionately deny the possibility. The scholar Janet Sharistanian has written, "Cather did not label herself a lesbian nor would she wish us to do so, and we do not know whether her relationships with women were sexual. In any case, it is anachronistic to assume that if Cather's historical context had been different, she would have chosen to write overtly about homoerotic love." Which seems jumping to a self-supporting conclusion; just because Cather didn't cast homosexual characters in her books, does that make her straight? Oscar Wilde, whose gay flamboyance colored the image of male homosexuals in America for decades, went to prison for being gay but created many heterosexual characters, not least among them the nymphomaniacally straight Salome. And fueling the debate, there exists a photograph in the University of Nebraska archives showing Cather at the age of eighteen or nineteen, dressed as a young man (which apparently she did throughout her college years, during which she also went by the name of "William"). In the picture her hair is also shingled—at a time when women wore their hair long and some thirty years before the style became fashionable for flappers in the 1920s.

Perhaps the dispute is rooted in Cather's silence about her private life; she was always an intensely private person. Before her death, she destroyed many of her personal papers and letters, as well as some original drafts of her works. And like many raised on the Great Plains, she remained politically conservative all her life.

Cather was christened Wilella Siebert Cather when she was born December 7, 1873, the first of seven children of a farming family that had lived near Winchester, Virginia, for six generations. When Willa (as she quickly became known) was nine, the family moved to Red Cloud, Nebraska, to join her father's parents. It was there, in the center of the Great Plains, that she grew up loving the still-frontier lifestyle, the dramatic weather, and the interplay of the various cultures, both native and immigrant, which she would later write about so evocatively. While attending the University of Nebraska, where she earned a BA in English in 1894, she also honed her writing talents by becoming a regular contributor to the *Nebraska State Journal.*

After moving to Pittsburgh soon after graduation, she spent a decade teaching high school English and Latin, while also working as the drama critic for the *Pittsburgh Leader*. In 1906 she moved to New York City, moved in with Edith Lewis, and took a job with *McClure's Magazine,* where she soon became controversial for a book—first serialized in *McClure's*—about Mary Baker Eddy, the founder of Christian Science. Christian Scientists were infuriated and, similarly to Scientologists today, who try to suppress anything negative about their religion, tried to buy up every copy (the book was reprinted by the University of Nebraska Press in 1993).

Six years later, *McClure's* serialized Cather's first novel, 1912's *Alexander's Bridge*. On the advice of friends to concentrate her writing efforts on her Nebraska background and experiences, she quit *McClure's*.

Fame came swiftly. The "Prairie Trilogy" (*O Pioneers*, 1913; *The Song of the Lark*, 1915; and *My Antonia*, 1918) were the first examples of a plainspoken writing style about ordinary people; it was immediately spotted and praised by such national critics as H. L. Mencken as new and refreshing. With *One of Ours*, a 1922 novel set in World War I, Cather won what many consider the ultimate writing accolade, the Pulitzer Prize. (Sinclair Lewis said, when accepting the Nobel Prize for Literature in 1930 for his body of work, that it really should have gone to Cather.) Among the most popular of her twelve novels and several collections of short stories and essays is one that has become a sort of cultural icon of Southwestern history, her 1927 biography of the pioneering Santa Fe cleric, Jean Marie Latour, *Death Comes for the Archbishop.*

Willa Cather's reputation suffered during the 1930s when, with the nation devastated by the Great Depression, critics attacked her for a seeming lack of interest in economics and her conservative politics. Apparently depressed by the criticism, she became essentially a recluse for the rest of her life, until death came for her on April 24, 1947.

In 1973, the centennial of her birth, the U.S. Post Office issued a stamp honoring her.

Although the contributions of lesbians to New York in the 1920s were not as profound as that provided by their presence in Hollywood during its great star-making years, without their influence and talent—from Broadway to the look of interior design to the very lifestyle of Harlem, described in the next chapter—nothing would have been the same.

In the 1920s, Harlem became not only America's most important African-American metropolis as a result of the cultural ferment remembered as the "Harlem Renaissance," but also a celebrated site for the era's most defining music—jazz. The music's most famous venue was the mob-owned and operated Cotton Club where legends from Duke Ellington to Cab Calloway, Louis Armstrong, and Dizzy Gillespie made their mark. Few remember today that it was also, as clearly shown in this rare flyer from 1931, originally a "whites only" club where blacks were the entertainers and the help.

Photographs and Prints Division, Schomburg Center for Research in Black Culture, The New York Public Library, Astor, Lenox and Tilden Foundations

CHAPTER 18

The Harlem Renaissance

The Cotton Club, Bessie Smith, and the Harlem Renaissance

What happened to a dream deferred?
Does it dry up like a raisin in the sun? . . .
Or does it explode?
— Langston Hughes, on African-American aspirations in the 1920s

So it's 1925, and you're ready for a great night on the town. Where to go? If you were like thousands of your fellow citizens—straight, gay, rich, poor, creative, or a time clock puncher—there was no question: Harlem. But Manhattan Island's East Side above 125th Street was by then much more than an entertainment destination; it was also the nexus of one of the most dynamic cultural changes in American history.

Harlem dates from 1658, when it was organized by Dutch settlers and named after Haarlem in the Netherlands. In the nineteenth century it was a middle- and upper-class white suburb whose residents abandoned it to the huge influx of European immigrants at the end of the century when middle-class African-Americans also started moving in. Their presence then made it a particularly friendly destination for the thousands of African-Americans who, in the early years of the twentieth century, headed to New York from the South to fill the huge demand of Northern industry for unskilled laborers; it then quickly evolved into a major African-American community.

But it soon became much more than a black suburb. In 1919 or thereabouts a cultural ferment commenced in Harlem that was first labeled the "New Negro Movement" but was soon known as the Harlem Renaissance, as it was called by writer James Weldon Johnson. Like most cultural movements—and this one involved art, music, theater, and, especially, literature—there were many contributing elements. In this case it was a combination of an industrial boom in the Northeastern states and the tremendous social and cultural changes created by the recently ended World War I (which, as we have noted, were largely responsible for the ferment of the Jazz Age as well).

Many of the African-Americans who were part of the renaissance were heirs of a Southern generation that had lived through the post–Civil War social gains and the subsequent disillusionment of Reconstruction, when the white establishment regained power and reestablished Jim Crow segregation. Some were the children or grandchildren of slaves. Some also came from the Caribbean, where society was racially stratified as well. A contemporary called it "our own black city as big as Rome."

The artists and intellectuals of the Harlem Renaissance would also echo the new spirit of progressivism in American life, with its associated democratic reform, a belief in art and literature as agents of change, and an almost childlike belief in progressivism itself. This would, of course, be shattered by the reality of the Great Depression. Nevertheless, the ideas it spawned, the talent it nurtured, and the belief in self that centered it, effected a major change in the way millions viewed African-Americans in our multicultural society.

It is difficult to pick the exact dates for the Harlem Renaissance because there was no single event for easy reference, but it basically spanned the decade of the 1920s. There is no question, however, that for recognition of the literary output of the phenomenon, the high point was in 1924, when the magazine *Opportunity: A Journal of Negro Life,* a monthly published by the National Urban League, hosted a landmark party that, for the first time, put black writers together with many white, establishment publishers.

The beginnings of the Harlem Renaissance can actually be dated as early as 1917, when *Three Plays for a Negro Theatre*, written by a white playwright named Ridgely Torrence, premiered. Instead of portraying African-Americans as two-dimensional minstrel show characters, the plays, for the first time in American literature, presented them as men and women with complex emotions and desires. James Weldon Johnson, whose own fiction began describing the reality of contemporary African-American life in America, called the premieres of these plays "the most important single event in the entire history of the Negro in the American Theatre." Two years later a militant sonnet, "If We Must Die" by Claude McKay, sounded a rare note of defiance against racism and the nationwide race riots and lynchings then taking place.

The presence of jazz, with its roots in the Southern black and African music traditions, had also begun to captivate America, its popularity spread both in clubs and soon on the fast-rising communications phenomenon of the age, radio. Nevertheless, in Harlem and other African-American communities, many middle- and upper-class blacks believed that their race would be best served by assimilating into what was called "the white business culture" of the large American cities and were initially hostile to the new music. But it was a losing battle in a decade that F. Scott Fitzgerald famously defined as "the Jazz Age."

One of the most eminent personalities identified with the Harlem Renaissance was the poet, playwright, and novelist James Langston Hughes (born James Mercer Langston Hughes in Joplin, Missouri, in 1902), who was of African-American, European, American, and Native American descent. His work would be suffused by pride in the African-American identity and its diverse culture: "My seeking has been to explain and illuminate the Negro condition in America and obliquely that of all human kind," Langston, once dubbed the "people's poet," explained.

In 1926 Hughes wrote a piece for the *Nation* entitled "The Negro Artist and the Racial Mountain," which, even today, essentially stands as the manifesto of the Harlem Renaissance:

> *The younger Negro artists who create now intend to express our individual dark-skinned selves without fear or shame. If white people are pleased we are glad. If they are not, it doesn't matter. We know we are beautiful. And ugly, too. The tom-tom cries, and the tom-tom laughs. If colored people are pleased we are glad. If they are not, their displeasure doesn't matter either. We build our temples for tomorrow, strong as we know how, and we stand on top of the mountain free within ourselves.*

While in grammar school, Langston, who would later invent a new literary form called "jazz poetry," was elected class poet, but afterwards he thought it was probably because he was black. "I was a victim of a stereotype," he later wrote. "There were only two of us Negro kids in the whole class, and our English teacher was always stressing the importance of rhythm in poetry. Well, everyone knows, except us, that all Negroes have rhythm, so they elected me as class poet." In high school he discovered a lifelong love of books and wrote his first jazz poem, "When Sue Wears Red."

Hughes entered Columbia University in 1921 as an engineering student, a compromise reached with his father, who was neither comfortable with his own black heritage nor with his son's seeming effeminacy. After dropping out of Columbia the following year because of a perceived racism, Langston worked at various odd jobs and spent several months traveling in Africa and Europe where, for a while, he was part of London's black expatriate community.

In 1924 he returned to the United States and lived with his mother in Washington, D.C., where, while working as a busboy, he met the poet Vachel Lindsay, who, after reading some of Hughes's work, proclaimed him an important new black poet. The following year Hughes enrolled in the historically black Lincoln University in Chester County, Pennsylvania, where a classmate was the future Supreme Court associate justice Thurgood Marshall. After graduating in 1929 Langston moved to Harlem, which would be his home for the rest of his life and where his literary activity would be marked by the rhythms of blues, jazz, and the African-American speech in which he was immersed.

As with the questions about Willa Cather's sexuality, despite the trove of unpublished poems to an alleged black male lover, experts are divided over whether Langston was homosexual or not. It is a fact that he remained closeted all his life, probably thinking it was necessary to maintain the support of black church groups as well as potential publishers.

Primary among those publishers was the *Crisis*, for which he started writing while at Columbia University. The *Crisis*, the official magazine of the NAACP, was founded in 1910 by W. E. B. DuBois, who remained its editor for years. Although eventually a current affairs journal, it also published reviews, essays, and poems, of which Hughes contributed many.

On May 22, 1967, Hughes died of complications following an operation for prostate cancer. His ashes were interred beneath a floor medallion in the Schomburg Center for Research in Black Culture located at 515 Malcolm X Boulevard in Harlem. Above those ashes are the words "My soul has grown deep like the rivers," taken from his signature poem, "The Negro Speaks of Rivers," first published in 1921. The poem reads:

I've known rivers
I've known rivers ancient as the world and older than the flow of human blood in human veins.
My soul has grown deep like the rivers.
I bathed in the Euphrates when dawns were young.
I danced in the Nile when I was old
I built my hut near the Congo and it lulled me to sleep.
I looked upon the Nile and raised the pyramids above it.

I heard the singing of the Mississippi when Abe Lincoln
went down to New Orleans, and I've seen its muddy
bosom turn all golden in the sunset.
I've known rivers: Ancient, dusky rivers.
My soul has grown deep like the rivers.

One aspect of the Harlem Renaissance's celebration of the African-American cultural heritage (certainly its most popular) was live musical entertainment. It was offered in abundance on and above 125th Street, opening the doors for the careers of many African-American legends. And jazz was its signature.

In New York the best jazz was found in Harlem, especially at the Savoy Ballroom, the Apollo Theatre, and The Cotton Club. The Savoy became famous for both its jazz fare and swing dancing (commemorated in Edgar Sampson's 1934 song, "Stompin' at the Savoy." The Apollo, originally opened as a burlesque house in 1914, would later become famous as the place where such legends as Billie Holiday, Ella Fitzgerald, and Sarah Vaughan began their careers (and, having been continually in business since its founding, remains the only direct theatrical link to the Harlem Renaissance).

But the Cotton Club, both because of the huge talent that played there as well as its links to the mob and the popularity of Francis Ford Coppola's 1984 film of the same name, is the place most people think of as *the* Harlem nightspot of the 1920s. During its thirteen-year existence, the Cotton Club was everything for everyone, but it also was a manifestation of the dark side of New York life that had little to do with Harlem's progressive movement. For one thing, it was initially a "whites only" club. For another, it was also owned by a leading underworld figure; to make the situation even clearer, the Chicago branch of the Cotton Club was owned by Al Capone's older brother, Ralph. With the deep pockets gained by the mob during Prohibition, and the prevalence of vice cops on the take, it isn't surprising that during the decade before alcohol became legal again in 1933, the Cotton Club was only shut down once (in 1925) for selling liquor, and then only briefly.

It seems odd today, but the club that showcased many of the greatest African-American entertainers of the 1920s, and after, generally denied admission to blacks and, even worse, in its shows often depicted African-Americans as clichéd savages in exotic jungle settings or as "darkies" on a Southern plantation. Duke Ellington, whose band was the house band from 1927 until 1931, was required, as part of his contract, to compose "jungle music" to titillate the white audience. This actually had an upside of sorts, which would make him famous. The requirement of composing "jungle music" gave him the freedom to experiment with his music, and during his time with the club, he not only hosted weekly radio broadcasts originating from the site, but also made more than a hundred recordings (eventually pressure from Ellington caused the club to somewhat relax its color ban).

There was also a color standard for employees, at least when it came to the chorus girls, who—in addition to being at least five feet six inches tall and under twenty-one years of age—had to be light-skinned.

Fletcher Henderson's band was the first to play at the Cotton Club, and over the years the place showcased the talents of Cab Calloway (whose band replaced Ellington's in 1931), Count Basie, Fats Waller, Louis Armstrong, and Dizzy Gillespie, as well as singers that included Nat King Cole, Ella Fitzgerald, Ethel Waters, Billie Holiday, and Bessie Smith, later dubbed the "Empress of the Blues."

It also showcased some of the era's most famous white entertainers as part of its regular Sunday "Celebrity Nights," including Jimmy Durante, Al Jolson, Eddie Cantor, Mae West (whose naughty double-entendres were especially applauded), New York City's mayor Jimmy Walker (chapter 1), and George Gershwin, whose African-American folk opera, *Porgy and Bess*, composed in 1934–35, would draw on his Harlem experience. The club also drew from white popular culture of the day. The prominent songwriters Dorothy Fields, Jimmy McHugh, and Harold Arlen provided the songs for the revues at the club; their *Blackbirds of 1928* featured the song "I Can't Give You Anything but Love," soon a national hit.

The Cotton Club started as the Club De Luxe, which was founded at 142nd Street and Lenox Avenue by the boxing champion Jack Johnson in 1920. At the time Johnson was far more than a footnote to black progress (as he seems to be today) and is an example of the high-profile African-Americans who were choosing to live and work in Harlem in the Twenties. Johnson won the world heavyweight title in 1908—appropriately, on December 26, "Boxing Day" in Sydney, Australia, where the bout took place—but his win so angered many white boxing fans that the celebrated writer Jack London called for a "Great White Hope" to retake the title. After successfully defending his title for seven years—most memorably in the "Fight of the Century" in 1910, an event celebrated by black poet William Cuney in his poem "My Lord, What a Morning"—Johnson lost the title in 1915 to Jess Willard, a Kansas cowboy. His story was retold in Howard Sackler's 1967 play *The Great White Hope* and in the 1970 movie of the same name, both of which starred James Earl Jones as Johnson.

In 1923 Johnson was bought out by Owney Madden, a leading underworld figure at the time (his nickname was "the Killer"), who relocated the club to 125th Street, renamed it, and reopened it as a "whites only" venue. Walter Brooks, who had directed 1921's successful Broadway show *Shuffle Along*, the first African-American musical in which Eubie ("I'm Just Wild About Harry") Blake played the piano, was the nominal owner.

Born in Leeds, England, in 1891, Madden, his older brother, and his younger sister followed their widowed mother to Manhattan in 1902, a year after she had left them in a children's home and emigrated to America to seek work. (Madden was sentimental about his British citizenship, refusing to give it up until 1950, when he had to do so to avoid deportation.) They settled in Hell's

Kitchen, the area in Manhattan between Thirty-Fourth Street and Fifty-Ninth Street, from Eighth Avenue to the Hudson. There Owney, described at the time as "that banty little rooster from hell," joined the then-notorious, five-hundred-member Gopher Gang based in the Irish neighborhood of Manhattan's West Side.

He quickly gained a reputation as a fierce street fighter and earned his "Killer" nickname for publicly gunning down a rival gang member. It was the first of several killings attributed to Madden, who by 1910, when he was eighteen, was earning some $200 daily (in buying power, about $4,500 today) from the Gophers' protection rackets. As was the case with that first killing, when Madden shot a local store clerk who had asked out one of his girlfriends, none of the many witnesses to the murder (which took place in daylight on a crowded street) came forward, and the case against him was dismissed.

In 1912 he survived being shot eleven times by members of the rival Hudson Dusters gang but refused to identify them to the police, saying "Nothing doing. The boys'll get 'em. It's nobody's business but mine who put these slugs in me!" Within a week of his release, "the boys" did just that, and several members of the Dusters were killed. Two years later he killed a Dusters gang leader for ratting him out to the police and was arrested and sentenced to twenty years at Sing Sing prison, where he joined buddies including Jimmy "the Shiv" DeStefano, who was the prison's death-row barber.

After serving nine years of his sentence, Madden was released in 1923 and immediately teamed up with Larry Fey, founder of the famous El Fey Club, today remembered as "the granddaddy of all speakeasies" (chapter 6). He needed Madden's muscle to gain control of the best cab stands on Broadway for the Manhattan taxi business he had set up (with mob money) and was using to run whisky from Canada in the first years of Prohibition. Madden soon branched out, attempting to turn New York's milk delivery into a racket before going on his own as a bootlegger whose gang became notorious for highjacking liquor shipments.

Madden and a former gang rival turned partner, Big Frenchy DeMange, began to open or buy some of the flashiest and busiest speakeasies and nightclubs of the time, owning at least twenty at one time (they were involved with Sherman Billingsley's Stork Club, which, after Prohibition ended, became New York's most famous nightclub; see chapter 2). In 1931, probably because he realized that alcohol would soon be legal, and he needed to find other income, Madden got out of bootlegging, and, in partnership with several boxing promoters, controlled the careers of some famous champions. Among the boxers he managed was Primo Carnera, for whom Madden fixed fights, soon making the Italian strongman the 1933 National Boxing Association heavyweight champion. (After Madden reportedly deserted Carnera over rumors of fixed bouts, the Italian was defeated by Madden client Max Baer the following year.)

In 1933 Madden retired to Hot Springs, Arkansas, then a popular haven for criminals, where he opened a hotel and casino; Charles "Lucky" Luciano hid out there for a while. He finally became an American citizen in 1943, married the daughter of the Hot Springs postmaster, and lived the good life until his death in 1965, when he was said to have $3 million in assets, not a dollar of which has ever been found. His life was fictionalized in Michael Walsh's *And All the Saints*, and he was played by Bob Hoskins in Coppola's *Cotton Club* film.

After Madden's departure it was never the same for the Cotton Club. Temporarily closed after a Harlem race riot in 1936, it reopened downtown in the theater district at Broadway and Forty-Eighth Street. It finally closed for good in 1940, and the Latin Quarter nightclub that opened in its space was torn down in 1989 to make way for a hotel. The present Harlem venue bearing the Cotton Club name opened in 1978, but as far as our shared cultural memory is concerned, it was the Cotton Club of the 1920s that was *the* Cotton Club.

Associated with the cultural ferment of the Harlem Renaissance was an extremely permissive attitude about sex; putting it bluntly, Harlem was a place where it was easy to get laid whether you were straight or gay—but especially if you were gay.

Because of its reputation for Bohemianism, most people would think that the gay bars of the era were all in Greenwich Village, and indeed, during the 1920s, homosexuality was as much a part of the community's life as radical politics.

But there were many gay bars in Harlem, and they operated far more openly than the Village bars, which, although generally clandestine, apparently so embarrassed the politicians of the era that Mayor Hyland's vice squad closed most of them.

This wasn't the case in Harlem, nor would the situation last long in Greenwich Village. In 1925 *Variety* reported that the number of Village restaurants and clubs hosting the "temperamental" element (code for gay or lesbian) was back up to about twenty (because clubs serving alcohol had to do so behind closed doors, there is no way to be absolutely sure of the number). But it is known that there were drag shows at the Jungle on Cornelia Street, and the Red Mask and the Flower Pot at the corner of Christopher and Gay Streets were popular speakeasies.

A woman named Eve Addams, called "the queen of the third sex," ran the Black Rabbit, a "tearoom" on MacDougal Street that was a popular lesbian gathering place. It was raided in 1929, and Addams was convicted on a charge of disorderly conduct and sentenced to a year in jail. She was later deported and ended up on the Left Bank in Paris, where apparently she lived out her life quite happily. Webster Hall, at 119 East Eleventh Street, was the downtown setting for extravagant, cross-dressing costume balls similar to those held in Harlem. An invitation to the fifteenth annual such ball on January 26, 1926 (billed as the Greenwich Village Ball; tickets were three dollars), cautioned attendees: "Unconventional? Oh, to be sure—only do be discreet!"

But as noted much of this was discernible only to those in the know. "It was quite a handicap to be a young guy in the Twenties," lamented one gay man who arrived in the city during the era. "It took an awfully long time to find a gay speakeasy."

Uptown, however, Harlemites "in the life" (as being gay was then called) built a gay- and lesbian-friendly world that far surpassed Greenwich Village's in size, scope, and sexual license. And they (and apparently the vice squad) didn't care who knew about it.

According to playwright, poet, and painter Richard Bruce Nugent, "You just did what you wanted to. Nobody was in the closet. There wasn't any closets." (Nugent also decorated with homoerotic scenes the walls of the apartment complex then known as "Niggeratti Manor" at 267 West 136th Street, where he lived with his lover, the writer Wallace Thurman, from 1926 to 1928.)

On August 23, 1926, Rudolph Valentino died in Manhattan of peritonitis following an appendectomy. Millions were plunged into grief; he was, at the time of his death at the age of only thirty-one, arguably the most famous man in the world, thanks to his three dozen films (over half unaccredited), which included 1921's *The Sheik.* So it is not surprising that his image also impacted the image of male sex appeal, both for women and for gay men. Gone was the image of the bruiser, the standard epitomized by the celebrated boxer Jack Dempsey. The new look was more androgynous, "prettier," and was exploited in everything from soap advertisements to the movies, where MGM raced to find a similar-appearing replacement after Valentino's death, finally settling on his one-time lover Ramón Novarro. The new "hot" male was a sailor in uniform, an African-American, or, especially, a swarthy, Valentino-appearing Italian youth. Each of them could be found in Harlem, especially, of course, the African-American.

According to essayist Margaret Graham in a fascinating analysis of Harlem's sexual environment of the era, "Negroes" were considered as particularly flexible sexually, a common pickup line among those available being "I'm a one-way man; now, which way would you like?" It is largely forgotten today, but at the time—thanks again to Graham's meticulous research—the Mafia, then becoming powerful in New York as well as elsewhere in the country, considered the African-American male—like they considered the straight populace's demand for alcohol or gambling—just another weakness to exploit. As odd as it seems, considering the Mafia's tough-guy image, some members of New York's Mafia families exploited the availability of male partners for themselves; the (black) writer and poet Parker Tyler claimed he had been approached by numerous gangsters. (It is also little remembered today that Al Capone's cousin was gay.)

Not surprisingly, Harlem became the center of much of the homosexual as well as straight nightlife, which was celebrated in more high-profile venues such as the Cotton Club. Drag events were commonplace, the biggest of which were the huge balls held at the Savoy Ballroom, the Renaissance, and others, where hundreds of women would come dressed in dark men's suits and men would dress as Spanish senoritas, early film stars, or society debutantes outfitted in white chiffon and rhinestones.

Gay bars and cabarets crowded the streets, especially 133rd Street, referred to as "jungle alley." Among them was the Ubangi, where the hostess was a sepia-skinned lesbian who styled herself as "Gloria Swanson." There were always "rent parties" available in private homes and apartments, where one basically had the option of choosing as the companion for an hour or so a drag queen outfitted as, perhaps, Mae West, or a boy-next-door type. If one was interested, it was a place where, as the title of the Cole Porter musical put it in 1934, "anything goes."

But the ultimate destination for lesbians and, especially, gay men, was Harry Hansberry's Clam House, where a three-hundred-pound singer and pianist named Gladys Bentley, dressed in her signature white tuxedo and top hat, regaled customers by belting out popular songs such as "Sweet Georgia Brown," to which she substituted obscene lyrics. *Vanity Fair* called it "a popular place for revelers, but not for the innocent young," and although the innocent probably dropped in from time to time, it was packed nightly with not-so-innocent revelers, both celebrity and otherwise, including the actors Tallulah Bankhead, Jeanne Eagels,

Beatrice Lillie, and, outfitted in matching bowler hats, the bisexual torch singer Libby Holman, with her rich lover, the DuPont heiress Louisa d'Andelot Carpenter.

But far more prominent than Gladys Bentley were a group of lesbian or bisexual entertainers whose names have become legendary, among them Jackie "Moms" Mabley, Ma Rainey (later known as "the Mother of the Blues"), her protégé Bessie Smith (the most popular female blues singer of the 1920s and '30s and known as "the Empress of the Blues"), and Ethel Waters. In Ma Rainey's then-celebrated song monologue "Prove to Me Blues," she sings, "Went out last night a crowd of my friends. They must've been women, cause I don't like no men . . . they say I do it, ain't nobody caught me . . ." Nevertheless, she was caught and caught often. Most notoriously, she was nabbed in 1925 when she was arrested in her home during an orgy with members of her chorus. Bessie Smith bailed her out of jail.

Bessie Smith knew a lot about jail and bail as well. In 1922 she married a Philadelphia security guard named Jack Gee, which didn't stop her from disappearing into "the life" for weeks on end and occasionally ending up in jail herself and needing Gee to bail her out. She claimed it was all part of life on the road covering concert dates and none of anyone's business—including her husband's. She, like many other African-American singers and entertainers of the time, was sponsored and booked by the powerful Theater Owners Booking Association (TOBA) agency, which could make or break a black singer's career.

Born in Chattanooga, Tennessee, in 1892 (or 1894 as she claimed), Bessie Smith and her brother were orphaned when she was nine, and they earned a living as street musicians; she danced and sang, and he accompanied her on a guitar. When she was eighteen, she joined a small traveling group as a dancer because the company already had a major singer in the person of Ma Rainey and spent several years touring East Coast cities. In 1923 she married Gee and at the same time began making recordings for Columbia, which, like other record labels, had discovered there was a big, new market for recordings that appealed to African-Americans.

Her first release was a coupling of "Downhearted Blues" with "Gulf Coast Blues"; it would be the first of 160 releases by the label, many accompanied by the biggest black musicians of the time, including Louis Armstrong and Fletcher Henderson. Among those other recordings were her so-called "Nobody" songs which, although written by men, were particularly evocative of a black woman's place in a male-controlled world: "Nobody in Town Can Bake a Sweet Jelly Roll Like Mine" by Clarence Williams; "Tain't Nobody's Business If I Do," a Depression-era lament of a former big-spender (as Bessie herself would become) composed by her pianist Porter Grainger; and her own song, "Nobody Knows You When You're Down and Out."

In 1923 Smith joined TOBA, where she soon became the headliner of a group of forty troupers that worked theaters in the winter and tent shows the rest of the year. She eventually became the highest paid black entertainer of the time and traveled in her own railroad car. It was then that a TOBA publicist upgraded her nickname from "Queen of the Blues" to "Empress."

Despite her success—actually probably because of it—her marriage was tempestuous. Bessie and Gee cheated on each other; reportedly, Gee never accepted Bessie's bisexuality nor her here-today-gone-tomorrow show business life. When she caught him in an affair, she ended the relationship (but never got a divorce). She then took up with a friend, Richard Morgan (who was Lionel Hampton's uncle), became his common-law wife, and remained so until her death.

The good times ended for Bessie—as they did for millions of Americans—with the Great Depression; few recordings, on which Bessie depended for much of her income, were being made, and audiences were drawn away from vaudeville both by the Depression and the advent of talking pictures. She somehow managed to continue touring and occasionally singing in clubs. In 1929 she appeared on Broadway in *Pansy*, a musical about which the critics claimed she was the only good thing. That year she also made her only film appearance, singing W. C. Handy's "St. Louis Blues" in a two-reeler of the same name.

In 1933 she recorded four sides for Okeh Records, the company that pioneered recordings for the African-American market in 1920 and had become part of Columbia. She was paid a nonroyalty fee of $37.50 for each side. Two of the recordings, all made with a band that included trombonist Jack Teagarden and Benny Goodman (who had been making a recording with Ethel Waters in an adjoining studio and dropped by), remain among her most successful: "Take Me for a Buggy Ride" and "Gimme a Pigfoot."

On September 26, 1937, while driving between Memphis, Tennessee, and Clarksville, Mississippi, her car sideswiped a slow-moving truck. Her common-law husband, Richard Morgan, was driving and was uninjured, but Smith, sitting in the passenger seat, took the full impact of the truck's tailgate, which sheared off the roof of the car and virtually severed her right arm from her body. By the time two ambulances came—one from a black hospital and one from a white facility—she had gone into shock and later died after surgery at the black hospital in Clarksville.

Two months after her death, the writer/producer John Hammond (who had produced her Okeh recordings) claimed in a *Downbeat* article that she had been refused admission to a "whites-only" hospital in Clarksville. The story was soon proven false by the doctor who first reached her following the accident, who explained that "the Bessie Smith ambulance would *not* have gone to a white hospital, you can forget that. Down in the Deep South cotton country, no ambulance driver, or white driver, would even have thought of putting a colored person off in a hospital for white folks." Nevertheless the story inspired Edward Albee's 1959 play *The Death of Bessie Smith.*

The funeral was held in Philadelphia, Pennsylvania, Smith's adopted hometown, and she was buried at Mount Lawn Cemetery in Sharon Hill. Although money was raised from friends and fans for a tombstone, Gee simply pocketed the funds and did nothing, leaving her grave unmarked for thirteen years. Then finally, in 1970, singer Janis Joplin and Juanita Green, who as a child had done housework for Bessie, paid for a tombstone.

Since then a number of Bessie Smith's recordings have been inducted into the Grammy Hall of Fame, and in 2001 her recording of "Downhearted Blues" was included in a "Songs of the Century" list by the Recording Industry of America. The following year the single was selected by the National Recording Preservation Board for inclusion on the Library of Congress's Recording Registry as "culturally, historically, or aesthetically significant," and since then it has been picked by the Rock and Roll Hall of Fame as one of the five hundred songs that shaped rock 'n' roll.

The Mississippi Blues Trail organization has also honored her memory with a historic marker at the hospital where she died, now the Riverside Hotel.

The "Sultan of Swat," the "Bambino" Babe Ruth, with a young admirer at the Polo Grounds in 1923, just before his team, the New York Yankees, moved into Yankee Stadium—instantly dubbed "the House that Ruth Built." There he would hit the venue's first home run, demonstrating a talent that with his reckless lifestyle, would both rewrite baseball's record books and make him America's most famous and beloved (if controversial) sports figure.
Library of Congress

CHAPTER 19

SPORTS

Bill Tilden and Babe Ruth

"[Babe Ruth] is our Hercules, our Samson, Beowulf, Siegfried. No other person outside of public life so stirred our imaginations or so captured our affections."
—*Marshall Smelser,* The Life That Ruth Built

From the 1920s, there have been five sports heroes whose fame has remained legendary: the heavyweight boxing champ Jack Dempsey, the golfer Bobby Jones, the tennis superstar Bill Tilden, the football phenomenon "Red" Grange and, of course, baseball's immortal Babe Ruth. While each was very much in the consciousness of sports fans in New York, only two called New York City home—at least for a while—but they were more than enough to make the city known as a sports capital, in addition to being America's capital of culture and capitalism. Bill Tilden lived in the city during much of his glory years, and Babe Ruth was the glory of the hometown team, the New York Yankees.

Sport, through its win-or-lose nature, inevitably creates heroes, those winners whose attainments can seem superhuman. And as we have seen only too often, some of those heroes—Pete Rose comes to mind—have fallen off their pedestals.

But there has rarely been a fall as dramatic—and tragic—as that of William Tatem Tilden II, who during the Jazz Age, when he completely dominated international tennis and for some time thereafter, called New York's Algonquin Hotel home.

In 1950, when an Associated Press poll selected the greatest performer in each sport during the century's first fifty years, Tilden emerged with the widest margin of victory, one greater even than Babe Ruth's in baseball or Bobby Jones's in golf. For seven years he was ranked as the world's number-one player. During his eighteen years of amateur play (1912–1930), he won 138 of 192 tournaments. He won Wimbledon three times (1920, 1921, and 1930), the U.S. Championship (the equivalent of today's U.S. Open) seven times, and led the U.S. Davis Cup team to seven consecutive victories, a record that has not been matched since. In 1925 Tilden won fifty-seven games in a row; a feat that biographer Frank Deford wrote was "one of those rare, unbelievable athletic feats—like Johnny Unitas throwing touchdown passes in forty-seven straight games or Joe DiMaggio hitting safely in fifty-six games in a row—that simply cannot be exceeded in a reasonable universe no matter how long and loud we intone that records are made to be broken."

Even in a sports-mad decade like the Twenties, during which fans became accustomed to superlatives, Tilden's match record of 907–62—a 93.6 percentage—silenced criticism over his occasional grandstanding. Now and then he would deliberately lose opening matches to prolong contests, making the game more interesting for himself and, of course, for the spectators. Sometimes when he was serving a match against a lesser player, he would show off by picking up four balls in his large hand and serving four aces in a row. He also disdained women's tennis; once in an exhibition game he gave the leading female player of the day, Suzanne Lenglen, three points in each game and still won 6–0, 6–0 (he started each game from minus 40 to love, not love–40).

Tilden, who was a serious student of the game as well as its star player, wrote two books: in 1922 *The Art of Lawn Tennis* (as the game was then called) and *The Common Sense of Lawn Tennis* (1924). Despite his grandstanding he possessed a remarkable level of sportsmanship, ceding points to an opponent if he thought the umpire miscalled a shot in his favor. He also became probably the only player in any sport to have refunded money to a promoter when the gate was poor. And by his preeminence "Big Bill" Tilden (as he was known to everyone) almost single-handedly changed the image of tennis from that of a country-club sport played by rich white people in long white pants or ankle-length skirts to that of a major sport played by world-class athletes.

The journalist John Kieran, then a sportswriter for the *New York Times*, was later quoted as saying, "Big Bill was more than a monarch. He was a great artist and a great actor. He combed his dark hair with an air. He strode the courts like a confident conqueror. He rebuked the crowds at tournaments and sent critical officials scurrying to cover. He carved up his opponents as a royal chef would carve meat to the king's taste. He had a fine flair for the dramatic; and, with his vast height and reach and boundless zest and energy over a span of years, he was the most striking and commanding figure the game of tennis had ever put on court."

And then everything came crashing down.

Bill Tilden was born February 10, 1893, into a wealthy Philadelphia family that was emotionally crippled by the deaths of his three older siblings in a diphtheria epidemic. His semi-invalid mother died when he was eighteen, and even though his father maintained their large home, he moved a few houses away to live with a maiden aunt. There is a story that Bill's mother, Selina, called him "June" until her death.

Three years later his father died of kidney failure and his remaining brother died of pneumonia. At twenty-two Bill's once-large immediate family was gone. He quit the University of Pennsylvania, where he was studying economics, and, with the encouragement of his aunt, focused on tennis as a way back from severe depression to a living an apparently normal life. Frank Deford, in his biography, also suggested that Tilden spent the rest of his life trying to establish a father-son relationship with a succession of ball boys and young tennis protégés. Of them, Vinnie Richards, Tilden's long-time doubles partner, was probably the most visible (with Richards Tilden won the U.S. amateur doubles title in 1918 when Vinnie was fifteen years old and, twenty-seven years later in 1945 when Bill was fifty-two, the professional doubles championship).

Considering the social conservatism of the time, he should have been more circumspect. Tilden possessed undisputed athletic prowess; Allison Danzig, the *New York Times*'s main tennis writer from 1923 to 1969, considered Tilden the greatest tennis player he had ever seen and said "he could run like a deer." Still, tennis was considered by many Americans as an effete, "sissy" sport (code at the time for "homosexual"—"gay" wouldn't come into common usage until the 1960s). The great comic actor W. C. Fields remarked in one of his films that he knew two brothers: "one's a tennis player, the other's a manly sort of fellow." It didn't help that Tilden's mannerisms, picked up while playing in Europe's more sophisticated environment, were perceived by American sports fans as effeminate.

To make more money than he was making from prize money and teaching during the 1920s, Tilden turned professional in 1931 and joined the pro tour that had recently been organized; for the next fifteen years, he, with a few other professionals, barnstormed across America and Europe in one-night stands. Tilden came from a wealthy family, and he spent money lavishly, maintaining a suite at the Algonquin Hotel (where he undoubtedly knew many members of the famous Round Table [chapter 14], who lunched there during the 1920s). The place was conveniently near the theater district where, considering himself a writing and acting talent, he lost large sums of money financing Broadway shows that he wrote and produced, among them an abortive, 1940 version of *Dracula*, which he financed with a thirty thousand dollar inheritance and in which he also played the lead. He starred in a number of silent films as well and wrote a couple of novels inveighing against the use of alcohol. One critic called them "droopy."

On November 23, 1946, Tilden was arrested for having his hand in the pants of a fourteen-year-old boy while in a parked car on Sunset Boulevard in Los Angeles. The boy turned out to be a prostitute whom Tilden had solicited, but there is also testimony that Tilden claimed they had just come from seeing *Lassie Come Home* at the Wiltern Theatre—unlikely, as the movie had been released three years earlier—and that they were just fooling around. He also claimed that the boy was not a prostitute but the son of a famous (unnamed) producer who subsequently beat Tilden senseless in his den.

In any event Tilden was charged with the misdemeanor of "contributing to the delinquency of a minor." At the trial he claimed that because he didn't have his reading glasses with him, he signed a confession without reading it. He was sentenced to a year in a road camp (of which he served seven and a half months), and five years' probation, the terms of which limited his profitable private-lesson business.

On January 28, 1949, he was arrested again after making advances to a sixteen-year-old hitchhiker whom he had picked up; the boy identified Tilden as the offender by the middle finger of his right hand, the tip of which had been amputated following a fingernail infection in 1922. The new charge could have been prosecuted as a felony, but the judge merely sentenced Tilden to a year on his probation violation and let the punishment for the new molesting charge run concurrently. He served ten months.

After all this, it was not surprising that his friends, particularly his Hollywood friends, who were always worried about any hint of homosexuality—illegal in California until the state's sodomy law was repealed in 1976 as well as being box-office poison—began to avoid him. At one point he was disinvited from participating in a professional tennis tournament being held at the Beverly Wilshire Hotel. The University of Pennsylvania removed his name from their attendance records, and the Forest Hills Tennis Club and the Germantown Cricket Club, where he had played two of his Davis Cup matches, removed his pictures from their walls.

His Hollywood friends, whom he had often coached, included Ramón Novarro (Valentino's gay "Latin lover" screen successor); Louise Brooks; the "It" girl, Clara Bow; Greta Garbo; Katharine

Hepburn; Tallulah Bankhead; Errol Flynn; and Spencer Tracy. Only Charlie Chaplin rallied to his buddy's needs by inviting Tilden to use his private tennis court to give lessons to help pay for his legal bills. There are some observers who believe the issue behind Tilden's dramatic fall from fame, rather than simply the homophobia of the era, was due to the revelation that some sports heroes were homosexual, a concept that seemed incomprehensible at the time. It was the collision of those two worlds that turned Tilden's personal tragedy into a national cause cèlébre.

Tilden, who was convinced that his arrests were socially, rather than criminally motivated, discussed his homosexuality publicly only once. That was in a veiled passage in his 1948 memoir, *My Story*, written after his first arrest. "Throughout all history there has been a record of occasional relationships somewhat away from the normal," he wrote. "One knows that this condition exists, that it is more or less prevalent and always will be. History further demonstrates that in frequent instances, creative, useful and even great human beings have known such relationships."

Friendless and penniless at the end, Tilden had to pawn his old trophies and lived in a tawdry rented room near Hollywood and Vine, where, on June 5, 1953, he died of a heart attack. A friend contributed a tennis sweater for him to wear in his casket.

In his famous book *Lolita*, Vladimir Nabokov used Tilden as inspiration for Lolita's tennis coach, "Ned Litam," ("Ma Tilden" spelled backwards), a former ace who had a "harem of ball boys."

Despite that previously noted Associated Press poll showing Bill Tilden beating out Babe Ruth as the greatest performer in sport during the first half of the twentieth century, no one praises a great new athlete by calling him "the Bill Tilden of _______." But the "the Babe Ruth of _______" is a frequently heard compliment. The reason is somewhat obvious. After his fall from grace, Tilden's name and memory were erased by the tennis establishment with much the same ferocity as a dictator attempting to remove a rival's name after a successful coup; as far as tennis was concerned, he might as well have never lived. And baseball is baseball. America's national sport is an intrinsic part of our culture, drawing millions more fans than tennis, however popular a Roger Federer or a Rafael Nadal may be. Other reasons, of course, included Ruth's charismatic personality (something woefully lacking in Tilden's makeup), a true rags-to-riches story, and his awesome talent for hitting home runs—as well as his reckless lifestyle—which never failed to garner headlines.

After joining the Yankees in 1919, Babe Ruth became the mainstay of the team that won seven pennants and four World Series titles while he was with the team. In 1927 he became the first player to hit 60 home runs in a single season, a record that remained for thirty-four years until Roger Maris broke it in 1961. Similarly, his career record of 714 home runs lasted for nearly forty years until Hank Aaron bettered it in 1974. He led the league in home runs during a season twelve times, slugging percentage and on-base plus slugging percentage (OPS—not a statistic used then, but an important one now) thirteen times each, runs scored eight times, and runs batted in (RBIs) six times. Except for the RBIs, each of these is an all-time record.

Unlike Tilden, who was born into wealth, George Herman Ruth Jr. was born on February 6, 1895, in a working-class section of Baltimore, Maryland, known then as "Pigtown." His parents owned a succession of saloons in the city. The neighborhood's name derived from the pigs that once were herded through its streets on the way to the nearby slaughterhouses. George's parents had eight children, only two of which, he and his sister, Mamie, lived past infancy. Other than describing his childhood as "rough," Ruth rarely spoke about his early years. When he was seven, he was sent to St. Mary's Industrial School for Boys, a local Catholic reformatory and orphanage, where he lived until he was eighteen. Early in his time there, the school's head of discipline, one Brother Matthias Boutilier, became a father figure to the young man, teaching him not only to read and write but training him in all aspects of baseball, from hitting and fielding to pitching (he also learned shirtmaking and was a member of the school's band and drama club).

In 1913, while Ruth was pitching in a game against Mount St. Mary's College (now University), he was spotted by a former student who was then a pitcher for the Washington Senators. Together with a teacher at Ruth's school, he introduced Ruth to Jack Dunn, the owner and manager of the then–minor league Baltimore Orioles. After passing a pitching audition, Ruth was signed to a $250 contract ($5,400 today) on Valentine's Day, 1914. He was immediately nicknamed "Jack's newest babe" by his teammates, and the nickname, as we know, stayed with Ruth the rest of his life (although most teammates called him George or "Jidge," and many fans called him simply the "Bambino," Italian for "baby"). Only five months after signing Ruth, Dunn offered to trade him along with two other players to Connie Mack of the Philadelphia Athletics for $10,000 ($218,000 today). After Mack and the Cincinnati Reds passed on the trade, Dunn sold the trio to the Boston Red Sox for a still disputed sum.

After five years with the Red Sox, Ruth was sold by the team's owner to the Yankees on December 26, 1919, apparently less because of his performance (which was splendid) than because of Ruth's demand for more money and his volatile temper, which caused Ruth on at least one occasion to throw a punch at the umpire after a disputed call. In 1918, during which he hit a league-leading eleven home runs, Ruth actually walked off the team following an argument with the manager. His final World Series appearance as a pitcher took place in the opener of the 1918 Series.

Legend has it that the Red Sox owner, George Frazee, sold Ruth to the Yankees because he needed the money to finance the production of the musical *No, No, Nanette*, resulting in the "Curse of the Bambino," which, according to local superstition, kept the Red Sox from winning the World Series from 1918 to 2004. As the musical wasn't produced until 1925, it doesn't add up; recent research has confirmed that Ruth and several other players were sold, at least in part, to finance the production of a play, *My Lady Friends*, on which the later musical was based.

But there was more. After the 1919 season Ruth demanded a salary increase to twenty thousand dollars, double what he was getting. Frazee refused, and Ruth threatened not to play until he got the raise. So considering all the factors—Ruth's temper, his salary demands, and Frazee's own need for money—Frazee decided to sell him. The Yankees owners, deciding that they needed something to revive a moribund team, initially offered $100,000 (the equivalent of $1.3 million today) for Ruth but settled on $200,000 ($2.5 million today) in cash and promissory notes plus a $300,000 loan to Frazee, with Boston's Fenway Park as collateral. The rest, as they say, is history.

After moving to the Yankees, Ruth completed his transition from pitcher to the power-hitting outfielder who would, during the subsequent fifteen years (and more than two thousand games), rewrite the record books.

In 1920, his first season with the Yankees, Ruth hit fifty-four homers and batted .376. His .847 slugging average was a Major League record until 2001. But the Bambino considered the next year his best, during which he hit fifty-nine home runs and batted .378 while leading the Yankees to their first league championship. Although they had high World Series hopes (for a subway contest with the New York Giants), they lost primarily because Ruth injured his elbow and knee and was out for several of the games.

In 1923 the Yankees moved from the Polo Grounds, which they were subletting from the Giants, into their new Yankee Stadium. It was soon dubbed "The House That Ruth Built"; he also hit the new stadium's first run in a game with, ironically, the Red Sox.

And so it went. Year after year, the superlatives mounted, with his records occasionally playing second fiddle to his personal life. During spring training in 1925, Ruth became ill with "the bellyache heard round the world." One sports writer claimed his illness was caused by bingeing on hot dogs and soda pop before a game, but it is far more likely that he had been poisoned by bad liquor, a common problem during Prohibition (chapter 2). In any event, it was his worst season with the team until the end of his career.

Matters were much improved the next couple of years, highlighted by his highly publicized promise in 1926 to a seriously ill eleven-year-old, Johnny Sylvester, that he would hit a home run for him (he did) and his sixty-homer record in 1927.

In 1929 the Yankees failed to make the World Series for the first time in four years, and their next appearance would not be until 1932. Ruth, however, led or tied for the league home run records during those years, and once, as a stunt in the 1930 season, pitched for the first time since 1921 (the Yankees won). When asked by a reporter if he felt guilty that his salary ($80,000, the equivalent of $975,000 today) was $5,000 more than President Hoover's, his response has been rendered as either, "I know, but I had a better year than Hoover," or, more likely, considering Ruth's pride in his own achievements, "How many home runs did *he* hit last year?"

In the third game of the 1932 World Series against the Chicago Cubs (which the Yankees swept), one of baseball's legendary events occurred when Ruth hit what has come to be called "Babe Ruth's Called Shot." During the at bat he pointed his bat at the deepest part of Wrigley Field's centerfield some 440 feet away, predicting a home run. And he delivered. The ball, a home run to straightaway center, ended up in the temporary bleachers nearly 500 feet away. It would be the thirty-seven-year-old's last Series homer and, in fact, his last Series hit. In the years since, many have disputed the veracity of this story. However, in 2010 retired Supreme Court Justice John Paul Stevens confirmed in an interview that it happened exactly as related. He would know; he was there.

After years of neglecting his health, Ruth knew he had little time left as a major league player. His heart was set on becoming the manager of his beloved Yankees, but Jacob Ruppert, owner of the team (as well as of New York's once famous Ruppert Breweries) refused to replace his manager and, insultingly, offered Ruth the job with the Yankees' top minor league team, the Newark Bears. On the advice of his second wife and manager, Claire Hodgson, Ruth rejected the offer, so on February 26, 1935, Ruppert traded him to the Boston Braves. He lasted only a year. After a game against the Giants, Ruth called reporters into the locker room and told them he was retiring.

The next year he was one of the first five players elected to the Baseball Hall of Fame and two years later, after a season as first-base coach of the Brooklyn Dodgers, left the profession in 1943 following an appearance at a charity game at Yankee Stadium.

His life, compared to his career, had been less of a success. Much was made over the introduction of the Baby Ruth candy bar in 1921. The Curtis Candy Company, the bar's maker, claimed it had been named for President Grover Cleveland's daughter, but as it had been years since Cleveland left office and fifteen years since the daughter had died, it was clearly a ploy to avoid paying Ruth any royalties.

Ruth had married a waitress named Helen Woodford in 1914, and they separated in 1926 after his infidelities became known. She died in 1929 in a fire at the home of a dentist she was then living with in Watertown, Massachusetts. They had adopted a daughter, Dorothy, who wrote a book, *My Dad, the Babe*, in which she claimed she was his biological child by a woman named Juanita Jennings. After Helen's death Ruth married Claire Merritt Hodgson, an actress and model, and adopted her daughter, Julia (who threw out the first ball in the final game at the old Yankee Stadium on September 21, 2008).

In November 1946 doctors discovered that Ruth had a malignant tumor in his neck, which was removed in an operation. Afterward, he received radiation treatments and eventually an experimental drug. But the cancer returned, poignantly apparent in Nat Fein's Pulitzer Prize–winning photograph of Ruth using a bat as a cane during a twenty-fifth anniversary reunion of the 1923 Yankees team at the stadium on June 13, 1948. The following July 26, after attending the premiere of the film *The Babe Ruth Story,* a biopic about his own life starring William Bendix, he returned to the hospital, where he died on August 16 at the age of fifty-three.

"He wasn't a baseball player. He was a worldwide celebrity, an international star," ESPN broadcaster Ernie Howell has claimed. It was Babe Ruth's home run batting skills coupled with a flamboyant personality that, in the 1920s, made him a celebrity and also changed baseball forever.

Baseball had been around in one form or another since the mid-1700s in England and a century later was being accepted as America's national game. But until Ruth arrived, bringing power hitting to the game—sometimes hitting more home runs than some *teams*—it had been a lower scoring contest dominated by pitchers. By his heroics Ruth also brought fans who had been disillusioned by the "Black Sox" scandal of 1919 back to believing in the game. League batting averages jumped thirty-five points, and home runs increased from an annual average of nine thousand in 1910 to over twelve thousand in the 1920s. For good or bad Ruth's salary demands eventually altered the financial structure of baseball itself.

All in all, the nation was captivated, forcing the enlargement of stadiums to accommodate thousands of newly energized fans; in 1920 the Yankees became the first club to reach one million in home attendance.

In the 1930s and early '40s, Babe Ruth was as big a presence off the baseball diamond as he was on it, as a frequent guest on radio, as host of his own radio show, and in movies beginning with an appearance in the 1920 silent film *Headin' Home*. In 1943 he played himself in *Pride of the Yankees*, the biopic of his teammate, Lou Gehrig. Several other films involved him playing himself or actors playing characters based on a Ruth-like persona; for instance, 1984's *The Natural* (based on a 1952 novel by Bernard Malamud), which starred Robert Redford as Roy Hobbs (the Gehrig character) and Joe Don Baker as the Ruth character ("the Whammer").

In his lifetime he was so popular, so much of the warp and woof of American life, that one of the worst things Japanese soldiers would shout (in English) as a taunt to Americans during World War II was, "To Hell with Babe Ruth!"

It's June 13, 1927, and New York is celebrating Charles Lindbergh's history-making solo flight from nearby Roosevelt Field on Long Island to Paris—a daring effort that made him one of America's greatest folk heroes—with the city's own, unique honor . . . a ticker-tape parade. Here, while flags fly and tons of confetti shower down on the parade, twenty-five-year-old "Lucky Lindy" and New York's beloved, top-hatted mayor Jimmy Walker perch on the back of the processional Packard while the mustached Grover Whalen, the city's "official" greeter, looks upward at the cloud of paper snow tossed from office buildings along the "Canyon of Heroes" parade route through the downtown financial district.
Library of Congress

CHAPTER 20

The Ticker-Tape Parade

Grover T. Whalen

I don't understand America. Someone becomes famous and you throw tons of trash down on them.

— British tourist watching the 1927 parade honoring Charles Lindbergh

In 1923 the New York Yankees won the World Series, two years after the Series began. Media praise poured in, ticket sales continued to climb, and thousands of fans clamored for seats in their new stadium. Nevertheless, they were denied the one accolade which today is considered New York City's ultimate public celebration of their feat: a ticker-tape parade. Time has taken care of that oversight; on November 6, 2009, the Yankees took their ninth trip down lower Manhattan's skyscraper-lined route since their first ticker-tape parade on April 10, 1961, which honored them for winning the American League pennant the year before, making them the event's most celebrated sports franchise.

Why did it take thirty-eight years for them to be showered with confetti along the so-called "Canyon of Heroes"? In the beginning, and this is largely the case today, New York's ticker-tape parades have mostly honored individuals or, in the case of multiple honorees, those who have competed on an international level (such as the U.S. Olympic teams in the 1920s). (With three ticker-tape parades, Admiral Richard Byrd holds the individual record.)

The ticker-tape parade is New York City's longest-standing public celebration and one that, because of the towering skyscrapers, only New York could stage. These days when an individual or a group—such as the 2009 New York Yankees—is honored by a ticker-tape parade from the tip of Manhattan Island to City Hall, some fifty tons of confetti and shredded paper are showered upon them. It may seem strange when you think about it, but there is no denying that the image of a hero or celebrity passing through a shower of paper, which harkens to an ancient custom of showering human icons with flower petals (or the newly wedded with rice), nearly deifies the person.

And maybe the urge to throw things out of high windows is part of human nature. Like the ticker-tape parade, there is—or at least, was—a tradition in Italy to throw anything you didn't want (including furniture) out the window to celebrate the New Year. And like the ticker-tape parade, it also created a heck of a mess to clean up the next day.

Such an urge certainly saw its downside after Black Friday, October 29, 1929, when the boom of the Jazz Age crashed into the pit of what would become the Great Depression, and some of those who were financially ruined ended it all by "defenestrating" themselves.

Such endings, of course, weren't limited to the ticker-tape parade route; any window more than five or six stories above the street would provide an effective means to end it all. In fact, a macabre cartoon of the time depicted a man asking a hotel receptionist for a room. The receptionist replies, "Do you want it for sleeping or jumping?"

But thankfully, it's the far less lethal aspect of throwing confetti out the windows along lower Broadway that has become a New York institution, and it really got serious in the 1920s.

The practice actually began more than a generation earlier when in 1886, two decades after the invention of the stock ticker, a use for the used ribbonlike paper, called ticker tape (for the sound the machine made), on which the machine stamped stock and bond sales was discovered by denizens of New York's financial district: Throwing the stuff out of windows was a fun way of celebrating.

The first time it happened was on October 29 of that year, the day after the dedication of the Statue of Liberty, a gift from France, whose financiers were probably more decorous. Three years later New Yorkers did it again, this time for the George Washington centenary (no record of who stood in for the honoree). The practice was still a novelty ten years later, when the *New York Times* reported that office workers had "hit on a new and effective scheme of adding to the decorations" at a parade for presidential candidate William McKinley.

In 1899 two million people joined the falling confetti to cheer Admiral Dewey for his Spanish-American War victory at the Battle of Manila Bay in 1898. Ex-president Theodore Roosevelt was similarly honored on his return from an African safari on June 18, 1910, and in 1919 General Pershing, commander of the American forces in the recently ended World War I, was honored, as was the twenty-five-year-old Prince of Wales. Years later he would become King Edward VIII, only to give up his throne for the American divorcée Wallis Warfield Simpson and, by then known as the Duke of Windsor, would end up living in exile in France and New York. New Yorkers always loved their royals anyway, and keeping the royal standards flying in the 1920s were parades for Crown Princess Louise of Sweden and Queen Marie of Romania.

The decade was really highlighted by perhaps the most famous ticker-tape parade in the history of the celebration. On June 13, 1927, Charles Lindbergh, fresh from his solo flight from Long Island to Paris, was honored (he had returned to the United

States, as did his airplane, the *Spirit of St. Louis*, two days earlier aboard the U.S. Navy cruiser *Memphis*). Such excitement was to be expected, considering the hysteria that surrounded "Lucky Lindy," who would soon become one of America's greatest folk heroes.

The first honoree of the 1920s, however, was certainly the least likely. He was also the only scientist to receive a ticker-tape parade: Albert Einstein, fresh not from a daring airplane flight but from winning the Nobel Prize for Physics, despite the fact that most of the people throwing the confetti out of the windows could not make head or tail of his relativity theory.

After honoring Pershing in 1919, the early Twenties' ticker-tape parades were taken up with honoring wartime allies such as the French marshals (Foch in 1921, Joffre the following year), former French premier Clemenceau (November 18, 1922), and in October 1923 England's former prime minister David Lloyd George.

Many of the people who were semiburied under the paper during the decade were sports heroes. Among them was the 1924 U.S. Olympic team on its return from the Paris games, where they had won thirty-two medals, twice as many as the next nation (Finland). A member of the team in that parade was Johnny Weissmuller, who won three swimming gold medals and one bronze medal (for water polo). Weissmuller also paraded up Broadway four years later with our 1928 Olympic team; he had won two more gold medals in Amsterdam and would soon move on to Hollywood, where he would become the silver screen's most famous Tarzan.

Other sports stars honored in the '20s included Gertrude Ederle, the first woman to swim the English Channel (in 1926). That year golfer Bobby Jones, the winner of the British Open, got a parade; actually he was one of the few people to become double honorees after he again won the British title in 1929. Another double honoree was Richard Byrd, then a U.S. Navy commander (later admiral), who was cheered in 1926 (with air hero Floyd Bennett) for flying over the North Pole and again the following year with the crew of his Fokker aircraft *America,* for their transatlantic flight. Other flyers honored were Amelia Earhart (who would also be honored again) and Hugo Eckner and his crew of the German airship *Graf Zeppelin* for initiating the new transatlantic air service. Though at the time much ballyhooed, such lighter-than-air transportation would end tragically in 1937 with the explosion of the *Hindenburg* as it prepared to land in Lakehurst, New Jersey, following its regularly scheduled flight from Berlin.

The ticker-tape parades became popular in the 1920s because of a talent for boosterism possessed by a man who reigned for a generation as the city's official "greeter." In 1919 New York City was not only playing host to homebound soldiers and sailors but also, as we have noted, to many of our allies' leaders in the war. The city's mayor, John F. Hylan, knew he wasn't good at the public events that civic welcomes demanded, so he appointed his gregarious secretary, Grover T. Whalen, as executive director of both of the two reception committees that Hylan formed (one for welcoming the troops, one for celebrities). Between 1919 and 1953 Whalen would organize eighty-six ticker-tape parades, many of them at the urging of the U.S. State Department.

One didn't even have to be famous to get the glad hand from the top-hatted Whalen. If you weren't considered important enough for a ticker-tape parade, well, there were lesser events—he staged more than a thousand—where, on behalf of the people of New York City, he welcomed everyone from Miss Brazil and the French Boy Scout Singers to the president of the Vienna Board of Health and the Irish and Scottish Damask Linen Advertising Association.

New York then was, politically, even more of a Democratic party stronghold than it is today, and from this standpoint Whalen was more than qualified for the job. Born on the Lower East Side, he was a "cradle Democrat," named for President Grover Cleveland, who was married in the Blue Room of the White House to Frances Folsom on the day Grover was born, June 2, 1886. As Whalen grew up he became fiercely committed to the Democratic Tammany Hall machine. When Tammany decided to retake City Hall from the reform mayor John Purroy Mitchel by running Hylan in 1917, Hylan, who knew of Whalen's political commitment, called Rodman Wanamaker, president of Wanamaker's department store where Whalen was then working, and borrowed him to be his aide.

Above and beyond his greeting duties, Hylan also appointed Whalen commissioner of Plants and Structures and chairman of the Board of Purchase, and he served the mayor's City Hall until 1924, when he returned to Wanamaker's. But he stayed on as the city's greeter under Hylan's Tammany successor, Mayor Jimmy Walker, and three years later threw the biggest celebration of them all for Lindbergh, a ticker-tape parade that would remain in the record books as the biggest ever until the August 14, 1945, celebration of the end of World War II.

In fact, it was apparently because of Whalen's connections that the Lindbergh flight was possible at all. His old boss, Rodman Wanamaker, was an early aviation buff who was financing Richard Byrd's planned attempt to fly the Atlantic nonstop in his huge trimotor Fokker aircraft *America.* As Wanamaker's agent Whalen gave the permission for Lindbergh's plane to be moved from Long Island's Curtiss Field to the Wanamaker-owned Roosevelt Field, which boasted one of the longest runways in the world (Whalen may have had an ownership interest in the airfield as well; the records are vague on this point). The longer runway was considered essential because of the extra takeoff weight of the added fuel supply that Lindbergh's Ryan aircraft, the *Spirit of St. Louis*, was forced to carry to complete the 3,600-mile, thirty-three-and–a-half-hour, nonstop flight to Paris.

After the plane was moved, it was also Whalen who gave the go-ahead for Lindbergh to use the runway on May 20, 1927, for his flight into immortality. (Byrd didn't get off the ground for another two weeks, so Lindbergh got the parade that Whalen and Wanamaker had originally planned for Byrd. As earlier noted, Byrd got his own parade the following month, but it would be an anticlimax.)

In December 1928 Mayor Walker appointed Whalen to another new job, that of the city's police commissioner. Cynics say Walker did it to deflect investigation into what his enemies said, with some justification, was a scandal-blighted administration, but Whalen's appointment probably had more to do with his links to Tammany Hall. In any event, Whalen was eventually victimized by the media as being more interested in taking vacations than in running the police department, despite the fact that, while commissioner, he founded the city's police academy.

After resigning from the Walker administration, he returned to Wanamaker's and then, after Rodman Wanamaker died, became head of Schenley Distilling Corporation in the heady post-Prohibition repeal days. He then left to become president of the 1939 World's Fair, which, primarily through Whalen's salesmanship, is remembered as one of the best.

The World's Fair, held in a converted dump at Flushing Meadow, was planned to celebrate both the 150th anniversary of George Washington's inauguration and "The World of Tomorrow." Soon after he took the job, Whalen went on an international tour to sell it to the world, and he was amazingly successful. Nearly sixty nations participated. While all this was going on, he was asked by Tammany to be their candidate to run against the reform mayor Fiorello LaGuardia in 1937, but Whalen decided running the fair would be more fun. He also had some pretty high-powered help in selling the fair: In July 1938 Howard Hughes used a hugely publicized round-the-world flight to promote the event. When he returned, Whalen saw to it that he had a ticker-tape parade, too.

On April 30, 1939, 150 years to the day after Washington took his oath, President Franklin D. Roosevelt opened the World's Fair. Symbolized by the soaring seven-hundred-foot Trylon and the eighteen-story Perisphere, the Fair—as advertised—offered a vision of the future: RCA publicly introduced television, and AT&T demonstrated long-distance telephones. Air-conditioning, an early fax machine, color film, the dishwasher, and nylon all made their debuts, and General Motors stunned the visitors with its World of Tomorrow diorama.

Despite all the excitement, the fair was a financial failure, returning only thirty-three cents on each of its investors' dollars; nevertheless, today it remains in our culture's collective memory as one of the most spectacular of such events, and even cheap souvenirs from it can sell today for hundreds of dollars. After the fair closed, Whalen went back to City Hall as the chairman of the Mayor's Reception Committee, but during the subsequent World War, there wasn't much reason to throw ticker tape around. When the conflict ended, though, the city made up for lost time with the biggest-of-them-all victory parade. It took three thousand street sweepers to clean up the 5,500 tons of stuff thrown at the celebrants (more than one hundred times the average amount of paper and confetti thrown on other parades).

Whalen next became an executive with the perfume maker Coty, where he worked to establish New York as a fashion rival of Paris by creating the American Fashion Critics' Award for clothing design (called the Winnie). His last official greeting was in November 1953, when he welcomed the king and queen of Greece.

Several months later the new mayor, Robert Wagner, appointed a new greeter without bothering to tell Whalen that he was being dumped after thirty-four years.

On April 20, 1962, the man often referred to as "Mr. New York," Grover Whalen, died at seventy-five.

Over the years there have been more than two hundred ticker-tape parades, but it was during the 1920s, thanks in no small part to the event honoring Charles Lindbergh, that they became established as New York's (and the nation's) most famous honor.

Today, June 20, 1932, it's all smiles as, following her second ticker-tape parade honoring her solo transatlantic flight (the first for a woman), the celebrated aviatrix Amelia Earhart and "Gentleman Jim" Jimmy Walker, New York's popular mayor, receive plaudits on the steps of City Hall. Ten weeks later, Walker would resign his office amid scandal and disgrace, and five years later, Earhart would tragically disappear somewhere over the Pacific Ocean on a round-the-world flight attempt. But today that's all in the future as the pair bask in their fame and the love poured out for both, a love for Walker which, despite the scandals and charges of corruption, would remain long after his death in 1946.
Library of Congress

CHAPTER 21

"Gentleman Jim," Part II, The Party's Over

Mayor Jimmy Walker

There are summer skies in your eyes
The bloom in your cheek
Makes winter retreat.
There'll be no December
If you'll just remember,
Sweetheart, it's always May.
— Lyrics to Jimmy Walker's song "Will You Love Me in December (as You Did in May)?"

With the shooting of Arnold Rothstein on November 4, 1928, at Manhattan's Park Central Hotel, the city's underground network of graft and corruption began to unravel, and one of the most vulnerable was the mayor, Jimmy Walker. The reason A. R.'s murder was such a body blow to the city government as well as Walker's political mentor, the Tammany Hall machine, was that Rothstein, most famous in legend for fixing the 1919 World Series and known as "the Brain," was not only a world-class gambler but also the major mob financier, a bootlegger, drug dealer, and, as well, a major financier of the Broadway theater. He had his hands in so many areas of city politics that when his clandestine criminal activities—including bribery of judges and payoffs to police officials—began to be revealed following his assassination, everyone remotely connected to him began pointing fingers at everyone else. Most often those fingers were pointed at the city's most visible political figure, Jimmy Walker.

Even the media scrambled for the high ground, trumpeting the "official" story that Rothstein was hit because he had run up a debt of $320,000 in a three-day poker game and then refused to pay, claiming that the game was fixed (supposedly, his last words just before he was shot were, "What's the matter, did I make a wrong bet?"). A number of suspects were named, among them Dutch Shultz, whose presumed motive was the murder of a mob buddy by Rothstein ally Joe "Legs" Diamond. Gambler George "the Hump" McManus and his associate Hyman Biller were actually arrested for the crime but soon were cleared of the charge. For his part, before dying in the Stuyvesant Polyclinic Hospital, Rothstein refused to identify his killer (almost certainly Vincent "Mad Dog" Coll), telling the police: "You stick to your trade. I'll stick to mine."

One of the first things Mayor Jimmy Walker did after hearing that Arnold Rothstein had been assassinated was to replace the city's police commissioner with his friend Grover Whalen, who told the mayor he would only take the job if he were given the freedom to clean up gambling and reorganize the police force, regardless of whom his actions might touch. Nevertheless, the moment Whalen told a city clerk to close a gambling club operating under the guise of a political office, Walker called his friend and threatened to fire him.

In November 1928 Al Smith lost his bid for the presidency to Herbert Hoover. In light of the economic chaos to come, he was lucky to lose, but at the time it certainly didn't seem so to the man whom the new governor of New York, Franklin D. Roosevelt, had dubbed "the Happy Warrior" at the Democratic presidential nominating convention. Smith's loss was due less to Democratic/Republican rivalry than to prejudice over his Roman Catholic faith, a political blight that wouldn't be erased in American politics until John F. Kennedy was elected a generation later.

Smith, who would go on to be the president of the corporation that ran the newly built Empire State Building, was also angry with Walker, who won his second term of mayor a year later. For one thing, even though they had feuded over Walker's partying, Smith now felt that Walker, once his protégé, had deserted him. Grover Whalen had fired several of Smith's friends and, to Smith, that wasn't being loyal. Walker had also won his reelection bid in large part because of his support of the five-cent subway fare over the efforts of the Transit Authority to raise it, which was supported by Smith and a public relations campaign run by the early public relations professional Ivy Lee. When the New York Supreme Court upheld the five-cent fare over the noisy protests of the transit owners, Jimmy famously quipped: "Subways are built by pickaxes, not thoraxes."

Walker's opponent for his job in 1929 was Fiorello LaGuardia (as well as a third party candidate, socialist Norman Thomas). Unlike Walker's opponent in his first mayoralty campaign, LaGuardia played it down and dirty—and there was some dust to be cleaned up. During the campaign he accused Walker of overlooking graft in many of the city's departments and claimed that Walker was planning to increase his salary, already a hefty $25,000 ($319,000 today). He also accused Walker of giving a friend the lease of the sixty-year-old Central Park Casino and sponsoring its reconstruction as the swankiest restaurant in the city, with two bandstands and interior decoration (personally approved by Jim and his mistress Betty Compton) by the then-famous Viennese designer Josef Urban. (Located at Seventy-Second Street and Fifth Avenue, the casino billed itself as "a country club in the city.")

It all reminded voters of Walker's playboy image at the worst time possible: The great stock market crash presaging the Great Depression took place on October 29, only days before the November election, and breadlines were soon to appear on the "Sidewalks of New York" (Smith's presidential campaign song the previous year). Walker, who by then had moved into the Mayfair Hotel on Park Avenue at Sixty-Fifth Street, appeared to take it all casually, accusing LaGuardia, soon to be popularly known as "the Little Flower" (a direct translation of his given name, Fiorello), of "shouting and screaming while playing with his toys." Jimmy was, however, reelected with an even larger margin than four years earlier.

Public criticism of his affair with Betty Compton then began. Cardinal Hayes, raised in the same lower-Manhattan neighborhood as Walker, summoned him to his residence and told him in no uncertain terms to mend his ways. So, apparently, did Walker's own family, especially his favorite brother, George, then terminally ill with tuberculosis. Walker, who had always had a morbid fear of illness (his niece, Rita, once said one of his closets at the St. Luke's Place house was so filled with prescription and patent medicines that it looked like a pharmacy), now, at forty-nine, began to have serious health problems. He was constantly catching colds, had heart palpitations, and, because his stomach was bothering him, became quite thin. His judgment was faltering also; at a time when he was working long hours to find ways to aid the thousands of out-of-work New Yorkers, he and the members of the Board of Estimate increased their own salaries (Jim donated his fifteen thousand dollar raise to charity, but his gesture was lost against his high-living, playboy image).

It has been said that Franklin Roosevelt disliked Walker, and, beginning in 1930, when the mayor's troubles began to mount, Roosevelt threw him to the wolves. FDR was always a political opportunist, but for the most part this story is untrue.

In 1929 Governor Roosevelt refused to bring charges against the Walker administration, but confronted by a Republican legislative majority the following year, he warned Tammany leaders that an investigation might be inevitable. Eventually, FDR was attacked in the state senate for refusing to order an investigation (an unlikely Roosevelt ally was the Socialist party, which also demanded an official look into Tammany's dealings). Then in July the *New York Times,* soon followed by the city's other leading newspapers, began demanding a Grand Jury investigation of corruption in the city's Magistrate's Court system.

Like confetti in a ticker-tape parade, resignations began to fall, the most famous of which was that of State Supreme Court Justice Joseph Crater, an FDR appointee. After selling his stock holdings and withdrawing all the cash in his bank account, Crater simply vanished in August 1930, and his disappearance—unexplained to this day—became a punch line for comics for a generation. That month the state finally decided to do something about the corruption charges flying about Walker's administration and summoned a former New York Supreme Court judge (and former Democratic gubernatorial candidate) named Samuel Seabury to head up an investigation of the Magistrates' Courts of Manhattan and the Bronx. Seabury, who has been described as a brilliant jurist but "as aloof as the ice cap of Mount Everest," was a champion of the downtrodden. Ominously in this case, he was unable to allow for human frailties . . . all too well personified by the man he would soon go after, Mayor James J. Walker.

Judge Seabury immediately assembled a team of young lawyers to help in his investigation and organized it in a very modern pattern. First, the bank accounts of everyone under investigation would be looked at; then, if the deposits seemed large, he would first hold private, followed by public, hearings. Fireworks came quickly when it was found that numerous police vice squad members had paid off stool pigeons to frame hundreds of women as prostitutes (who would then be forced to bribe the vice squad members to let them go). It was during this time that Polly Adler, then New York's top madam (chapter 5) was summoned to testify about the payoffs she had made to the police to leave her business alone; she fled to Florida for many months, and when she eventually returned and appeared before Seabury's court, as earlier noted, she refused to implicate anyone.

All the while, Judge Seabury's group was releasing news of irregularities within the court systems and decided to try the city's first woman judge, Jean Norris (a Hylan appointee who had been kept on by Walker at the request of Tammany). The charge was primarily for altering transcripts of hearings in her court to clear her of any bias in sending many women to jail for "immoral" acts after they were denied their right to present evidence of their innocence. Judge Norris was removed from the municipal bench as "unfit for judicial service."

Although Walker stated that he welcomed an investigation, it didn't help his reputation when Betty was caught in a gambling raid at a casino in Montauk, Long Island, while he hid out in the kitchen eating beans. The term *casino* is Italian for "little house," and such places could, as the Central Park Casino did, offer solely food and entertainment, but some also offered clandestine gambling.

Several months before Walker's death in November 1946, Gene Fowler asked him if he thought that FDR disliked him. "No," said Walker, who subsequently said the only person responsible for his troubles was himself. "Although he had many reasons to dislike me. I was careless and inconsiderate of both Governor and Mrs. Roosevelt [it is said that when Walker at one point lived less than a half block from the Roosevelts' Manhattan townhouse, he never called on them]. Frank Roosevelt certainly proved in the long run that he not only forgave but forgot my rudeness and neglect."

Complicating matters, Betty had discovered that Tammany was pressuring Jim to get rid of her, and instead of trusting the relationship, she impulsively eloped with a movie dialogue director named Ed Dowling. The moment they were pronounced man and wife, she realized it was a mistake.

The political pressure on Jimmy was mounting, compounded by the unrelated but headline-making murder of a Seabury witness, Virginia Gordon (who was to testify that she was illegally arrested by a vice cop), and the subsequent suicide of her daughter. The stress of reacting to the corruption charges, combined with the turmoil over Betty's marriage, made Walker's always-frail health collapse. His blood pressure was alarmingly low, and his weight dropped to 115 pounds. He went to Palm Springs, California, to recover at the home of a lawyer friend. But it was no vacation, as he tried to keep up with the mounting charges three thousand miles away via twenty or more long-distance telephone calls daily.

Among the new revelations breaking around his head were specific charges of negligence and incompetence contained in a four-thousand-word document given to Governor Roosevelt by Rabbi Steven Wise, a close friend of FDR (earlier, in 1914, cofounder of the NAACP), and John Holmes, the pastor of Manhattan's huge Community Church. (Holmes, as part of the personal attacks on Walker that were getting uglier and uglier, shouted during a City Affairs Committee meeting, "How much longer shall we be amused by this little man?") As he was returning from California, Walker learned that Betty had established residence in Mexico, enabling a quick end to her short marriage to Dowling.

Back on his home turf, Walker was heartened when, after reading his fifteen-thousand-word answer to the Wise/Holmes charges, FDR dismissed them. On June 19, 1931, Jim celebrated his fiftieth birthday at three banquets, the biggest of which drew two thousand guests to Brooklyn's St. George Hotel. Among them was the man soon to be known as "America's Toastmaster," George Jessel, and the actor Maurice Chevalier.

That August, however, Walker was served with a subpoena to appear before the Seabury Commission along with all documents relating to his personal finances and bank accounts. He postponed the appearance by embarking on another European vacation. His reasons were to see Betty, who was vacationing abroad with her mother, and to improve his health at European spas, the chic thing to do at the time. Betty, however, apparently angry over Jim's reluctance to end his twenty-year marriage to Allie, refused to take his calls or see him during his six-week trip, during which he was made a Commander of the French Legion of Honor. The reason for the honor, at least according to a story prevalent at the time, which further damaged his reputation, was that he had waived back taxes on land used by the French to store ammunition in New York City during the war.

By now Judge Seabury's commission—expanded to twenty-one investigators—was looking into both Walker's and his accountant's brokerage accounts. Then, two days before Walker's last public event, leading the so-called "Beer Parade" of tens of thousands of marchers protesting Prohibition, a broker for a taxi company testified that in 1929 he had given Walker bonds valued at over $26,500 ($338,000 today) before passage of the bill that created the city's Board of Taxicab Control. On March 24, 1932, after stalling Seabury for more than a year, Jim arrived at the courthouse in Foley Square to tell his side of the story.

It was not a happy event. There were numerous outbursts from the audience—all Walker supporters—as well as endless objections as Walker defended his actions in numerous instances, most notably regarding the claimed payoff from a bus company and details of the joint brokerage account established by his friend Paul Block. And so it went.

The following month fifteen charges against Walker were sent by Seabury to FDR. On June 22, the day before Walker was to leave for the Chicago convention that would nominate the governor as the Democratic standard bearer in the 1932 presidential election, Roosevelt, after stalling for nearly a month (he felt anything he did would offend someone, the last thing he needed to do before the nominating convention) notified Walker that he had to answer the Seabury charges. After the convention (where Walker stayed Tammany-true by voting for the nomination of Al Smith), the mayor composed a long answer to the Seabury charges and subsequently met with FDR a dozen times in the state house in Albany.

Throughout his public life FDR was always closemouthed about what he was going to do in any situation. That of course opened the door for all kinds of speculation, and Walker apparently had decided that the governor was going to remove him. So Jim decided to beat him to the punch and on September 1 told his sister Nan while they were attending his brother George's funeral at Calvary Cemetery that he was going to resign. He did so that evening.

In retrospect it was a mistake. Although Al Smith had told him that he had no choice but to resign, FDR, in fact, didn't think there was enough concrete evidence in the Seabury report to force him to do so. FDR said at the time that if Walker was guilty of anything it was "nonfeasance"—not paying enough attention—rather than "malfeasance." In a White House interview in 1941, FDR told Associated Press reporter Walter Brown that he didn't believe the Seabury evidence justified Walker's resignation, although Eleanor Roosevelt later commented that her husband was relieved that Walker resigned. Many believe that if the mercurial Walker had not resigned and had run for mayor again in 1933, by winning—an almost certain outcome—he would have vindicated himself.

An hour after his late-night resignation (four years before his retirement income would kick in), Walker cabled the news to Betty in Paris, who was delighted. Ten days later he sailed for Europe and Betty. Although he returned to the city (with Betty, to deal with harassing creditors—he commented at the time: "People woo you on the way in and sue you on the way out."), when they left again for Europe, it would be for what amounted to a three-year exile.

Before settling on the French Riviera, they visited Naples, where Jim received a tumultuous reception. The prospect of an autobiography was touted (by *Variety*) but abandoned, although Jim needed the money. Then in March 1933 the long-suffering Allie filed for divorce on the grounds of desertion. It was apparently Jim's idea, if her comments are to be believed. "After he went to Europe, Jim wrote that it would be best for me, as well as him, that I divorce him. . . . He was the light of my life, and still shines in my heart." They never met again.

The following month Jim and Betty were married in Cannes: Jim was fifty-one and Betty, twenty-eight. That summer, while the couple were visiting Betty's mother in England, Walker was found innocent of tax evasion after a three-month investigation by a federal grand jury. A friend, a stage and screen actor named William Gaxton (who would the following year star in Cole Porter's *Of Thee I Sing* on Broadway), ran into Jim sitting on a piece of driftwood on Venice, Italy's Lido Beach. Clearly homesick, Jim told him, "Billy, I think about old friends all the time . . . Cohan, Jolson, Cantor, Fanny Brice, Jessel, and the rest. . . . I'd like to be home. There must be a way somewhere, somehow, for a man to get back. I don't mean politically, I mean with himself."

Jim and Betty settled into a cottage owned by her mother near Dorking in Surry, England, which they called "the Thatch." Jim seemed to be getting over his melancholia and began going into London weekly to meet friends, such as Sophie Tucker and the financier Otto Kahn at the Savoy Hotel—friends whom he never forgot and who never forgot him. According to Gene Fowler, Jim

Farley, FDR's campaign manager and by then Postmaster General, wrote him: "Jim, if there is anything in the world that I can do to help you in the slightest degree, it will be my pleasure and privilege to do so. And you may be assured that I will not forget you."

About this time Walker learned that the house on St. Luke's Place had been sold ahead of foreclosure for property taxes unpaid in 1934. The price was $18,000 ($293,000 today), much of which went to creditors. Later that year, while Jim and Betty were in London, the Thatch, containing all Jim's books and keepsakes, was destroyed by fire. Jim-haters claimed that he had ordered the fire to destroy incriminating papers stored in the cottage's attic. It was true that Walker had a lot of material stored in the Thatch, but all his official papers had been left in New York, as Gene Fowler, his executor and friend, later testified. On August 27 a second grand jury investigation of Jim's income tax reports showed no discrepancies; now, twice vindicated, he was free to return home to take advantage of any business or professional offers that were coming his way.

At noon on October 31, the *Manhattan*, carrying Jim, Betty, her mother, the Sterlings (friends from Europe), twenty bags, ten trunks, and two kennels with Jim's dogs, was greeted in New York harbor by boat whistles, a tug broadcasting his December/May song on a loudspeaker, and thousands of greeters on the pier. Although Jim needed an income, for the next couple of years he refused all the offers that came his way, although Betty tried (and failed) with a flower store. The pair finally leased a small farm on Long Island, where they raised prize chickens and bred Irish terriers but failed to make a profit.

In March 1936 Jim and Betty adopted a six-week-old girl and named her Mary Ann. The following year they adopted an infant boy, whom they named John Jr. but called Jim-Jim. In 1937 Walker began a late-life career as a toastmaster, his first "real" job since resigning as mayor. He also became assistant counsel of the State Transit Commission at a salary of $12,000 ($182,000 today).

In 1938 Jim's old political enemy Fiorello LaGuardia, now mayor of New York, appointed Jim to become the impartial czar of industrial and labor relations in the $250 million women's coat and suit industry at $20,000 ($309,000 today), plus $5,000 for expenses. Apparently, this was at least in part due to pressure from President Roosevelt.

Early in 1941 Betty, who knew that Jim wanted to return to the Catholic church but could not while married to a divorcée, filed for divorce in Key West, Florida, citing that "demands made on her as the wife of a prominent figure" had caused her intense mental pain resulting in sickness. Jim did not contest the divorce; custody of their children—Mary Ann was five and Jim Jr., four—was to be shared jointly.

Soon after the divorce became final, Betty, who was becoming somewhat unstable emotionally and was seeing a psychiatrist, asked Jim to take her back, but he refused, claiming that a personal relationship such as the one they shared can't be restored once it has gone away. On a vacation trip to South America "to forget Jim," Betty met an engineer, Theodore Knappen, whom she married (but only after both asked and received Jim's permission). Soon afterward she simultaneously became pregnant and was diagnosed with breast cancer. Although doctors recommended that the pregnancy be terminated, as such cancers can spread rapidly during pregnancy, she decided to have the child (a boy, born January 19, 1944) and died the following July 12 at forty, as she had always claimed she would.

Before dying, Betty asked Jim and Ted to agree that the three children would be raised together and that they, Jim and Ted, would live together so it could be carried out. Although the arrangement started off well, with the strange family living together at her old family home in Westbury, Long Island, Knappen, who was a decade younger than Walker, found the situation more and more difficult to live with. So in October Jim leased a ten-room apartment for all of them at 110 East End Avenue, two blocks south of Doctors Hospital, where Betty had died.

Now that that era was gone, Jimmy Walker lived a far more modest life, although when he was back in Manhattan, he still fastidiously dressed to the nines and was the center of attention whenever he went out. However, his bedroom furnishings said much about the former mayor at this point in his life,

He would sometimes spend all day and night in his bedroom, playing solitaire at a battered card table with an old, dog-eared deck of cards. Walker drank one highball a night from an old, chipped glass—one he prized, as it had been given to him by Betty. A lithograph of Jesus Christ hung over his double bed, and on the opposite wall were framed silhouettes of his adopted children. Other photographs were displayed on modernistic chests placed on a side wall, including pictures of Betty and the children and a tintype of Jim's mother. On the other chest was Jim's collection of 160 cigarette holders in various colors, each equipped with a filter.

On shelves hung between the two windows that overlooked the East River were a number of books, many of a religious nature, and souvenirs he prized: a football autographed by an early Notre Dame football team (the legendary Notre Dame football coach, Knute Rockne, had been a close friend) and a baseball signed by New York Giants players. His closet was still filled with clothing of his own design, and in the corner stood the old mannequin from St. Luke's Place on which hung his silk dressing gown.

Early in 1945 Jimmy resigned as the Garment Workers' czar and became president of Majestic Records (he was succeeded in the garment workers job by FDR intimate Harry Hopkins).

Over the next few months, Walker's health continued to deteriorate. During a visit to Los Angeles, he had to be rushed to Cedars of Lebanon Hospital with pneumonia. While there he took a call from his friend, the New York restaurateur Toots Shor, who put Sir Alexander Fleming, the discoverer of the "miracle drug" penicillin (which had cured Walker's pneumonia), on the phone. Jim's only comment was "thanks."

Back in New York he one day banged on the wall of his bedroom, summoning his sister Nan, who was visiting.

"Sis, I want to talk to you about something," he said.

"Yes?"

"I'm halfway across the river . . . and I can't swim back. I want you to take care of the little ones."

The doctors weren't quite sure of his problem. His temperature and blood pressure were normal, but they suspected that something was happening in his brain. That was confirmed when he had a seizure and slipped into a coma and was taken to the nearby Doctors Hospital. Mayor O'Dwyer arranged for a policeman to guard the door to his room, where the curtains were drawn after a photographer with a telescopic lens was seen trying to shoot pictures of the dying Walker though his window. That night of Monday, November 18, 1946, Jim's heart started to give out, and soon it was over.

Walker's body was moved to Frank Campbell's Funeral Church, where restaurateur Toots Shor and the journalist Arthur "Bugs" Baer decided to visit at four in the morning. "Toots was crying," Baer remembered, "and cried out, 'Jimmy! Jimmy! When you walked into the room, you brightened up the joint!'" Thirty thousand people visited the funeral home; few believed the truth, that he died a relatively poor man with less than fifteen thousand dollars to his name.

His funeral was held at St Patrick's Cathedral, where more than a thousand wreaths and bouquets were banked around the casket, which had been delayed in arriving because of traffic. A member of the police detail at the cathedral entrance murmured, "Our Jimmy is late again." Afterward he was taken to Gate of Heaven cemetery in Hawthorne, New York; there the casket was opened and the star sapphire cuff links given him by Betty were removed to be sold to benefit his children.

In his biography of Jimmy Walker, Gene Fowler wrote of his last years, "He still displayed the magic that had endeared him to an era . . . that starry time, before a great hush came over the world. For he stayed Beau James, the New Yorker's New Yorker, perhaps the last of his kind."

For many, New York City's Chrysler Building, with its transcendental Deco architecture and cloud-piercing spire, is a unique presence in the city's skyline. By being started in the boom year of 1928 and finished in Depression-shrouded 1932, it also was an unintended tribute to the prior decade. Here, soon after its completion, the building's architect, William van Alen, attends a costume ball wearing a hat shaped like the top of his most famous and iconic creation. More than two dozen other architects attending the ball dressed like their buildings, too.
Author's Collection

EPILOGUE

The Crash and the Sign of a Better Tomorrow

The Chrysler Building and Architect William Van Alen

Once I built a tower, up to the sun, brick and rivet and lime,
Once I built a tower, now it's done. Brother, can you spare a dime?

— Lyrics to "Brother, Can You Spare a Dime" (1931); music by Jay Gorney, lyrics by Yip Harburg

Throughout history, people—from princes to paupers—have sought clues as to what fate had in store for them. They still do, as witnessed by the enduring popularity of astrological predictions available everywhere from your local newspaper to your computer server.

Even more powerful over the millennia have been portents, those once-unexplained appearances of comets and solar eclipses, as well as the arrangement of such objects as a sheep's entrails or tea leaves, that were said to predict that something momentous or terrible would happen.

Toward the end of the 1920s, there were signs that the unprecedented boom that most everyone seemed to be enjoying was coming to an end. Some—not many—financial experts repeatedly cautioned investors of the dangers of speculation and also warned that the boom might have been too leveraged on borrowed money. Few paid any attention. As President Coolidge had said, "After all, the chief business of the American people is business," and they continued to buy more and more "sure bet" stocks and bonds.

Then, after a few warning drops in the Dow, it all came tumbling down in a series of financial body blows called "Black Thursday" ("Black Friday" in Europe) and, finally, "Black Tuesday," October 29, 1929, when the stock market collapsed. It was but one part of the bursting of a worldwide economic bubble, but few Americans cared about what was going on in Germany or Italy or anywhere else at the time. It was the crash centered at the New York Stock Exchange that hit hardest at home, when billions of paper dollars were lost in one day, bringing on an era of bread lines, "Brother, Can You Spare a Dime?," and despair.

It didn't end there, either. The stock market kept dropping, and on July 8, 1932, the Dow reached its lowest level of the twentieth century and did not return to pre-1929 levels until November 1954.

At the next presidential election, in 1932, the nation vented its frustration by throwing the business-friendly Republicans out of the White House (Herbert Hoover's dallying while the market crashed was the final gasp of the party's commitment to letting big business do its own thing) and turned the country over to the Democrats for the next twenty years.

Among the first things the new president, Franklin Delano Roosevelt (". . . the only thing we have to fear is fear itself") did was to end Prohibition (making even the newly bankrupt happy for a while). He started bringing some order and responsibility to Wall Street and initiated a host of jobs programs to put the unemployed back to work. Many conservatives loathed him; the man and woman in the street adored him.

More dramatically portentous because of its timing—Roosevelt's economic fixes would take years and a world war to bring about recovery—was the construction of a building begun in the boom year of 1928 and finished in the deepening economic crisis of 1930 that was a near-perfect metaphor for the dramatic events of the era. Few imagined that, when it was finished in the gloom of the Great Depression, it could be seen as a portent for America's future, a shining arrow transcendentally pointing toward the time when all would be well again, even though it would take half a lifetime for many people just to get back to even.

The Chrysler Building, financed by auto tycoon Walter P. Chrysler, at seventy-seven stories was planned to be the tallest skyscraper in the world—and it was for eleven months, until the Empire State Building was finished in May 1931.

Peter Gössel and Gabriele Leuthäuser, in their book *Architecture in the Twentieth Century*, wrote, "The design, originally drawn up for building contractor William H. Reynolds, was finally sold to Walter Chrysler, who wanted a provocative building which would not merely scrape the sky but positively pierce it."

Part of the building's enduring appeal, an attribute that made it an instant star of New York City's skyline and an enduring landmark, is its crowning spire. It was an inspiration of both the architect, William Van Alen, and the contractor, who, following Van Alen's plan, stunned the city in 1932 with what Gössel and Leuthäuser call "a deliberate strategy of myth generation."

Van Alen planned a dramatic completion for his art deco skyscraper by first assembling most of the entire seven-story pinnacle, complete with special steel facing, *inside* the building. It was then hoisted into position through the roof opening and anchored on top in just one and a half hours. "All of a sudden it was there—a sensational fait accompli," measuring, from the ground to the tip of its spire (often joked about as "a parachutist's nightmare"), 1,048 feet. Ironically, the first part of the pinnacle, which would one day become a symbol for New York's dynamism, was worked into place on October 23, 1929. The next day, October 24, has been remembered in history as "Black Tuesday," the day of the first major break in stock prices that presaged the final tumultuous crash five days later.

William Van Alen was born in Brooklyn on August 10, 1883, only three months after the opening of the Brooklyn Bridge linked his neighborhood to a Manhattan whose skyline, then limited to four or five stories, he would help dramatically change. While attending school, he worked for the architect Clarence True, then studied for three years at the Atelier Masqueray, the first independent architectural workshop in the United States. Afterward he worked for several firms in Manhattan before being awarded a scholarship in 1908 that allowed him to study in Paris at, among other venues, the École des Beaux-Arts.

After returning to New York in 1911, Van Alen formed a brief partnership with H. Craig Severance; after it broke up, both continued to design the distinctive multistory commercial buildings that, together, they had become known for. In the late 1920s both designed what would be heralded as the tallest buildings in the world. Severance planned the Manhattan Trust Building at 40 Wall Street and Van Alen, the Chrysler Building.

Initially, people greeted the Chrysler design with mixed feelings. Van Alen was called the "Ziegfeld of his profession" after the 1920s showman (chapter 8), and some called the whole thing a "stunt" with "no significance as serious design" (certainly, his coup de théâtre in surprising the city with that spire *was* a stunt). What they missed, however, was, stunt or not, the design's sheer, transcendental exuberance, which enabled the Chrysler Building to become an icon of the city, while other, more mundane buildings erected at the time have faded into the background.

Unfortunately, Van Alen had no contract with Walter Chrysler. When, after completion, he requested a payment of the standard 6 percent architect's commission of the building's construction cost—$14 million, today the equivalent of $217 million—Chrysler refused. Van Alen sued him for it and won, but between his action's scaring off other builders and the impact of the Great Depression, he was effectively out of the architecture business and spent his remaining years teaching sculpture.

His name still lives on in New York City through the presence of the Van Alen Institute, a nonprofit organization dedicated to improving design of public works through exhibitions, competitions, and the like.

But his real monument is the beloved building at the corner of Forty-Second Street and Lexington Avenue that, for more than eighty years, has inspired New Yorkers to look upward always. That same upward gaze, that same exuberance and awe, is as much a symbol of New York City during the 1920s, when it became the capital of the world, as the building itself.

ACKNOWLEDGMENTS

Writing this book was immeasurably enabled by Roseanne Wells, Keith Wallman, Francis Milliken, Dale Olson, Marianne Strong, Marc Wanamaker, Thomas Lisanti, Margot Martin, Linda Rees, and the still lively ghosts of New York's most defining decade.

BIBLIOGRAPHY

Adler, Polly. *A House Is Not a Home*. Amherst: University of Massachusetts Press, 2006.

Alexander, Michael. *Jazz Age Jews*. Princeton, NJ: Princeton University Press, 2001.

Allen, Frederick Lewis. *The Big Change: America Transforms Itself*. New York: Bantam, 1961.

Allen, Frederick Lewis. *Only Yesterday: An Informal History of the 1920s*. New York: Harper & Row, 1959.

Allen, Frederick Lewis. *Since Yesterday, 1929–1939*. New York: Bantam Matrix, 1965.

Baughman, James. *Henry R. Luce and the Rise of American News Media*. Boston: Twayne Publishers, 1987.

Behr, Edward. *Prohibition: 13 Years That Changed America*. New York: Arcade Publishing, 1996.

Berry, Faith. *Langston Hughes, Before and Beyond Harlem*. Westport, CT: IIill, 1983.

Birmingham, Stephen. *Our Crowd: The Great Jewish Families in America*. New York: Dell, 1967.

Black, Stephen. *Eugene O'Neill: Beyond Mourning and Tragedy*. New Haven, CT: Yale University Press, 1999.

Blumenthal, Ralph. *Stork Club: America's Most Famous Night Spot and the Lost World of Café Society*. Boston: Little Brown & Co., 2000.

Brown, E. K. *Willa Cather: A Critical Biography*. New York: Knopf, 1953.

Buxton, Frank, and Bill Owen. *The Big Broadcast, 1920–1950*. New York: Avon Books, 1973.

Chotzinoff, Samuel. *Toscanini, An Intimate Portrait*. New York: Knopf, 1956.

Christopher, Matt, and Glenn Stout. *Babe Ruth*. New York: Little Brown & Co., 2005.

Churchill, Allen. *The Improper Bohemians*. New York: Ace Books, 1959.

Farrar, Geraldine. *Such Sweet Compulsion*. New York: Greystone Press, 1938.

Fitzgerald, F. Scott. *The Great Gatsby*. Edited by Matthew Bruccoli. New York: Scribner, 1995.

Fitzgerald, F. Scott. *The Love of the Last Tycoon*. Edited by Matthew Bruccoli. New York: Scribner, 1994.

Fitzgerald, F. Scott. *This Side of Paradise*. New York: Scribner, 1948.

Follian, John. *The Last Godfathers: Inside the Mafia's Most Infamous Family*. New York: Thomas Dunne Books, 2009.

Gelb, Arthur and Barbara. *O'Neill*. New York: Applause, 2000.

Gosch, Martin A., and Richard Hammer. *The Last Testament of Lucky Luciano*. Boston: Little Brown and Co., 1974.

Graham, Martha. *Blood Memory*. New York: Washington Square Press, 1991.

Graham, Sheilah. *Beloved Infidel*. New York: Holt, 1958.

Grossman, Barbara. *Funny Woman: The Life and Times of Fanny Brice*. Bloomington: Indiana University Press, 1991.

Hemingway, Ernest. *The Sun Also Rises*. New York: Scribner, 2006/1926.

Higgins, Jack. *Luciano's Luck*. New York: Stein & Day, 1981.

Johnson, Paul. *Modern Times: The World from the Twenties to the Eighties*. New York: Harper & Row, 1983.

Kaiser, Charles. *The Gay Metropolis*. New York: Grove Press, 1997.

Keats, John. *You Might As Well Live: The Life and Times of Dorothy Parker*. New York: Simon & Schuster, 1970.

Kunkel, Thomas. *Genius in Disguise: Harold Ross of the* New Yorker. New York: Random House, 1995.

Lee, Hermione. *Willa Cather: Double Lives*. New York: Pantheon Books, 1990.

Le Vot, André. *F. Scott Fitzgerald*. New York: Doubleday & Co., 1983.

Lewis, Alfred Allen. *Ladies and Not-So-Gentle Women*. New York: Viking, 2000.

Lewis, Thomas S. W. *Empire of the Air: The Men Who Made Radio*. New York: Burlingame/Harper Collins, 1991.

Loos, Anita. *Kiss Hollywood Goodbye*. New York: Viking Press, 1974.

Lord, Walter. *The Good Years, 1900 1914*. New York: Bantam Pathfinder, 1969.

Marek, George. *Toscanini*. New York: Atheneum, 1975.

McGarry, Molly, and Fred Wasserman. *Becoming Visible: An Illustrated History of Lesbian and Gay Life in Twentieth Century America*. London: Penguin Putnam, 1998.

Meade, Marion. *Dorothy Parker*. London: Penguin Books, 1989.

Meade, Marion. *Dorothy Parker: What Fresh Hell Is This?* New York: Villard Books, 1988.

Meyers, Jeffrey. *Scott Fitzgerald*. New York: Harper Collins, 1994.

Miller, Neil. *Out of the Past: Gay and Lesbian History, 1860 to the Present*. New York: Random House First Vintage Books, 1995.

Mitgang, Herbert. *Once Upon a Time in New York*. Lanham, MD: Cooper Square Press, 2003.

O'Neill, Eugene. *Anna Christie*. New York: Modern Library, 1937.

O'Neill, Eugene. *Desire Under the Elms*. New York: Literary Classics of the U.S./Viking, 1988.

O'Neill, Eugene. *Strange Interlude*. New York: Literary Classics of the U.S./Viking, 1988.

Rampersad, Arnold. *The Life of Langston Hughes, Vol. I, 1902–1941: I, Too, Sing America*. New York: Oxford University Press, 1988.

Rudnick, Lois P. *Mabel Dodge Luhan: New Woman, New Worlds*. Albuquerque: University of New Mexico Press, 1984.

Rupp, Leila J. *A Desired Past: A Short History of Same-Sex Love in America*. Chicago: University of Chicago Press, 1999.

Smelser, Marshall. *The Life That Ruth Built*. Lincoln: University of Nebraska Press, 1993.

Smith, Jane S. *Elsie de Wolfe: A Life in the High Style*. New York: Atheneum, 1982.

Stern, Robert A. M., Gregory Gilmartin, and Thomas Mellins. *New York 1930: Architecture and Urbanism Between the Two Wars*. New York: Rizzoli, 1987.

Swanberg, W. A. *Luce and His Empire*. New York: Scribner, 1972.

Teichmann, Howard. *Smart Aleck: The Wit, World, and Life of Alexander Woollcott*. New York: Wm. Morrow, 1976.

Thomas, Bob. *Winchell*. New York: Doubleday, 1971.

Thurber, James. *The Years with Ross*. Boston: Little Brown, 1959.

Wallace, David. *Lost Hollywood*. New York: St. Martin's Griffin, 2001.

Wharton, Edith. *The Age of Innocence*. New York: Barnes & Noble Classics, 2004.

Wharton, Edith. *The House of Mirth*. New York: Scribner, 1905.

Wilson, Edmund. *The Thirties*. New York: Farrar, Straus and Giroux, 1980.

Wilson, Edmund. *The Twenties*. New York: Farrar, Straus and Giroux, 1975.

INDEX

ABOUT THE AUTHOR

David Wallace is a writer/journalist whose popular histories of Hollywood have been hailed as "inspired" (the *New York Times*), "delicious" and "irresistible" (columnist Liz Smith), and "a whirlwind of storytelling" (King Features). Here, with enthralling anecdotes and profiles of the city's most influential people of the time—from politicians to artists to gangsters—he tells the captivating story of New York City in the 1920s, its most glamorous and defining decade. Formerly the national correspondent for *People*, Wallace lives in Palm Springs, California.